July 00.

To Bill, with best wishes
from Frank [illegible]

ALSO BY DAVID REMNICK

Lenin's Tomb: The Last Days of the Soviet Empire
The Devil Problem and Other True Stories
Resurrection: The Struggle for a New Russia

KING OF THE WORLD

DAVID REMNICK

KING
OF THE
WORLD

Muhammad Ali and the Rise
of an American Hero

PICADOR

First published 1998 by Random House, Inc., New York

First published in Great Britain 1999 by Picador
an imprint of Macmillan Publishers Ltd
25 Eccleston Place, London SW1W 9NF
Basingstoke and Oxford
Associated companies throughout the world
www.macmillan.co.uk

ISBN 0 330 37188 6

Grateful acknowledgment is made to the following for
permission to reprint previously published material:

James Baldwin Estate: Excerpt from "The Fight: Patterson vs. Liston" by James
Baldwin, originally published in *Nugget*. Copyright © 1963 by James Baldwin.
Copyright renewed. Reprinted by arrangement with the James Baldwin Estate.

Playboy: Excerpt from "The Playboy Interview: Cassius Clay" (October 1964).
Copyright © 1964 by Playboy; excerpt from "The Playboy Interview:
Muhammad Ali" (November 1975). Copyright © 1975 by Playboy. Reproduced
by special permission of *Playboy* magazine.

Simon and Schuster: Excerpts from *Muhammad Ali: His Life and Times* by Thomas
Hauser. Copyright © 1991 by Thomas Hauser and Muhammad Ali. Reprinted by
permission of Simon and Schuster.

Gay Talese: Excerpt from "The Loser" by Gay Talese. Originally published in
Esquire magazine. Copyright © 1962 by Gay Talese. Excerpt from "In Defense of
Cassius Clay" by Gay Talese. Originally published in *Esquire* magazine.
Copyright © 1966 by Gay Talese. All excerpts reprinted by permission of the author.

The Wylie Agency: Excerpt from "Ten Thousand Words a Minute" by Norman Mailer.
Copyright © 1963 by Norman Mailer, first printed in *Esquire* magazine. Reprinted
with the permission of The Wylie Agency.

7 9 8

A CIP catalogue record for this book is available from
the British Library.

Printed and bound in Great Britain by
Mackays of Chatham plc, Chatham, Kent

For my brother, Richard,
and for my friend Eric Lewis

CONTENTS

PROLOGUE:
IN MICHIGAN

Cassius Clay entered the ring in Miami Beach wearing a short white robe, "The Lip" stitched on the back. He was beautiful again. He was fast, sleek, and twenty-two. But, for the first and last time in his life, he was afraid. The ring was crowded with has-beens and would-bes, liege men and pugs. Clay ignored them. He began bouncing on the balls of his feet, shuffling joylessly at first, like a marathon dancer at ten to midnight, but then with more speed, more pleasure. After a few minutes, Sonny Liston, the heavyweight champion of the world, stepped through the ropes and onto the canvas, gingerly, like a man easing himself into a canoe. He wore a hooded robe. His eyes were unworried, and they were blank, the dead eyes of a man who'd never gotten a favor out of life and never given one out. He was not likely to give one to Cassius Clay.

Nearly every sportswriter in the Miami Convention Hall expected Clay to end the night on his back. The young boxing beat writer for *The New York Times*, Robert Lipsyte, got a call from his editors telling him to map out the route from the arena to the hospital, the better to know the way once Clay ended up there. The odds were seven to one against Clay, and it was almost impossible to find a bookie willing to take a bet. On the morning of the fight, the *New York Post* ran a column written by Jackie Gleason, the most popular television comedian in the country, that said, "I predict Sonny Liston will win in eighteen seconds of the first round, and my estimate includes the three seconds Blabber Mouth will bring into the ring with him." Even Clay's financial backers, the Louisville Sponsoring Group, expected disaster; the group's lawyer, Gordon Davidson, negotiated hard with Liston's team, assuming that this could be the young man's last night in the ring. Davidson hoped only that Clay would emerge "alive and unhurt."

It was the night of February 25, 1964. Malcolm X, Clay's guest and mentor, was at ringside, in seat number seven. Jackie Gleason and Sammy Davis were there, and so were the mobsters from Las Vegas, Chicago, and New York. A cloud of cigar smoke drifted through the ring lights. Cassius Clay threw punches into the gray floating haze and waited for the bell.

"SEE THAT? SEE ME?"

Muhammad Ali sat in an overstuffed chair watching himself on the television screen. The voice came in a swallowed whisper and his finger waggled as it pointed toward his younger self, his self preserved on videotape: twenty-two years old, getting warm in his corner, his gloved hands dangling at his hips. Ali lives in a farmhouse in southern Michigan. The rumor has always been that Al Capone owned the farm in the twenties. One of Ali's dearest friends, his cornerman Drew "Bundini" Brown, had once searched the property hoping to find Capone's buried treasure. In 1987, while living in a cheap motel on Olympia Avenue in Los Angeles, Bundini fell down a flight of stairs. A maid finally found him, paralyzed, on the floor; he died three weeks later.

Now Ali was whispering again, "See me? You see me?" And there he was, surrounded by his trainer, Angelo Dundee, and Bundini, moon-faced and young and whispering hoodoo inspiration in Ali's ears: "All night! All night! Float like a butterfly, sting like a bee! Rumble, young man, rumble!"

"That's the only time I was ever scared in the ring," Ali said. "Sonny Liston. First time. First round. Said he was gonna kill me."

Ali was heavy now. He had the athlete's disdain for exercise and ate more than was good for him. His beard was gray and his hair was going gray, too. I'd come up to Michigan to see him because I wanted to write about the way he'd created himself in the early sixties, the way a gangly kid from Louisville managed to become one of the most electric of American characters, a molder of his age and a reflection of it. As Cassius Clay, he entered the world of professional boxing at a time when the expectation was that a black fighter would behave himself with absolute deference to white sensibilities, that he would play the noble and grateful warrior in the world of southern Jim Crow and northern hypocrisy. As an athlete, he was supposed to remain aloof from the racial and political upheaval going on around him: the student sit-ins in Nashville in 1960 (the year he won a gold medal in Rome), the Freedom Rides, the march on Washington, and the student protests in Albany, Georgia, and at Ole Miss (as he was making his way up the heavyweight ladder). Clay not only responded to the upheaval, he responded in a way that outraged everyone from white racists to the leaders of the National Association for the Advancement of Colored People. He changed his religion and his name, he declared himself free of every mold and expectation. Cassius Clay became Muhammad Ali. Nearly every American now thinks of Ali with misty affection— paradoxically, he was a warrior who came to symbolize love—but that transformation in the popular mind came long after Ali's period of self-creation in the early sixties, the period covered in this story.

Ali and I talked that afternoon about the three leading heavyweights of the time—Floyd Patterson, Sonny Liston, and Clay himself—and the uncanny way they seemed to mark the political and racial changes going on just as they were fighting one another for the title. In the early sixties, Patterson cast himself as the Good Negro, an approachable and strangely fearful man, a deferential champion of civil rights, integration, and Christian decency. Liston, a veteran of the penitentiary before he came to the ring, accepted the role of the Bad Negro as his lot after he discovered that he would not be permitted any other. For most sportswriters, Liston was monstrous, inexplicable, a Bigger Thomas, a Caliban beyond their reckoning. So this story begins with Patterson and Liston, their lives and their two quick and dramatic fights in 1962 and 1963. Each man, in his own way, represented the world that Ali would encounter and then transcend. Ali would declare himself independent of the stereotypes Patterson was beholden to; he became independent of the mobsters who, for years, had dominated boxing in general and Liston in particular.

"I had to prove you could be a new kind of black man," Ali told me. "I had to show that to the world."

At times, Ali was taken with the subject of himself, but sometimes his heavy lids would blink a few times and then stay shut and he would sleep, mid-conversation, for five, ten minutes or so. He used to do that when he was young. Now he did it a lot more often. Sometimes the present world, the life going on all around—the awards dinners, the championship games, the visits to the king of Morocco or the aldermen of Chicago—sometimes it all bored him. He thought about death all the time now, he said. "Do good deeds. Visit hospitals. Judgment Day coming. Wake up and it's Judgment Day." Ali prayed five times a day, always with death in mind. "Thinking about *after*. Thinking about paradise."

The fight began. In black and white, Cassius Clay came bounding out of his corner and right away started circling the square, dancing, moving around and around the ring, moving in and out, his head twitching side to side, as if freeing himself from a neck crick early in the morning, easy and fluid—and then Liston, a great bull whose shoulders seemed to cut off access to half the ring, lunged with a left jab. Liston missed by two feet. At that moment, Clay hinted not only at what was to come that night in Miami, but at what he was about to introduce to boxing and to sports in general—the marriage of mass and velocity. A big man no longer had to lumber along and slug, he could punch like a heavyweight and move like Ray Robinson.

"It's sweet, isn't it?"

Ali smiled. With great effort, he smiled. Parkinson's is a disease of the nervous system that stiffens the muscles and freezes the face into a stolid mask. Motor control degenerates. Speech degenerates. Some people hallucinate or suffer nightmares. As the disease progresses, even swallowing can become a terrible trial. Parkinson's comes on the victim erratically. Ali still walked well. He was still powerful in the arms and across the chest; it was obvious, just from shaking his hand, that he still possessed a knockout punch. No, for him the special torture was speech and expression, as if the disease had intended to strike first at what had once pleased him, and pleased (or annoyed) the world, most. He hated the effort that speech now cost him. ("Sometimes you won't understand me," he said when we first met. "But that's okay. I'll say it again.") He rarely risked a word in front of a camera. And usually it was an enormous effort to show a smile. I said I knew what he was talking about. My father has Parkinson's. He can no longer walk more than a few steps, and his speech, depending on the time of day, can be a trial. So I knew. What I couldn't tell him was that my father is over seventy. His speech is better than Ali's. But my father had not spent decades getting hit hundreds, thousands of times, by the best heavyweight fighters of his era.

Ali was smiling now as his younger self, Cassius Clay, flicked a nasty left jab into Liston's brow.

"You watchin' this? Sooo fast! Sooo pretty!"

Liston seemed hurt and confused. He had no answer to this new species of athlete.

Ali's fourth wife, Lonnie, came up the stairs and put her hand on Ali's shoulder. She is a sturdy and handsome woman with a face full of freckles. Lonnie is fifteen years younger than Ali. She grew up near the Clay family in Louisville's West End. She went to Vanderbilt and used to work as a sales rep for Kraft in Los Angeles. When Ali's third marriage, to Veronica Porsche, was on its way out, he called her to come be with him. Eventually, Ali and Lonnie married. Lonnie is precisely what Ali needs. She is smart, calm, and loving, and she does not treat Ali like her patient. Besides Ali's closest friend, the photographer Howard Bingham, Lonnie is probably the one person in his life who has given more than she has taken. In Michigan, Lonnie runs the household and the farm, and when they are on the road, which is more than half the time, she keeps watch over Ali, making sure he has rested enough and taken his medicine. She knows his moods and habits, what he can do and what he can't. She knows when he is suffering and when he is hiding behind his symptoms to zone out of another event that bores him.

Ali didn't look up from the television. He reached out and rested his hand on the small of Lonnie's back.

"Muhammad, you've got to sign a couple of pictures, okay?" Lonnie said. She put a couple of eight-by-ten glossies in front of him. Cassius Clay was dancing around the ring, stopping only to needle a tattoo on the meat of Sonny Liston's face.

"Ali, can you make that 'to Mark'? M-A-R-K. And 'to Jim.' J-I-M. And later on, you've got to sign some pictures and some boxing gloves."

This is how Ali makes much of his living these days. Ali made plenty of money in boxing, but he didn't keep as much of it as he could have. There were alimonies, hangers-on, the IRS, good times, the Nation of Islam. But the advantage of being the most charismatic sports figure of the century is that even in his reduced state, slow and nearly speechless, he can show up at a banquet or a convention and walk away with a big check. Of all the sixties icons—the Kennedys, King, Malcolm X, John Lennon, Elvis Presley, Bob Dylan, Mickey Mantle—only a few are left, and Ali is, by far, the most adored among them.

"I sign my name, we eat," he said sheepishly.

The tape kept rolling. Cassius Clay was in complete control of the fight. There were welts under both of Liston's eyes. He had aged a decade in fifteen minutes. Ali loved it then and he was loving it now. "People shouted every time Liston threw a punch," he whispered. "They was waitin'. But now they can't believe it. They thought Liston'd knock me into the crowd. Look at me!" Clay danced and jabbed. By the sixth round Clay was a toreador filling a bull's back with blades.

At the end of the sixth, Liston sat down on his stool and stayed there. He quit. Ali smiled as he watched his younger self dancing around the ring, shouting "I'm the king of the world! King of the world!" and climbing the ring ropes and pointing down at all the sportswriters: "Eat your words! Eat your words!" The next day, Clay would announce that he was not merely the heavyweight champion, but a member of the Nation of Islam. Within a few weeks he would have a new name. And within a couple of years, he would make out of himself, a fast and funny kid from Louisville, Kentucky, one of the most compelling and electric American figures of the age. He became so famous that in his travels around the world Ali could gaze out of airplane windows—down at Lagos and L.A., down at Paris and Madras—and be assured that almost everyone alive knew who he was. He'd fantasize about hitching around the world, knowing that everyone would take him in, feed him, adore him. In those early days, as Cassius Clay, he was often reviled in the press and elsewhere, but with time those voices were barely audible. He hit people for a living, and yet by middle age he would be a symbol not merely of courage, but of love, of decency, even a kind of wisdom.

A cleaning woman walked into the room, put aside her vacuum cleaner, and sat down to watch the screen. Cassius Clay was still screaming "King of the world!"

"Ain't I pretty!"

"Oh, Ali," she said, "you had a big mouth then."

"I know," he said, smiling. "But wasn't I pretty? I was twenty . . . twenty what? Twenty-two. Now I'm fifty-four. Fifty-four." He said nothing for a minute or so. Then he said, "Time flies. Flies. Flies. It flies away."

Then, very slowly, Ali lifted his hand and fluttered his fingers like the wings of a bird.

"It just flies away," he said.

PART ONE

Floyd Patterson, 1954.

CHAPTER ONE

Underground Man

SEPTEMBER 25, 1962

ON THE MORNING OF THE FIGHT, THE HEAVYWEIGHT CHAMPION of the world packed a loser's suitcase. Floyd Patterson, for all his hand speed, for all the hours he put in at the gym, was the most doubt-addled titleholder in the history of the division. There were always losers, professional opponents, set-'em-ups, unknowns who suffered as he did, men who took no pleasure in winning except as the periodic escape from loss and humiliation. But he was champion, the youngest man ever to win the title.

In the last weeks of training, Patterson lay on his bed at night, out in a cabin in the Illinois countryside, half asleep, listening to his recording of "Music for Lovers Only," and, if he was lucky, he saw himself winning, he saw himself leaping out of a crouch and striking Sonny Liston with his famous "kangaroo punch," a flying left hook delivered with so much vaulting thrust and ambition that there was always a chance that Patterson would go sailing past his target and through the ropes and into the flannel laps of press row. If the punch landed, as it had against so many, Patterson was golden. He might wait a while to take such risks, at least a few rounds until Liston started to feel the fatigue, but he would leap soon enough. Then he'd follow up, relentless, dropping the bigger man with a right uppercut, a cross, another hook. Patterson could not count on the power of a single punch, not against Liston, whose countenance suggested the strength of iron. He would rely on his gift, his speed.

Patterson knew he had to beware: Liston's left jab was as power-ful as another man's cross; in one fight, Liston had beaten a plod-ding contender named Wayne Bethea so badly with his jab that at the end of the bout Bethea's cornermen dragged their fighter to the dressing room and removed seven teeth from his mouthpiece. Blood was dripping from his ear. The fight had lasted fifty-eight seconds. So Patterson would have to keep his head. He would box, he would duck inside Liston's jab and beat the body.

"I really thought I could beat Liston," Patterson told me nearly forty years later. "I think about it even *now* and I figure I'll find a way to win. That's funny, isn't it?"

But the odds were against Patterson. Cus D'Amato, his mentor since he began boxing at fourteen, had spent years avoiding this fight, preferring instead to set Patterson up with softer opponents. D'Amato, who looked like a cross between the emperor Hadrian and Jimmy Cagney, used his authority and standing among the columnists to deliver righteous pronouncements about Liston's connections to the Mafia, and, like someone from the department of social welfare, he spoke of the need for rehabilitation, for Sonny to prove himself civilized and stay that way if he wanted a chance at the title. But Patterson knew perfectly well that D'Amato thought he had little chance against Liston. And in this, D'Amato was not alone. Some of Patterson's predecessors as champion, Rocky Marciano and Joe Louis among them, arrived in Chicago for the fight, and no sooner had they stepped off the plane than they began telling reporters that the challenger was too strong, too mean, to lose to Patterson.

Almost everyone, of course, was backing Floyd, rooting for him, but this support was purely sentimental: the writers liked Patter-son because he was always so cooperative, he was so open and po-lite; the National Association for the Advancement of Colored People was behind Patterson because he was a civil rights man, an integrationist, a reform-minded gentleman, while Liston, the ex-con, projected what one newspaper after another called "a poor ex-ample for the youth of America." Jackie Robinson's prediction that Patterson would "demolish" Liston had more to do with political hopes than boxing smarts.

Patterson was determined, as always, to be fair, to accommo-date, to do the right thing. Liston had been ranked the top contender for a long time. He had been to jail for armed robbery, true enough, but he had served his time, he deserved a chance. Patterson was doing his bit for the cause of social mobility. "Liston paid for his crimes," he said. "Should he be able to win the championship, these qualities will rise to the surface. I think you'd see a completely new and changed Liston."

At least for the time being, Liston did not wish to betray any appreciation. "I'd like to run him over with a truck," he said.

And so, with losing on his mind, Floyd made arrangements. He carefully stuffed his bag and an attaché case with clothes, food, and a disguise—a custom-made beard and mustache. If he won, of course, he'd meet the press and head back to the hotel for a victory party. If not, he would leave Comiskey Park in his false whiskers and drive through the night to his training camp in upstate New York.

That was always the way it was with Floyd. Fear, especially the fear of losing, ate at him. He was entitled to call himself the toughest man on the planet, yet he didn't much believe it. He was champion in the sense that Chester A. Arthur had been president. "I'm not a *great* champion," he would say, "I'm just a champion." There were those who wondered if Floyd was beyond sensitive, if he was a neurotic in shorts. Some of the reporters from England took to calling him *Freud* Patterson.

He had ample reason to doubt himself. Until now, Patterson had been a lucky man, winning the title in November 1956 against Archie Moore. Moore was the craftiest of fighters, but like Patterson, he was small for a heavyweight, and, by the time of his fight with Floyd, a geriatric case in his early forties. Once Patterson won the title, he never projected the arrogance of a heavyweight champion. He never had the proper disdain. His eyes were sad and vulnerable, the dreamy eyes of a jilted teenager, and his physique was sinewy, the body of a road laborer, an utterly *plausible* body, but one that did not convey invincibility.

At best, Patterson was a fine light heavyweight, bulked up for the marquee division. At fight time, Liston would outweigh Patterson 214 to 189. In boxing, if both men are equally skilled, more or less, the rules of physics usually obtain, and, as in the straight-on collision of two vehicles, the greater power goes to the greater force, to the bigger man, to the truck. Patterson's natural inclination was to get even smaller. "If we put him on a diet," his trainer, Dan Florio, said, "we'd soon have a middleweight on our hands."

Patterson had never defended his title against a fighter even remotely as powerful as Liston. D'Amato set him up with the likes of Pete Rademacher, an Olympian fighting for the first time as a professional, and Brian London, one of those knobby Englishmen who bleed rivers on a pale chest. Perhaps the most notable of Patterson's opponents before Liston was one Roy Harris of Cut and Shoot, Texas. As the papers were happy to point out (happy, because the fight itself didn't promise much except cornpone exotica), Harris grew up wrestling alligators in a swamp around his house known as the Big Thicket. He was also kin to an Uncle Cleve and cousins Hominy, Coon, and Armadillo. In short, Harris was a PR setup, and still it took Floyd thirteen rounds to end it. Liston destroyed Harris in one.

So, as much as he played out the winning scenario in his head, as much as he trained, Patterson was fully prepared to lose. Mentally or physically, he had no great advantage he could call his own. He had lost to lesser men than Liston, certainly—first to Joey Maxim in 1954, and then, as champion, to Ingemar Johansson in 1959. He reacted not with fury, as most heavyweights did, but with depression, prolonged withdrawal. After the Maxim defeat—a controversial decision—Floyd locked himself in his apartment and stayed there for several days. Against Johansson, the humiliation was far deeper because the stage was so much more visible. Defending his title at Yankee Stadium, he had been knocked to the floor, over and over, as in a particularly merciless alley fight. Patterson was a speed fighter, but against Johansson he never made his move. He froze, and Johansson, a burly Swede of modest talent, unloosed what his camp called, so annoyingly, his "toonder and lightning." After the first knockdown, Floyd got off the canvas and began walking dreamily toward his corner. Leaving the neutral corner, Johansson came in from Patterson's blind side and struck him down again; the assault looked less like boxing than an angry drunk splitting open another man's skull with a beer bottle. By around the fourth knockdown, as Patterson crawled around the canvas, staring through the ropes, his eyes locked on John Wayne, who was sitting at ringside, and, as he stared at the actor, Floyd felt embarrassed. Embarrassment was Patterson's signature emotion, and never more so than now. The fight was not even over before he started to wonder if everything he had fought for—his title, his belonging to a world greater than the one he grew up in—if all that was now at risk. Had he ever deserved any recognition, any belonging in the first place? What would John Wayne think of him? The referee, Ruby Goldstein, stopped the fight after Patterson had gone down for the seventh time.

Floyd wanted to hide, but there was no hole deep enough. He had no disguise, so he borrowed a cornerman's hat and tugged at the brim as if to disappear inside it. He let his friends and family hug him, console him, but he hated their pity. He could not wait to be alone. And when they all went away, the family and the friends and the reporters, Floyd went home to New York. Day after day, he sat in his living room with the curtains drawn. "I thought my life was over," Patterson told me. He was one step away from where he started, one step from Bedford-Stuyvesant, the slum of his childhood. It was as if he expected the repo man to trot up his walk at any minute and start stacking the television and the oven and the couch outside in the front yard, and all the neighbors, his white neighbors, would see that he was nobody now.

Floyd could not sleep, or, at least, not for long. Later that night, as he recounts in his autobiography, he climbed out of bed and headed down to the den. After a while, just before dawn, Sandra found him there.

"Floyd," she said, "Floyd, what good will it do sitting down here in the dark thinking?"

"Will it do more good lying up there in the dark?"

When he woke, he looked up from the couch to see his three-year-old daughter, Jeannie, staring at him. His face was still covered with welts, and so he held Jeannie close, trying not to scare her. Later, Sandra persuaded him to come upstairs and get some real sleep. But after a while, she looked down at her husband and was terrified.

"What's wrong with your ear?" she said.

Patterson's pillow was covered with blood. Johansson's punches had ruptured his eardrum.

His depression deepened. He sat alone for days, not reading, not talking, pushing everyone away. In three weeks, he left the house twice. He was, he said later, mourning his own death as champion.

"Daddy's sick," Jeannie kept saying. "Daddy's sick." Patterson's depression lasted nearly a year.

Fighters, Floyd was convinced, are always afraid, all of them, especially fighters at the top level. "We are not afraid of getting hurt but we are afraid of losing. Losing in the ring is like losing nowhere else," he said once. "A prizefighter who gets knocked out or is badly outclassed suffers in a way he will never forget. He is beaten under the bright lights in front of thousands of witnesses who curse him and spit at him, and he knows that he is being watched, too, by many thousands more on television and in the movies, and he knows that the tax agents will soon visit him—they always try to get their share before he winds up flat broke—and the fighter cannot shift the blame for his defeat onto his trainers or managers or anybody else, although if he won you can be sure that the trainers and managers would be taking bows. The losing fighter loses more than just his pride and the fight; he loses part of his future, he is one step closer to the slum he came from."

THERE HAD NEVER BEEN A HEAVYWEIGHT CHAMPION AS SENSI-tive, and as honest about his fears, as Floyd Patterson. He was the first professional athlete to receive what would become the modern treatment, a form of Freudian sportswriting that went beyond the ring and into the psyche. *Victory Over Myself,* Patterson's autobiography, as dictated to Milton Gross, a columnist at the *New York Post,* as well as his confessions to Gay Talese in *The New York Times* and later in *Esquire* magazine, had about them at least an echo of Richard Wright's "The Man Who Lived Underground" and Ralph Ellison's *Invisible Man.*

Patterson was surely not the first fighter to know fear, but he was the first to talk about it so freely in public. He was brought up that way in the gym. Cus D'Amato trained Patterson not only in the jab and the peekaboo defense, but also in introspection. D'Amato was the only modern psychoanalyst who carried a spit bucket in his hand and a Q-Tip in his teeth. In his lectures to his fighters, D'Amato taught that all things being relatively equal, the fighter who understands his own fears, manipulates them, uses them to his advantage, would always win; he taught young men like Patterson and José Torres, the brilliant light heavyweight from

Puerto Rico, to understand their fights as psychodramas, as contests of will more than of gristle.

Patterson grew up in a series of cold-water flats in Brooklyn's Bedford-Stuyvesant, a crumbling landscape of galling poverty. His father worked as a longshoreman, on construction gangs, as a laborer at the Fulton Fish Market. At night, Floyd's father came home so tired that he often forgot to eat and fell asleep in his clothes. Floyd would quietly take off his father's shoes and polish them, and wash his father's swollen feet. When Floyd's mother was not working at home, she was making a few dollars as a maid and working at a bottling plant. There were eleven children to feed. Floyd shared a bed with two of his brothers, Frank and Billy. Very early on, Floyd came to despise himself. He hated that he could do so little to help his father and mother. He felt stupid, powerless. "All I wanted to do was help my parents," Patterson told me, "and all I did was ending up in failure and making matters worse." He used to point at a photograph of himself at two years old and tell his mother, over and over again, "I don't like that boy!" When he was nine, he took down the picture and scratched a series of X's over his face. He had nightmares. More than once, neighbors found him out on the street, in the middle of the night, sleepwalking. He was a child who wanted to hide all the time, who sought the dark. Floyd prowled the alleyways, the dark corners, not because he was looking for trouble, but because he wanted to lose himself. He went to the movies in the morning and stayed through the last show. He rode the A train, back and forth, east to Lefferts Boulevard in the far reaches of Queens, back through Brooklyn, across the East River and up Manhattan to Washington Heights, and back again. From the time Floyd was nine, he would often stop his journeying at the High Street station in Brooklyn. He discovered there the ultimate hiding place. He walked through the tunnel to a semi-hidden tool shed the subway workmen used. He climbed up the metal ladder and locked himself into the darkness. This was his hideaway from the world. "I'd spread papers on the floor and I'd go to sleep and find peace."

During the day, he began to steal, little things, a quart of milk, a piece of fruit, something he could bring home to his mother. By the time he was a teenager, Floyd was in court all the time—for truancy, for stealing, for running away. He went to court, he guessed, thirty or forty times.

Finally, when Floyd was ten, a judge who had seen enough of him sent him to the Wiltwyck School for Boys, a farm for troubled youngsters upstate in Esopus, New York. It was September 1945 when Floyd went off to Wiltwyck. He thought he was being sent to jail, and he was furious with his mother, who had greeted the news with relief. It turned out to be the best thing that had ever happened to him. Wiltwyck was 350 acres of farmland, an old estate that had been owned by the Whitney family. There were no fences or bars. There were chickens and cows, a decent gym, a creek to swim and fish in. There were teachers on the staff, as well as psychiatric social workers and therapists. The children were never beaten or locked in their rooms. Slowly, Floyd began to learn to read, to speak with a little more ease, to get over his permanent sense of shame. When he became champion, Patterson dedicated his autobiography to the school, "which started me in the right direction." Wiltwyck was precisely the kind of break that Sonny Liston would never have.

THE TWO YEARS AT WILTWYCK TURNED FLOYD AROUND. HE WAS never a good student, but at least now he could function in the world. Back in New York, Floyd entered P.S. 614, one of the city's "600" schools for troubled kids, and later he went for a year to the Alexander Hamilton Vocational High School. By the time Patterson got back to the city, two of his brothers were working out at the Gramercy Gym on East Fourteenth Street. Cus D'Amato owned the gym and slept in the back room. His dog was his only companion. D'Amato was a boxing ascetic. He made his living from boxing, but he despised money, gave it away. Money, he said, "was for throwing off the back of trains." When Patterson won the title, D'Amato took most of his share of the take, more than thirty thousand dollars, and used it to order up a bejeweled championship belt as a gift for his fighter. "Cus was crazy about everything in life except boxing," José Torres said. D'Amato was a well-informed paranoid. Fear ruled him. He was especially fearful of the Mafia, which ran boxing in his time—and he slept with a gun under his bed. He would never ride the subways, for fear of being pushed onto the tracks. He feared snipers. He feared unfamiliar food and drink. He told people that he never married for fear of being duped by "enemies."

"I must keep my enemies confused," he once said. "When they are confused, then I can do a job for my fighters."

As a kid, growing up in the Bronx, D'Amato starved himself for days, the better to withstand the pain when someone tried to take food from him. He was probably the youngest fatalist in the borough. He used to watch funeral processions outside his building and say, "The sooner death the better." D'Amato was a street kid and a street fighter. One day another kid slammed him in the head with a stick, and he lost the vision in his left eye. D'Amato, however, believed in the regeneration of optic tissue, and throughout his life he made an effort to heal himself, closing his good eye so as to "force" the left eye to see once more. When he became a trainer, D'Amato told his fighters that security, financial and otherwise, would be the death of them. Security dulled the senses, and pleasure—pleasure was worse. "The more pleasures you get out of living," D'Amato said, "the more fear you have of dying."

Compared to most fight trainers and managers, who ritually described what the fighter ate for breakfast, how many miles he ran, and other such pabulum, D'Amato, with his sweat-scented philosophies and his strange habits, made for great copy, and writers came to his Gramercy Gym counting on a good story. D'Amato read, of all things, military history and Nietzsche, and out of that came a philosophy of pain and endurance. Norman Mailer began coming to the gym not long after his success with *The Naked and the Dead*. Young newspaper reporters—Gay Talese, Pete Hamill, Jack Newfield—came even when they had no story in mind. D'Amato, for them, was the moralist in Babylon, the one fight manager of importance who talked up against the gangsters who ran nearly every fighter and arena in the country. They wrote about him, sometimes idealized him, as a figure of authenticity, the decent cornerman in the film noir world of fifties boxing. D'Amato, Mailer once wrote, "had the enthusiastic manner of a saint who is all works and no contemplation. . . . He reminded me of a certain sort of very tough Italian kid one used to find in Brooklyn. They were sweet kids, and rarely mean, and they were fearless, at least by the measure of their actions they were fearless. They would fight anybody."

Patterson was fourteen when he walked up the two flights of wooden stairs to the Gramercy Gym. D'Amato always liked to see how kids came up the stairs for the first time. He watched their expressions, and then he'd wait and see how they came in the next day—if they came at all. Cus did not wait long to unleash his philosophy. He wanted Floyd, and the others, to begin digging into their own heads almost as soon as they hit their first heavy bag. For other managers, self-doubt was unthinkable; for D'Amato, a fighter had to understand himself or he would lose. A fighter isn't merely knocked out, he would say, he *wants* to be knocked out, his will fails him. "Fear is natural, it is normal," he said. "Fear is your friend. When a deer walks through the forest, it has fear. This is nature's way of keeping the deer alert because there may be a tiger in the trees. Without fear, we would not survive."

Patterson proved to be a quick fighter, with a good left hook. He could sneak inside his opponent's jab and, with a combination, take him out. As a middleweight, he won a gold medal at the 1952 Olympics in Helsinki. Red Smith, writing for the *New York Herald Tribune,* was impressed. Patterson, he wrote, "has faster paws than a subway pickpocket and they cause more suffering." That same year, Floyd went pro, and fighting in New York he got a lot of attention beating, in succession, Eddie Godbold, Sammy Walker, Lester Johnson, and Lalu Sabotin. For all his fears, Patterson had learned enough discipline and ring sense to take out all the top club fighters of his day, all the hard young men who fought at Eastern Parkway in Brooklyn and St. Nick's on the West Side. Floyd's older brother Frank told Lester Bromberg, the fight writer at the *New York World Telegram & Sun,* "I'd like to say that I always knew it was in Floyd, but I have to be honest about it. I can't get used to my kid brother being a name fighter. I remember him as the boy who would cry if you hit him too hard when we boxed in the gym and as the green kid who would blow up if I pressed him."

Floyd showed an unusual concern for his opponents. When he was training for a bout to be shown on television's *Wednesday Night Fights* against a Chicagoan named Chester Mieszala, D'Amato suggested that in the week before the bout Patterson work out at the same Chicago gym where Mieszala trained. Patterson refused. He said he didn't want to take "unfair advantage." In the fight itself, Patterson knocked out Mieszala's mouthpiece, and Mieszala, in a daze, went looking for it. Instead of stepping in and belting Mieszala, Floyd bent over and helped him. Eventually, Patterson went back to work, finishing Mieszala with a TKO in the fifth round. Even in a title fight, Floyd was capable of kindness. Against Tommy "Hurricane" Jackson, he kept trying to get referee Ruby Goldstein to step in and save the challenger from unnecessary punishment. Goldstein, touched to the core, complied.

Patterson's emotional makeup contained not one ounce of schadenfreude. Even on the sweetest night of Patterson's career, the night at the Polo Grounds in March 1961 when he came back to avenge his humiliating seven-knockdown loss to Johansson, he derived no great enjoyment from his opponent's pain. Going into the fight, Patterson felt rage for the first time. He hated the way Johansson had bragged after taking his title, and he wanted back what had been taken away. In the fifth round, Floyd clubbed Johansson with two terrifying hooks, dropping him to one knee for a nine-count. When Johansson got up, Patterson was right there with one of his great leaping punches, and the champion went down like a dropped board. Johansson lay on the canvas, blood trickling out of his mouth and his left foot vibrating, like a man in a grand mal seizure. For a moment, Patterson betrayed a smile as he faced the crowd, but when he turned to see Johansson, still out cold, his foot twitching, he was repulsed, terrified that he had killed a man. Patterson ripped himself out of the jubilant grasp of one of his cornermen, knelt on the canvas, and cradled Johansson in the crook of his arm. Patterson kissed Johansson on the cheek and promised him another chance, a third fight.

Later, Patterson admitted he had come to the arena with his beard and mustache, just in case. "He lacks the killer instinct," D'Amato said. "He's too tame, too nice to his opponents. I've been trying all the psychology I can think of to anger his blood up, but he just doesn't have the zest for viciousness. I have a big job on my hands."

ON DECEMBER 4, 1961, PRESIDENT JOHN KENNEDY WATCHED A televised boxing doubleheader held in different cities: Patterson's fourth-round knockout of Tom McNeely in Toronto and Liston's first-round destruction in Philadelphia of the fighter he called Albert "Quick Fall" Westphal. Like any other sports fan in the country (and even the non–boxing fan took notice of heavyweight title

fights), Kennedy had been saying that the real fight would be between Patterson and Liston. After the second Johansson fight,
Kennedy had even invited the champion to the White House,
partly to congratulate him on being the first man ever to regain the
heavyweight title, but also to encourage him. It was a seemingly
routine visit—sports stars had been visiting presidents for decades;
both won some easy and harmless publicity—but the session made
Patterson uneasy. The president asked the champion whom he
would be fighting next. Cassius Clay, the brash Olympic champion, was tearing his way to the top of the division, but no one was
demanding that fight yet. Clay was not yet twenty. Patterson knew
what the president meant.

"Liston," he said. "I'm gonna fight Liston."

Instead of merely wishing Patterson well, Kennedy said, "Well,
you've *got* to beat this guy."

Liston, for his part, was convinced that the White House meeting was the reason Patterson had finally agreed to a match.
"Frankly, I don't think Patterson would have fought me if he hadn't
promised the president," he said. "I believe Floyd found himself in
a position where he couldn't go back on his word. After all, you
don't tell the President of the United States that you are going to
do something and then fail to do it."

Floyd admitted to his own confusion in the Oval Office. "I felt
all alone in there, completely terrified," he said. "You've got to remember how young I was, what my background was, and now I
was getting advice in the Oval Office. What was I supposed to do?
Disagree? I had to take the challenge. I was always afraid of letting
people down and now I was in a position where I had to worry
about letting down the president."

Patterson was now fighting for the Good, and Sonny, whether he
liked it or not, was the Bad. Liston understood his role well. "A
boxing match is like a cowboy movie," he said. "There's got to be
good guys and there's got to be bad guys. That's what people pay
for—to see the bad guys get beat. So I'm the bad guy. But I change
things. I don't get beat."

It was far from automatic that Liston would even be allowed to
fight Patterson. Madison Square Garden, still the most prestigious
site in America for boxing, was out of the question. The New York
authorities were (rightly) convinced that Liston had never cut his

ties to the Mafia and refused him a license. Where could they go? Dr. Charles Larson, president of the United States National Boxing Association, said he would do all he could to prevent the match. "In my opinion Patterson is a fine representative of his race, and I believe the heavyweight champion of the world should be the kind of man our children could look up to as they have always done, as hero-worshipers," he said. "If Liston should become champion before he had rehabilitated himself, it might well be a catastrophe." The same camp said that a Liston victory would be worse for boxing than the horrible night six months before when Emile Griffith killed Benny "Kid" Paret in the ring. It took Sir David Harrington Angus Douglas, the twelfth Marquess of Queensberry, a descendant of the rule maker of boxing, to lift the whiff of moralism from the match. "I would have rather thought it wasn't all that relevant whether or not Liston was a good character. If he's not in prison at the moment, he must currently be legally straight. If he's a good boxer, he must be entitled to a fight with Patterson."

Patterson could endure or ignore the politics of boxing and its various commissions, but not the concerns of men like Ralph Bunche and Martin Luther King. The civil rights movement was gathering momentum in the South and was setting off a profound backlash, especially in the Deep South, and the leaders of the movement worried that, in a moment, they would lose an upstanding champion, a worthy standard-bearer, in Patterson and get Sonny Liston, a convicted felon, instead. The civil rights movement had problems enough—the fight came in the midst of James Meredith's attempt to integrate the University of Mississippi and the battle between the Supreme Court and Governor Ross Barnett, who vowed that the state "will not drink from the cup of genocide." Martin Luther King's rebellion represented the most powerful social upheaval since the war. To tens of millions of Americans, integration was unthinkable and every breakthrough of the civil rights movement, every court case, every march and sit-in, seemed an offense against nature. Fair or not, the last thing the movement's leaders needed was to have the most visible black man in America be a graduate of the Missouri penal system, a thug who'd been jailed for armed robbery. Percy Sutton, head of the Manhattan chapter of the NAACP, said, "Hell, let's stop kidding. I'm for Pat-

terson because he represents us better than Liston ever could."
They saw Patterson as one of theirs, a black man who had fought
his way up (literally, in his case); he was a race man, but one whom
enlightened white men could accept, could talk to. When Patterson's wife was refused an appointment by a masseuse near their
house on Long Island, he sued under the local antidiscrimination
code. When Patterson later bought a house in northern Yonkers,
near Scarsdale, his white neighbors made his life miserable; a dentist next door immediately threw up a six-foot fence. When Patterson built his own fence, the dentist, a Dr. Morelli, shouted to the
workmen, "Touch on my property and you had better have a court
order for it." Eventually, Patterson gave up the fight and moved out.

"I am just part of the social history of our time and our country,
and I can't lag behind it—or run too far ahead of it," he said later
in his autobiography. "If you keep walking around with the bitterness in you, sooner or later it's got to turn into a pain that makes
you want to strike out at the injustice. I would never want to do
that. If I can't go some place legally, I don't want to go there at all.
If I can't fight back legally, I don't want to do it viciously. At the
same time, you can't overlook it and pretend it doesn't exist."

Fame was no protection against humiliation. In the spring of
1957, after Patterson had become champion, he and two of his
sparring partners were refused seating at one restaurant after another on a Saturday afternoon in Kansas City. They bought cheese
and crackers instead and went back to their hotel. They heard that
Jersey Joe Walcott was in town to referee a professional wrestling
match and they called on him in his room. When they arrived they
noticed that Walcott was also eating his lunch in his room; all he'd
been able to come up with was a bag of cookies and a quart bottle
of milk. Walcott offered Patterson and his friends some cookies.

"We've just had a bite," Patterson said, "just the way you're having it."

"Ain't it something?" Walcott said. "The former world's heavyweight champion and the present champ, but in this town it's all
the same. The oldest champ and the youngest, but both have to eat
in their rooms. This is a nice town. Not too bad if you walk with
your eyes just looking ahead and don't listen to what folks are saying. That's why I stay in the room here. Less chance of being mis-
understood."

Liston and Patterson trained for several months—Liston in Philadelphia, Patterson at his camp in upstate New York. In the last weeks before the fight, they both set up camp in the Chicago area. The facilities they chose might have been predicted. Patterson's camp resembled a monastic retreat, a series of cabins in the town of Elgin called Marycrest Farm. Marycrest was a Catholic Worker settlement house, not much different from Wiltwyck. One building that had been converted into a press headquarters was decorated with religious mosaics and a set of crucifixes. The two doors to the room where the press agents worked were marked by Latin signs: *Veritas* over one, *Caritas* over the other. In ordinary times, *Veritas* and *Caritas* marked barns for cows. Patterson trained in a tent with a sign outside reading *So we being many are one body in Christ.* His press conferences took place in a refectory under a mural of saints. Patterson felt at home here. He had converted to the Roman Catholic Church and now he was being advertised as the fight game's St. Francis.

The promoters offered the Liston entourage a camp next to the prison in Joliet. They figured that the barbed wire and watchtowers would be the perfect backdrop for feature stories focusing on Liston's past. Liston thought otherwise. Instead, he trained at an abandoned racetrack in East Aurora, with wire gates and a uniformed cop stationed outside. The infield of the track was a bleak expanse of withered grass. A vicious wind whipped off the disintegrating grandstands. Liston pounded the heavy bag and sparred in a makeshift gym that had once been the parimutuel shed. It was as if Johnny Appleseed were training in one place and the Angel of Death in the other, one of the writers remarked.

The press shuttled between the two and drew out this contrast of Good versus Evil, of the Good Negro versus the Threatening Negro. This was 1962, and newspapermen were still dominant, above all white columnists from New York: Milton Gross of the *Post,* Jimmy Cannon of the *Post* (and then the *World-Telegram*), Red Smith of the *Herald Tribune,* Dick Young of the *News,* Arthur Daley of the *Times.* Liston trusted none of them. He could not read a road sign, much less a newspaper, but his wife, Geraldine, read the columns to him, and it was not long before he knew that he had few fans among the writers. Nor did Sonny have any great supporters among the white literati who had come from the various magazines: Budd Schulberg for *Playboy,* A. J. Liebling for *The New Yorker,* Ben Hecht for a Nyack paper, and Norman Mailer for *Esquire.*

The literary undercard of the Patterson-Liston fight in Chicago featured the meeting of Norman Mailer and James Baldwin, who was on assignment for *Nugget,* a men's magazine which would go out of business in 1965. (Liebling apparently did not care for the presence of visiting novelists. "The press gatherings before this fight sometimes resembled those highly intellectual *pour-parlers* on a Mediterranean island," he wrote. "Placed before typewriters, the accumulated novelists could have produced a copy of *The Paris Review* in forty-two minutes.") Mailer and Baldwin had been on friendly terms in the fifties, but by 1961, they were not getting along. Baldwin felt insulted by Mailer both personally and intellectually: personally because Mailer, in an essay critical of a range of contemporaries, had called him "too charming to be major"; intellectually because he thought that Mailer's essay on race, "The White Negro," was dangerous in the way it featured the black man as merely a collection of unbridled sexual and violent impulses. In a 1961 article for *Esquire* called "The Black Boy Looks at the White Boy," Baldwin said that Mailer was obsessed with power and was essentially an adolescent, a beatnik, arrogant and naive, and had committed the folly of advertising a perverse notion of black culture to titillate the bourgeois white hipsters.

Baldwin arrived in Chicago unsure of his subject. Unlike Mailer, who prided himself on his knowledge of boxing and knew many trainers and fighters, Baldwin was ignorant of the sport. He would never acquire Mailer's ease hanging out at a gym, he could not rely on a ready facility with boxing history and the metaphors of sporting glory. Baldwin would rely instead on his empathy for Patterson and Liston, his understanding of them as poor black kids with an ambition. "I know nothing whatever about the Sweet Science or the Cruel Profession or the Poor Boy's Game," he wrote. "But I know a lot about pride, the poor boy's pride, since that's my story and will, in some way, probably, be my end."

Baldwin, with Gay Talese of the *Times* as his guide, visited both camps and was bewildered by the fight-week scene: the reporters gossiping away the morning and then crashing their stories on deadline, the late dinners on expense account, the customarily farcical feud between the two fighters, the inane press conferences, the parties at the Playboy Mansion, the former champions—Louis, Marciano, Barney Ross, Johansson, Ezzard Charles—milling around, dispensing opinions for quotation as a form of stature maintenance. In the pressroom, the general feeling was that Patterson had become champion by default and, pity though it might be, had little chance against Liston. Look at how he had lost to a mediocrity like Johansson! Down seven times in a single round—a human yo-yo!

Baldwin went to Elgin, where Patterson's press aide, Ted Carroll, greeted him with great deference and gave him a tour of the camp. Carroll seemed to understand that Baldwin was a beginner in boxing.

"Mr. Baldwin, this is a training camp," he said. "And this countryside matches the personality of the champion. While his trade is violent, Mr. Baldwin, his personality is unruffled, *bucolic*. Is that a good word, Mr. Baldwin?"

Baldwin nodded. Yes, it was.

Carroll set up Baldwin to take a long walk with the champion and watch him train. Patterson allowed that he had not read any of Baldwin's books, but he had seen him once on television debating the race question.

"I *knew* I'd seen you somewhere!" Patterson said.

Baldwin clearly felt something for Patterson—he would even place a $750 bet on him. Patterson, for Baldwin, was an unlikely warrior, a complicated, vulnerable, troubled young man who seemed to yearn for privacy even as he uncorked yet another interview for another set of reporters. Baldwin watched Patterson jump rope, "which he must do according to some music in his head, very beautiful and gleaming and far away, like a boy saint helplessly dancing and seen through the steaming windows of a storefront church"; it was a scene that recalled Baldwin's boy saint Elisha, in his novel *Go Tell It on the Mountain*.

After the training session, one of the last before the fight, Baldwin watched Patterson meet with a few reporters. Patterson drank a cup of hot chocolate and wore a tight shy smile. He was asked, as he was every day, why he was fighting Liston.

"Well, it was my decision to take the fight," Patterson said. "You gentlemen disagreed, but you were the ones who placed him in the number one position, so I felt it was only right. Liston's criminal record is behind him, not before him."

"Do you feel you've been accepted as champion?"

"No," he said. "Well, I have to be accepted as champion—but maybe not a good one."

"Why do you say that the opportunity to become a great champion will never arise?"

"Because you gentlemen will never let it arise."

"I mainly remember Floyd's voice, going cheerfully on and on," Baldwin remembered later in his piece for *Nugget*, "and the way his face kept changing, and the way he laughed; I remember the glimpse of him then, a man more complex than he was yet equipped to know, a hero for many children who were still trapped where he had been, who might not have survived without the ring, and who yet oddly did not really seem to belong there."

Before Baldwin left, he gave Patterson copies of *Another Country* and *Nobody Knows My Name,* inscribing them, "To Floyd Patterson . . . because we both know whence we come, and have some idea of where we're going."

Baldwin also visited Liston's camp, and there he found the Liston almost no one else did. Some reporters, including Jack McKinney of the *Philadelphia Daily News,* Jerry Izenberg of the Newark *Star-Ledger,* and Bob Teague of *The New York Times* (one of the very few black reporters on the sports beat), had enjoyed a good rapport with Liston, even when he was still a contender, but the rest had not. The reporters asked questions that invariably referred to this arrest or that shortcoming, and Sonny would answer with a grunt or a yes or a no or a sustained glare.

Even when Liston was trying to be funny with a reporter, he could be intimidating. A. J. Liebling once went up to visit him in training camp and was told he would get an interview at a local restaurant after the day's workout. Liston arrived at the restaurant and everyone around the banquette ordered cups of steaming tea. Suddenly, Liston's expression soured and he began screaming at his cornerman, Joe Pollino, about the two dollars he owed him. The two men argued and then Liston lunged toward Pollino.

"You lie, you hound!" Liston shouted. "Gimme my two bucks!"

As Liebling remembered it, "A vast fist shot out, and I heard a tremendous smack as Pollino went down, amid a shower of teeth."

Liston then pulled out a pistol and started firing away at his cut man. Pollino slumped in the banquette. Then Liston turned the revolver on Liebling and fired. "I threw up my hands and, in doing so, spilled my tea." Liebling's self-description gives him more credit for calm than was genuinely due. He nearly died of heart failure on the spot. When he recovered, his overcoat now blotched with tea stains, Liebling heard Pollino explain that the teeth were actually white beans and Liston explain that the bullets were blanks.

"You come see us again, hear?" Liston told Liebling. "You come back!"

These public relations tactics, such as they were, got an ex post facto laugh from Liebling in print, yet they did not always charm. Many of the reporters approached Liston as they would a monster. The terms "gorilla" and "jungle cat" were common enough, but the texture of the racism became far more elaborate. Peter Wilson of *The Daily Mirror* wrote: "Sometimes he takes so long to answer a question, and has so much difficulty in finding the word he wants to use, that it's rather like a long-distance telephone call in a foreign language. But the man is fascinating. While his scarred face is immobile and his enormous painted-saucer eyes have the fixed glare of an octopus, his hands compel attention. The palms are soft and white, like the inside of a banana skin. His fingers are the unpeeled bananas."

Many of the reporters marked Liston's recalcitrance for stupidity or worse. Baldwin did not. "He is far from stupid; he is not, in fact, stupid at all," he wrote. "And while there is a great deal of violence in him, I sense no cruelty at all. On the contrary, he reminded me of big, black men I have known who acquired the reputation of being tough in order to conceal the fact that they weren't hard. Anyone who cared to could turn them into taffy. Anyway, I liked him, liked him very much. He sat opposite me at the table, sideways, head down, waiting for the blow: for Liston knows, as only the inarticulately suffering can, just how inarticulate he is. But let me clarify that: I say suffering because it seems to me that he has suffered a great deal. It is in his face, in the silence of that face, and in the curiously distant light in the eyes—a light which rarely signals because there have been so few answering signals. And when I say inarticulate, I really do not mean to suggest that he does not know how to talk. He is inarticulate in the way we all are when more has happened to us than we know how to express; and inarticulate in a particularly Negro way—he has a long tale to tell which no one wants to hear."

Liston, as it turned out, didn't mind talking to Baldwin. The son of a Harlem preacher, Baldwin, with his bulging sad eyes, was unlike any other writer who had visited him. Baldwin's soft manner was far different from the wised-up style of most of the journalists Liston had known, and so he spoke to Baldwin in a different tone, with his defenses down. "Colored people say they don't want their children to look up to me," Liston told Baldwin with great sorrow. "Well, they ain't teaching their children to look up to Martin Luther King, either." Liston seemed to be issuing a plea through Baldwin. "I wouldn't be no bad example if I was up there. I could tell a lot of those children what they need to know because I passed that way. I could make them *listen*."

Baldwin went away from his meeting with Liston liking him, but racked with confusion. In Patterson-Liston, the heavyweight championship was once more a morality play; what was unique was that the opponents were both black and represented opposing styles of rhetoric, of political style and action. Baldwin's essay for *Nugget* was not his best, but in it he was able to rehearse some of the themes he would develop the following year in what would be his most thorough statement on race, *The Fire Next Time*. "I felt terribly ambivalent, as many Negroes do these days," he wrote of Liston, "since we are all trying to decide, in one way or another, which attitude, in our terrible American dilemma, is the more effective: the disciplined sweetness of Floyd, or the outspoken intransigence of Liston. . . . Liston is a man aching for respect and responsibility. Sometimes we grow into our responsibilities and sometimes, of course, we fail them."

Baldwin's antagonist at the fight, his erstwhile friend Mailer, did not approach his chore with the same sadness or sense of burden. If Baldwin approached fight night with dread, Mailer looked forward to it with pleasure—the event was, after all, an opportunity both to witness something memorable and to perform. For all the ambition, energy, and self-advertisement he poured into the novels following *The Naked and the Dead*—*The Deer Park, Barbary Shore, An American Dream, Why Are We in Vietnam?*—his journalism for

Esquire and *Harper's* and *Life* was far more than a job done for money. His dispatches, written at great speed and length, from prizefights and political conventions, crackled with an energy that laid waste the conventions of fifties gentility. He was never more on the job than he was in Chicago for the Patterson-Liston fight. Patterson, he wrote,

> was a liberal's liberal. The worst to be said about Patterson is that he spoke with the same cow's cud as other liberals. Think what happens to a man with Patterson's reflexes when his brain starts to depend on the sounds of "introspective," "obligation," "responsibility," "inspiration," "commendation," "frustrated," "seclusion"— one could name a dozen others from his book. They are a part of his pride; he is a boy from the slums of Bedford-Stuyvesant who has acquired these words like stocks and bonds and income-bearing properties. There is no one to tell him it would be better to keep the psychology of the streets than to cultivate the contradictory desire to be a great fighter and a great, healthy, mature, autonomous, related, integrated individual. What a shabby gentility there has been to Patterson's endeavor. . . .
>
> But the deepest reason that Negroes in Chicago had for preferring Patterson was that they did not want to enter again the logic of Liston's world. The Negro had lived in violence, had grown in violence, and yet had developed a view of life which gave him life. But its cost was exceptional for the ordinary man. The majority had to live in shame. The demand for courage may have been exorbitant. Now as the Negro was beginning to come into the white man's world, he wanted the logic of the white man's world: annuities, mental hygiene, sociological jargon, committee solutions for the ills of the breast. He was sick of a whore's logic and a pimp's logic, he wanted no more of *mother wit,* of *smarts,* or *playing the dozens,* of battling for true love into the diamond-hard eyes of every classy prostitute and hustler on the street. The Negro wanted Patterson, because Floyd was the proof a man could be successful and yet be secure. If Liston won, the old torment was open again. A man could be successful *or* he could be secure. He could not have both. If Liston had a saga, the average Negro wanted none of it.

If, for Mailer, Patterson was the "archetype of the underdog, an impoverished prince," "Liston was Faust. Liston was the light of every racetrack tout who dug a number on the way to work. He was the hero of every man who would war with destiny for so long as he had his gimmick; the cigarette smoker, the lush, the junkie, the tea-head, the fixer, the bitch, the faggot, the switchblade, the gun, the corporate executive, anyone who was fixed on power. It was due to Liston's style of fighting as much as anything else."

A literary footnote to the Baldwin-Mailer presence in Chicago was a short essay written by a young poet, LeRoi Jones, who had been allied with Allen Ginsberg and the Beat writers in Greenwich Village and who was becoming more of a presence in the Black Arts movement. Unlike Baldwin, who loved the *tenderness* in Patterson, Jones was disgusted with the champion, calling him an "honorary" white man who craved acceptance in the bourgeois world. He celebrated Liston as a threat, "the big black Negro in every white man's hallway, waiting to do him in, deal him under for all the hurts white men, through their arbitrary order, have been able to inflict on the world." He was " 'the huge Negro,' 'the bad nigger,' a heavy-faced replica of every whipped up woogie in the world. He is the underdeveloped, have-not (politically naive), backward country, the subject people, finally here to collect his pound of flesh." When Jones printed the essay in a collection titled *Home,* he added a footnote saying that now his heart was with the young Cassius Clay, for only Clay could represent the new militant, the truly independent black man.

At the remove of nearly forty years, when boxing has become a marginal event in American life, all this symbol-mongering heaped on the shoulders of two men belting each other in a ring for money seems faintly ridiculous. But for decades, boxing had been a central spectacle in America, and because it is so stripped-down, one-on-one, a battle with hands and not balls or pads or racquets, the metaphors of struggle, of racial struggle most of all, came easily. Ever since Jack Johnson won the heavyweight title in 1908, white boxing fans and, most of all, white promoters required a white hope. Johnson avoided the black contenders of his era—Sam Langford, Joe Jeanette, Sam McVey. Instead, his fight was against a Caucasian retiree, the former champion Jim Jeffries. Until late in his career, all of Joe Louis's leading opponents were white:

Schmeling, Billy Conn, Tony Galento. Sugar Ray Robinson fought one white after another—Bobo Olson, Paul Pender, Gene Fullmer, Jake LaMotta, Carmen Basilio; the promoters rarely offered remotely the same money for bouts against equally tough black challengers. With Patterson-Liston, something had changed. Both men were black; both had grown up with the same hero (Joe Louis), and with similar deprivations and injuries. The narrative of boxing, however, requires an opposition as broad as slapstick. A fight between two members of the same ethnic group has always required a level of differentiation. When John L. Sullivan, the first modern heavyweight champion, defended his bareknuckle title in 1889 against Jake Kilrain, Sullivan was required to play the bad Irish immigrant who drank and took lots of women to bed while Kilrain was the good immigrant, the virtuous worker. Until Patterson-Liston, the press did not bother much with drawing differences between blacks.

Now the symbolic differences between the two fighters were obvious, and the resulting pressures on Patterson, especially, were making his life impossible. Patterson's fear was evident even in his carriage at the weigh-in, a ritual that has always required of fighters a molten stare or, at least, a chilling equanimity. But as Liston glared at Patterson, Patterson stared at his own feet. He never stared at an opponent before a fight. Couldn't risk it. After all, he said, "we're going to fight, which isn't a nice thing." Once, as an amateur, he made the mistake of looking his opponent in the eye and he saw that he had a nice face and the two fighters smiled at each other. From then on Patterson looked at the floor. Except now he had real reason to worry. Sonny Liston wanted to run a truck over him, and he felt if he let it happen he would have failed his family, his country, his president, and his race.

"I kept thinking about these things right up until the fight," Patterson said later. "When the bell rang and I came out, instead of seeing Liston, I seemed to have a vision of all these people; what they told me and wanted me to do. All I can remember is that I wasn't able to think of the fight at all."

Sonny Liston and Floyd Patterson.

CHAPTER TWO

Two Minutes, Six Seconds

THE EVENING OF THE FIGHT WAS MISTY AND RAW, TOPCOAT weather. It was a cold September even for Chicago. Comiskey Park could hold around fifty thousand, but though this was probably the biggest heavyweight fight since Rocky Marciano ended Joe Louis's career a decade earlier, the stadium was less than half filled with just under nineteen thousand paying customers.

The ring announcer introduced a parade of past champions, and one by one they climbed through the ropes: Louis, Marciano, Jim Braddock, Johansson, Ezzard Charles, Barney Ross, Dick Tiger. Archie Moore, who was still fighting for a living in his forties, entered the ring wearing a tuxedo and a long cape lined in white silk. "The Mongoose" carried a cane.

The only noncombatant met with boos was the young contender from Louisville, Cassius Clay. After winning the gold medal as a light heavyweight at the 1960 Rome Olympics, Clay had quickly become known for his mouth. By now he'd run off a string of victories over the middle level of the heavyweight division, and he was scheduled to fight Archie Moore in a few months. But mainly he was known as an outrageous character who reeled off rhyming ditties predicting the round in which he would prevail. When Patterson visited the athletes at the Olympic Village in Rome, Clay informed the champion, in a pitch of happy hysteria, that he would soon be wearing Floyd's crown. "You just keep at it," Patterson had said, laughing. And Clay did, declaring himself the prettiest, the greatest, the king of the world. The sportswriters, especially the older ones, did not find this funny. They hated Clay. Clay was a punk who kept his hands too low and had a punch that could not juice a grape. He had a fresh mouth. Whom had he beaten? He was an affront. Even the liberals among the writers had come to expect the politesse of Louis and Patterson in their champions. Clay's impudence was beyond imagining.

"Cassius was still a youngster, just a pretty good contender, when he jumped around that night," Patterson recalled decades later. "He seemed like a nice kid and all, but how could you take him too seriously? I looked over at him and had to smile, but the way you smile at a kid who's showing off for all the relatives."

The rows around the ring were filled with writers. Mailer and Baldwin were separated by an empty seat, and they were cordial enough. There was the usual gaggle of actors and crooners. And, most of all, there were the mobsters, the cigar chewers, the whisperers, the hawk-nosed men in dark suits who had been running boxing all along. And all of them—the men who ran the unions and the contracting businesses, the numbers rackets and the bookie joints, the garbage haulers and the pizza parlors—they were all for Liston. Part of it was natural allegiance, a nod in the direction of Alcatraz maximum security, where their honorary chieftain, Frankie Carbo, "Mr. Gray," was beginning a long sentence, first for illegal management (not least for the illegal management of Sonny Liston) and later for extortion. Carbo, for all anyone knew, was still running Liston. But the mob was not behind Liston merely out of allegiance. Loyalty is mob rhetoric, a code, but only sometimes a fact. No, it was also a matter of aesthetics. How could a heavyweight champion bow in the direction of the president, much less stomach a sanctimonious prig like Cus D'Amato? And how could a champion talk about his fears, his anxieties, like some . . . woman? "In their mind," Mailer wrote of the mobsters at ringside, "Patterson was a freak, some sort of vegetarian."

As challenger, Liston entered the ring first. He wore a white robe and a white hood that was peaked like a monk's. His shoulders, which were already the size of cantaloupes, were even bigger now; Liston had stuffed towels in his robe. The crowd out beyond the press rows booed him. Liston began warming up, stretching his neck, rolling his shoulders, flicking languid jabs at the floor, like a fop shooting his cuffs. He bounced on his toes, sliding back and forth. If ever a man looked collected, powerful, if ever a fighter looked *ready*, it was Sonny Liston at that moment.

Then came Patterson and his entourage. They came bobbing down the aisle, a bubbling stream of heads. D'Amato had been cast out as official manager—Patterson could not accept D'Amato's lack of confidence in him, nor was he pleased to read press accounts alleging that D'Amato, for all his denials, had played ball with "Fat Tony" Salerno to finance the first Johansson fight, an enormous scandal in New York—but, for all that, D'Amato was still there with him, leading the way toward the ring. With his white buzz cut and Roman jaw, D'Amato kept up a brave face, no matter what intimations of blood he was seeing now. Patterson, for his part, could not hide his terror. He bent through the ropes and into the ring, but he did it stealthily, nervously, with quick glances all around, like a thief climbing in a window on the night he knows he will be arrested at last. He was in a terrible state. His eyes flicked around the ring. Rarely had fear been so visible in a fighter's face. In later years you'd see it in Ken Norton before his fight with George Foreman, then later with Michael Spinks before facing Mike Tyson—both fights that lasted a few minutes. Fighters know.

All along, Liston had been possessed of an almost unseemly calm. The morning before, the two teams of seconds had argued over the gloves to be used for the fight; it was one of those fantastically comic scenes at sporting events that are customarily played out with angry expressions and threatening tones. Grown men arguing over sporting equipment. Such disputes give the reporters something to use for their "setups," their "these two men just plain don't like each other" stories for fight day. At one point, Liston's man, Jack Nilon, claimed the gloves were a whisper heavier than the called-for eight ounces, a difference, Nilon insisted, that might deprive his fighter of some fraction of his power. The shouting became fierce until, finally, Liston stepped in.

"What the hell's going on?" he said.

He was shown the gloves.

"Oh, they're all right," he said. "Let's use them. I'm going to hit him so hard that extra quarter of an ounce isn't gonna be any more than just an extra quarter of an ounce he's being hit with."

During the referee's instructions, Liston stared down at the champion. The champion stared at his shoes. They went back to their corners and waited. The bell rang. The fight was scheduled for fifteen rounds.

"YOU HAVE NO IDEA HOW IT IS IN THE FIRST ROUND," FLOYD would tell his confidant, Gay Talese. "You're out there with all those people around you, and those cameras, and the whole world looking in, and all that movement, that excitement, and 'The Star-Spangled Banner,' and the whole nation hoping you'll win, including the president. And do you know what all this does? It blinds you, just blinds you. And then the bell rings, and you go at Liston and he's coming at you, and you're not even aware that there's a referee in the ring with you. . . ."

Some great athletes experience a round, a play, even an entire contest, in slow motion, as if their superior speed, their gift of judgment and coordination, provides them with a more usable perception of time. The athlete who sees the contest this way has invariably won; he has beaten his opponent to the punch, run down the quarterback, read the seams on a curveball and hit it out of the park. But for the overmatched, time does not so much slow down as lose its coherence. Floyd experienced time in Chicago as a confusion of pressures and noise, as anxiety, like drowning, like falling out of a plane, and afterward he could barely remember what had taken place over the span of two minutes and six seconds. Even the pain would be a while in coming. He would complain of terrible headaches, for Liston hit harder than any other heavyweight alive, but that would not come until an hour later.

Patterson was frozen from the start. Like a singer who begins an aria in the key of A in B-flat and can't make the subtle transposition to the right key, Floyd had it all wrong from the bell. Anything that had ever made him effective in the past, his quickness, his jab, his ability to read the other fighter, was forgotten. Patterson set his gloves at his temples, the peekaboo stance taught him as a teenager by D'Amato, but all he did was wait to get hit. His strategy was inexplicable. Patterson went toe to toe with a slugger, with an opponent who had an incredible thirteen-inch reach advantage.

Liston began by banging an inquiring left jab into Patterson's face. Patterson's head shot back as if he'd been smacked by a bat.

Then, after a series of missed and pawing punches, Patterson ventured his lone experiment in the offensive, his one attempt to see if he had any chance at all. He tried one of his leaping hooks. Liston seemed to shock himself by how easy it was to dodge. He did it by taking an even step backward, as if to avoid a stream he'd just noticed at his feet. Nothing dangerous. From then on, Liston simply did what he wanted to do. He jabbed; he banged short hooks with both hands to Patterson's ribs and liver; then he started loading up with enormous hooks and uppercuts. In the clinches, he pounded at Patterson's kidneys. Patterson tried to grab Liston's arms, tie him up, but he could only muffle the right, while Liston poleaxed him with the left.

Only a minute had elapsed. But now the big punches started to land, first a right uppercut that made Patterson's face seem, in flash-frame, as contorted as putty dropped to the sidewalk from a fifth-floor window. He would never recover from that. The right was not the punch that put him down, but, as it happened, it was the one that ended all hopes of a contest. From then on, butterflies flew free in Patterson's brain. To clear his head, to rest, Patterson tried desperately to clinch. Liston shoved him away and hit him with two left hooks. The punches were not especially fast, they did not have that short, dense, quickness of Louis's best blows—Liston had a way of saying "Ahem" and then throwing a punch; he was not especially deft—but that made no difference at all, not against Patterson. Dazed, his eyes drooping, Patterson headed to the ropes and, with his left hand, he tried to find support there, some balance, a more sober friend. This was a very bad idea. With that hand draped over the ropes, Patterson was inviting the end; perhaps D'Amato was right: the fighter who gets knocked out *wants* to be knocked out. Liston put all his weight into a left hook that caught Patterson square on the jaw and suddenly Patterson's body described a right angle. His legs stiffened straight and he bent at the waist, but it was a posture that held only an instant and then the legs gave out.

"The way he fell I knew he wouldn't get up," Liston said later.

The referee, Frank Sikora, began the count. Patterson rolled over on his side. By nine, he was on one knee. He made it to his feet, but only after Sikora had counted ten and waved his arms.

"One minute I had a fight, the next I didn't," Sikora said. "I was all prepared to see them warm up. . . . Then came a tremendous right to the head and I had a new champion's hand to raise." At ringside, the reporters for the dailies were either barking lead paragraphs to dictationists at home or typing furiously and handing pages of copy to the runners for Western Union. They all knew their second paragraph: this was the third-fastest knockout in the history of heavyweight title fights. In 1908, Tommy Burns knocked out the challenger, Jem Roche, at 1:28, in Dublin, and in 1938, Louis beat Max Schmeling in 2:04 at Yankee Stadium.

Gay Talese had a daily deadline, but he could not help feeling overwhelmed with sadness for his friend. Very often young reporters will find a single object of attention and even affection—for Talese it was Floyd Patterson. He spent hours with the fighter, he interviewed him at home and in training camp, he watched him nap in dressing rooms before fights, he knew his fears, his secrets, and now he had witnessed his friend taken apart in a ballpark. "I felt that part of me had been destroyed," Talese said many years later. "Fighters are so alone. They can't spread the blame around. It's a humiliation witnessed by millions. Liston was the most menacing human being of my lifetime, a born destroyer of other people. I didn't think anyone could survive him. I thought Floyd had such courage, he almost seemed to welcome the punishment. He risked annihilation in public to a much bigger man. And then I watched the two men embrace. Only in boxing do you have that ritual, of two men, nearly naked, exhausted, the smell and taste of each other, after such serious battle, the strange intimacy of that. . . ."

As Liston and Patterson drew away from each other, Liston's cornermen rushed through the ropes to hug him. Willie Reddish, his trainer, put his palms on Sonny's cheeks.

Patterson walked toward his corner and, through his daze, spotted D'Amato coming toward him. D'Amato held out his arms and Patterson's legs nearly gave out again, but this time from grief, not pain. He found D'Amato and rested his forehead on his teacher's shoulder.

"What happened, Floyd?" D'Amato said.

Patterson could only say that he had seen all the punches except the last. He was still dazed. He could barely talk for the shame of it all. It was only months later that he started making sense of the moment: "It's not a *bad* feeling when you're knocked out," he said.

"It's a *good* feeling, actually. It's not painful, just a sharp groggi-ness. You don't see angels or stars: you're on a pleasant cloud. . . . But then this good feeling leaves you. You realize where you are, and what you're doing there, and what has just happened to you. And what follows is a hurt, a confused hurt—not a physical hurt— it's a hurt combined with anger; it's a what-will-people-think hurt; it's an ashamed-of-my-own-ability hurt . . . and all you want then is a hatch door in the middle of the ring—a hatch door that will open and let you fall through and land in your dressing room in-stead of having to get out of the ring and face those people. The worst thing about losing is having to walk out of the ring and face those people. . . ."

It was not long before Floyd's thoughts turned to his escape plan, his disguise. He could not avoid the press entirely. On his way out of the ring, he remembered to say something nice about Liston, and he asked people to let the new champion prove himself not just as a fighter, but as a man. "I think Sonny has inner quali-ties that are good," he said. "I think the public should give him a chance."

But there was more. In the dressing room, a reporter asked what had happened. What did they think had happened?

"I got caught with a good punch," Patterson said.

"A right hand, wasn't it?"

"I think it was."

"Did you hear the referee counting over you?"

"Not clearly at first. When I did begin to hear, I thought I heard him say 'eight' and I jumped up."

At one point, Patterson said, yes, he wanted to fight Liston again.

"Fight him again?" one reporter said. "Why didn't you fight him tonight?"

"Could you have gone on, Floyd?" another reporter asked.

"Sure, I thought I could go on. But then, I guess every fighter thinks that."

The reporters wanted to know what Liston was really like, how good a champion he would be, how brave.

"That remains to be seen," Patterson said. "We'll find out what he's like after somebody beats him, how he takes it. It's easy to do anything in victory. It's in defeat that a man reveals himself. In defeat I can't face people. I haven't the strength to say to people, I did my best, I'm sorry, and whatnot."

EVERYBODY AROUND SONNY LISTON SAID THE BEST THING ABOUT him was his wife, Geraldine. He was not the most loyal husband in the world, he played around everywhere he went, he drank, he gambled, but when Geraldine was with him, Liston was at ease, even gentle.

Geraldine couldn't bear to go to the stadium to see her husband fight. Instead she stayed up in their room at the Sheraton-Chicago, her hair in curlers and her face smeared with cold cream. In her bathrobe, she waited for a phone call from one of Sonny's cornermen.

"If it were up to me," she said, "I'd never have let Sonny do it. I'd take poverty over prizefighting. If we have kids, I won't let them fight either. True, we wouldn't have the money. But if I didn't have it, I wouldn't know about it. . . . I know Charles has done wrong, but if he weren't in the public eye, it would be forgotten. The sportswriters always keep bringing it up. It's like they don't ever want him to be good. How's a man going to be good, if folks won't let him? Many nights we talk it over. Sonny knows himself, and he knows if he becomes champ he only wants to live to make everybody realize he's a better person."

That was precisely Liston's intention. Now, in his dressing room, the reporters started to bombard him with questions.

"Hold it," one of the promotional hands said, silencing the room. "This is the heavyweight champion of the world. This is Mr. Liston. Let's treat him as you would the President of the United States."

Indeed. With the room now more in line with White House protocol, Liston made a special plea for himself, a request for forgiveness. He had served his time. He would try to stay out of trouble, do some good. "If the public allows me the chance to let bygones be bygones, I'll be a worthy champ," he said. "If they'll accept me, I'll prove it to them." He said that he had thanked Patterson after the fight for the opportunity. "Then I told him, 'I'll be as much of a man toward you as you were to me. And you were a heck of a good man.'"

Liston even defended Patterson as a fighter. When someone asked if Floyd lacked guts, Liston said, "That's got to be the stupidest thing I've ever heard. I felt enough of him under my glove on that last hook to know it was a good enough punch to put any man down hard. I looked at him close when he was going down and I took another good look when he hit the floor. He was gone. He surprised me for a tiny second when he got up on one knee, but then I could see he was like a man reaching for the alarm clock while he was still asleep."

Then someone asked if he'd been hurt at all in the fight.

"Only once," he said. "That was when the man said 'nine' and it looked like he might get up before 'ten.'"

WITH HIS DRESSING ROOM CLEARED, PATTERSON SHOWERED, dressed, and pasted on his beard. He waited awhile until he thought the stadium had emptied out and then found his friend Mickey Alan, the singer who had performed the national anthem that night. He and Alan got in a borrowed car that had been parked in an agreed-upon spot by Patterson's chauffeur, and they headed for the expressway—due east.

Patterson and Alan rode in silence. A couple of hours outside of Chicago, they stopped to stretch their legs by the side of the road. A police officer pulled up and asked Patterson for his driver's license. Floyd started to tear away his beard.

"What are you, some kind of actor?" the police officer said.

Then the cop looked at the license and realized he had stopped Floyd Patterson. He wished him luck and let him go.

Patterson did not drive home to his house in Yonkers. He went instead to his upstate training camp in Highland Mills. The trip took around twenty-two hours. When they arrived, Patterson asked Alan to leave. Patterson's head was throbbing. Liston had hit him hard and now he was feeling it. He started thinking that maybe he should start working out, get ready for another fight with Liston. He walked over to the gym. He flicked on the lights and realized most of his equipment was in Chicago.

Patterson's family and friends were still in Chicago, too. They never knew about his flight until news of it appeared in the papers. When reporters started asking Patterson's mother where her son had gone, she said she didn't know. "Floyd's a man that has a lot of pride, and I guess he just wants to be alone," she said. "I guess he just don't want to face the people because he always liked to give them his best." Cus D'Amato roamed the lobby of his hotel, wondering what would become of his fighter.

Not long after, Floyd decided to get away entirely. He went out to New York's Idlewild Airport carrying his passport, a suitcase, and his disguise. Before he got to the ticket counter, he put on his beard and mustache. He looked up at the departures board, scanned it for the next few flights, and bought a ticket to Madrid. It made no difference—anywhere but here. When he got to Madrid, he took a cab straight to a hotel and registered under the name Aaron Watson. For several days, Patterson wandered around the poorer sections of the city, faking a limp. The people stared at him. Patterson got the distinct impression they thought he was mad. He ate most of his meals in his hotel room. The one time he ate at a restaurant he ordered soup, not because he liked it—he hated soup—but because he figured that soup is what an old person would eat.

"You must wonder what makes a man do things like this," Patterson told Talese later. "Well, I wonder, too. And the answer is, I don't know. . . . But I think that within me, within every human being, there is a certain weakness. It is a weakness that exposes itself more when you're alone. And I have figured out that part of the reason I do the things I do, and cannot seem to conquer that one word—*myself*—is because . . . is because . . . I am a coward."

WHILE PATTERSON WAS ON HIS ROAD TRIP, LISTON WAS STILL IN Chicago. The morning after the fight, he appeared for the customary next-day press conference so that the writers would have some fresh quotes for their follow-up feature stories and profiles of the new champion.

Norman Mailer arrived after the press conference had started. He had been up all night drinking at the Playboy Mansion, and the more he had drunk, the more he had buttonholed people there about how to promote a rematch and make it a multimillion-dollar score. He himself would help promote the fight. He even insisted that he could prove Liston had not really won the fight in Chicago, that Patterson had gotten up off the floor and "existentially" beaten Liston in the ninth round. Mailer had had a great deal to drink.

"It was a revolutionary theory, I have to admit that," Jack Mc-Kinney, a sportswriter for the *Philadelphia Daily News* and a close friend of Liston's, told me. "We were at the Playboy Mansion practically all night, and every time Norman would lay this on me I'd move away a little further. I guess he saw me as a special conduit to the Liston people. I didn't want to insult him, but what can you say?"

Instead of getting some sleep between the party and the news conference, Mailer spent a couple of hours chatting up the chambermaid and then went to the hotel ballroom where Liston was scheduled to appear. He took a seat fairly close to the front of the room. But it turned out that he didn't have the proper credentials, or so the hotel officials believed, and they asked him to leave. Mailer insisted that he had been asked to speak at this press conference and began arguing.

"If you don't leave, we'll have to remove you by force," one of the security officers said.

"Remove me by force," Mailer insisted. Before they could do the job, a reporter for the *Times* asked Mailer (as if to compound the peculiarity of the moment) for a statement.

"Yes," Mailer said. "I came here prepared to make a case that I am the only man in this country who can build the second Patterson-Liston fight into a two-million-dollar gate instead of a two-hundred-thousand-dollar dog in Miami. I wish to handle the press relations for this second fight. For various and private reasons I need to make a great deal of money in the next two months."

And with that a security guard put his hand on Mailer's shoulder and asked, "Would you come with us?"

"No."

"We'll have to carry you out."

"Carry me out."

Norman Mailer was thus carried out of the ballroom on a chair looking like the Hebrew emperor of ice cream. By the time he argued his way back upstairs and into the ballroom, Liston had taken his place at the dais and was answering the usual sort of postfight questions. Was he ever hurt? (No.) Would he fight all comers? (Of course. Bring 'em on.) What about the past? (What about it?) Jack

McKinney felt that some of the reporters were trying to bait Liston, trying to get him to act the role of the boor, the thug. "Sonny'd been burned by these guys so many times," McKinney said. "He had what you call 'mother wit,' a black concept, meaning the innate sense you are born with, what you inherit from your mother. If there had been some way of measuring Sonny's IQ in that way, he'd be in the Mensa range. The whites would be shocked but in the West Philly poolrooms they knew it was true, though he could be stupid sometimes, naive. Every question seemed loaded to him and so he was being careful."

Then Mailer stood up to speak. Some of the sportswriters, red-meat conservatives like Dick Young of the New York *Daily News,* who were protective of their prerogatives as members of a confraternity and made nervous by Mailer's standing in the literary world, started muttering. They didn't consider Mailer one of them. He was a novelist, an art guy, not a fight guy. Some of them thought of Mailer as a Greenwich Village freak, a fool, the same guy who had stabbed his wife with a penknife just two years before. But Mailer was not about to be dissuaded, and he started to repeat the fancies of the night before, his notion of a Patterson victory, his plans for promoting a rematch. The muttering in the room grew louder. The champion, who didn't know Mailer, seemed curious, if not entirely amused.

"Well, I'm not a reporter but I'd like to say—" Mailer said.

Now someone tried to shout Mailer down.

"Shut the bum up!"

"No," said Liston, "let the bum speak."

"I picked Floyd Patterson to win by a one-punch knockout in the sixth," Mailer said, "and I *still* think I was right."

"You're still drunk," Liston said, reasonably.

While some of the reporters hooted at him, Mailer got up and walked behind the dais, as if to continue the conversation with Liston one-on-one. A couple of Liston's men blocked his way and advised the author never to approach Mr. Liston from the rear. Mailer waited while Liston attended to some other questions, then, circling around to the front of the champion, picked up where he had left off.

"What did you do," Liston said, "go out and get another drink?"

"Liston, I still say Floyd Patterson can beat you."

"Aw, why don't you stop being a sore loser?"

"You called me a bum," Mailer said.

Liston laughed. "Well, you are a bum," he said. "Everybody's a bum. I'm a bum, too. It's just that I'm a bigger bum than you are." Liston stood up and extended his right hand. "Shake, bum," he said.

Mailer pulled Liston in close by the hand and said, "I'm pulling this caper for a reason. I know a way to build the next fight from a two-hundred-thousand-dollar dog in Miami to a two-million-dollar gate in New York."

"Say, that last drink really set you up," Liston said. "Why don't you go and get me a drink, you bum?"

"I'm not your flunky," Mailer said.

Mailer thought he had gained Liston's respect, and the sound of Liston's laughter tickled him, too. "The hint of a chuckle of corny old darky laughter, cotton-field giggles, peeped out a moment from his throat," is the way Mailer put it in his *Esquire* article.

Actually, Liston was not tickled at all. After it was over, he kept referring to Mailer as "that drunk" and "the son of a bitch who was trying to ruin my press conference." He had wanted to make a decent impression on the reporters, but, as it happened, the memorable story, the one that would dominate the papers, was Mailer's, not his.

LISTON SPENT THE REST OF THE DAY RELAXING, EATING, AND watching television with Geraldine, his friend Jack McKinney, and his entourage. McKinney wouldn't say so, but he was worried about how Liston would be received back in Philadelphia. The mayor, James H. J. Tate, had sent a telegram full of congratulations but containing unmistakable hints of condescension, even a warning: "Your feat demonstrates that a man's past does not have to dictate his future. I know all Philadelphians join with me in extending best wishes for a successful reign and that you will wear the crown in the fine tradition of Philadelphian champions before you."

Liston had no reason to expect a great outpouring of affection from the people of Philadelphia. Not long before the Patterson fight, he had gotten himself in just enough trouble to solidify his jailbird image. Late one night, Liston was driving with a friend from the neighborhood in Fairmount Park. They saw a woman driving a black Cadillac, and Liston's friend assumed the woman was a prostitute. Liston caught up with the Cadillac. The woman, who was actually employed by the board of education, pulled over, thinking Liston was a police officer. Just then, a squad car pulled up. Liston panicked and took off at sixty-five miles an hour. Time and again, since moving to Philadelphia, Liston had gotten in minor scrapes with the police; he had even been arrested for standing around on a street corner. Every police officer in the city had a picture of Liston on his sun visor. As it turned out, the case against Liston for the "lark in the park" was a bust—the various charges were either dismissed or ended in acquittal—but the publicity, especially in the local papers, the *Inquirer,* the *Bulletin,* and the tabloid *Daily News,* made him out to be, once again, an unrepentant thug. And so, after the fight, when Liston called home for a report on the attention he was getting, a friend read him Larry Merchant's scathing column in the *Daily News:* "So it is true—in a fair fight between good and evil, evil must win. . . . A celebration for Philadelphia's first heavyweight champ is now in order. Emily Post probably would recommend a ticker-tape parade. For confetti we can use shredded warrants of arrest."

Liston was scheduled to leave Chicago for Philadelphia the next day, and while he slept, McKinney stayed up half the night working the phones, trying to arrange for a decent reception. But after talking to a series of sources in City Hall, he realized that Mayor Tate had decided to stiff Liston.

The next afternoon, on the plane, Liston asked McKinney to sit with him, and as they ate lunch, Liston described how he planned to conduct himself as champion and what he would tell the people and the press in Philadelphia. He talked about how he would listen to Joe Louis's fights on the radio as a kid and how the announcer would say Louis was a credit to his race, to the human race—the old Jimmy Cannon line—and how that made him feel warm inside. He said he wanted to meet the president and win over the NAACP even though they had all been rooting for Patterson to win.

"There's a lot of things I'm gonna do," Liston told McKinney. "But one thing's very important: I want to reach my people. I want to reach them and tell them, 'You don't have to worry about me disgracing you. You won't have to worry about me stopping your progress.' I want to go to colored churches and colored neighborhoods. I know it was in the papers that the better class of colored people were hoping I'd lose, even praying I'd lose, because they was afraid I wouldn't know how to act. . . . I don't mean to be saying I'm just gonna be champion of my own people. It says now I'm the *world's* champion and that's just the way it's gonna be. I want to go to a lot of places—like orphan homes and reform schools. I'll be able to say, 'Kid, I know it's tough for you and it might even get tougher. But don't give up on the world. Good things can happen if you let them.' "

In front of almost any other reporter, Liston would never dare be so reflective as he was now with McKinney. The others, he felt, always turned his past against him. But he was relaxed with McKinney. McKinney was a character around town, a kind of Philly Renaissance man, who wrote about sports and classical music, who took up boxing and even sparred once with Liston. As McKinney listened to Liston, he thought he was sincere, and it killed him to think of the hurt he was about to experience. By the time the plane was in its landing pattern, McKinney was at the point of tears, filled with rage and frustration.

The plane landed. The door opened. Liston came out first and looked down at the tarmac. McKinney saw Liston's Adam's apple move and his shoulders shudder. There was no crowd on the tarmac, no welcome at all, only a desultory ground crew doing its job. Liston adjusted his tie and put on his hat, a trilby with a little red feather in the band. "You could see Sonny literally deflate like a balloon with the air letting out," McKinney said. "It was a good forty-five seconds or a minute before he finished taking in the whole scene, confirming to himself that there was nothing there, and then the next thing you know, his back stiffened and his shoulders rose again, as if he was saying to himself, 'Well, if this is the way it's going to be . . .' It was amazing. There wasn't even a tertiary flunky from City Hall, much less the mayor and the key to Philadelphia."

Liston met briefly with a few reporters inside the terminal and headed for home. On the way to West Philly, he turned to McKinney and said, "I think I'll get out tomorrow and do all the things I've always done. Walk down the block and buy the papers, stop in the drugstore, talk to the neighbors. Then I'll see how the real people feel. Maybe then I'll start to feeling like a champion. You know, it's really a lot like an election, only in reverse. Here I'm already in office, but now I have to go out and start campaigning."

After a few weeks, it was clear to Liston that there would be no endorsement from the NAACP. There would be no parade. There would be no invitation to the White House. His hopes faded to bitterness. "I didn't expect the president to invite me into the White House and let me sit next to Jackie and wrestle with those nice Kennedy kids," he told his sparring partner Ray Schoeninger, "but I sure didn't expect to be treated like no sewer rat."

CHAPTER THREE

Mr. Fury and
Mr. Gray

YEARS LATER, WHEN LISTON WAS SPENDING HIS TIME WITH thumb-breakers and casino rummies in Las Vegas, he sensed his life heading toward oblivion. The history of fighters is the history of men who end up damaged: the great Sam Langford at the beginning of the century barred by the "color line" from fighting for the title and left blind and broke; Joe Louis strung out on cocaine and running from the IRS; Beau Jack shining shoes at the Fontainebleau Hotel; Ike Williams fleeced by the mob and in debt to the government; "Two Ton" Tony Galento wrestling an octopus and boxing a kangaroo to make a living. Liston knew he could expect no better. "Someday they're gonna write a blues song just for fighters," he once said. "It'll be for slow guitar, soft trumpet, and a bell." From start to finish, Liston's life was a mean one run by careless people, and so a mournful blues, an instrumental just as he arranged it, seems right.

The incident at the Philadelphia airport was no false harbinger of his reign as champion. Liston could forget about adoration, he could forget about recognition from all but hard-core boxing fans who now judged him indomitable. Muhammad Ali would rise above his sport after mastering it, but Liston was pure boxing and, in the eyes of the public, only boxing. He was also a source of mockery, the tabloid joke of his day. Many felt free to use the full range of racist tropes to have their laughs. He was the goon, the ape, the beast, the monster of nightmares; he was the dangerous

John Carbo (wearing glasses) at the Elizabeth Street police station
following his arrest. Detective Nicholas Barrett, of the
district attorney's office, is at right.

creature you paid to see in his roped-off cage. Jim Murray, a columnist at the *Los Angeles Times,* wrote that realizing Liston was now champion was "like finding a live bat on a string under your Christmas tree." Arthur Daley, the columnist on the *New York Times* sports page and a winner of the Pulitzer Prize for commentary, wanted his readers to know that Liston was even more horrible than they could readily imagine. "The public instinctively dislikes Liston, and that's grossly unfair," Daley wrote. "The average fan doesn't even know the man. One really has to know Liston to dislike him with the proper intensity. He's arrogant, surly, mean, rude, and altogether frightening. He's the last man anyone would want to meet in a dark alley." *Esquire* played with the idea of Liston-as-Antichrist when George Lois, the art director, dressed him up as a glowering Santa Claus—an image that became the most famous cover in the history of the magazine.

As feared as Liston was now in the ring (two minutes and six seconds!), he could be mocked without fear of reprisal. No one felt freer to do so than the tribe that owned him. Liston was once at a hotel in Los Angeles and ran into an acquaintance, Moe Dalitz, one of the most powerful mob figures in Las Vegas and late of the bootlegging business. As a joke, Liston made a fist at Dalitz and cocked it. This is an old and friendly convention of boxers, and yet, by way of reply, Dalitz turned to Liston and said, "If you hit me, nigger, you'd better kill me, because if you don't, I'll make one telephone call and you'll be dead in twenty-four hours." Liston did not reply. Dalitz was a Mafia god in Las Vegas, a link to the Teamsters. In such company, Liston knew his place.

One of the few columnists who tried to see Liston's ascent to the championship as anything other than an offense to American society and the tender sensibilities of its citizens was Murray Kempton of the *New York Post.* Kempton was a mandarin among the street columnists, schooled in subjects as various as Etruscan mosaics and the internal politics of the Five Families. Kempton visited sports rather as a duke descends on the fens; he did it rarely, but with panache and a sense of history. In Liston he saw a man "whose experience with American society has been confined to the Teamsters Union, prison, and the sport of boxing." With his nineteenth-century prose, Kempton managed a sneer at those who would judge prizefighting and its champions with the airs of a moralist. "The Negro heavyweights, as Negroes tend to do, have usually given that sense of being men above their calling," he wrote. "Floyd Patterson sounded like a Freedom Rider. We return to reality with Liston. . . . We have at last a heavyweight champion on the moral level of the men who own him. This is the source of horror which Liston has aroused; he is boxing's perfect symbol. He tells us the truth about it. The heavyweight championship is, after all, a fairly squalid office. . . ." Kempton was under no illusion that Liston was some sort of choirboy *manqué*; nevertheless, he managed to find reformist possibility in the champion's nastiness. Liston, he wrote, "has already helped us grow up as a country because he is the first morally inferior Negro I can think of to be given an equal opportunity. He will help us grow up further if he destroys the illusion that a man whose trade it is to beat another man senseless for money represents an image which at all costs must be kept pure for American youth."

Unlike some new champions, Liston did not assume his office a total stranger to the public. He had been on television often enough, beating up the likes of Eddie Machen, Cleveland Williams, and Roy Harris, but he had made his most vivid personal impression appearing as a witness in 1960 before the Senate subcommittee on antitrust and monopoly, chaired by Estes Kefauver, Democrat of Tennessee. Kefauver's political career had taken an enormous leap in 1951 after he chaired a series of hearings on organized crime. As a result of the clamorous publicity he attracted after those hearings, Kefauver made a run at the Democratic nomination for president in 1952 before losing out to Adlai Stevenson. In 1956, Kefauver joined Stevenson on the losing Democratic ticket.

Boxing was a more limited target than organized crime, certainly, but still a fairly obvious one, splashy, hard to miss. The perfidy of the business was well known. Throughout the fifties, to read Dan Parker in the New York *Daily Mirror* or Jimmy Cannon in the *Post* was to scan a bill of particulars against a dirty game run entirely by mobsters—mainly Italian and Jewish mobsters. After the war there was not a single champion who was not, in some way, touched by the Mafia, if not wholly owned and operated by it. Kefauver (with substantial help from his chief counsel, John Gurnee Bonomi) intended to prove the case and instigate a reform of boxing.

Liston's appearance before the committee was significant not so much for the details he provided about his particular circumstances—most of the time he either feigned ignorance or demonstrated it—no, what was more striking was Liston's presentation of himself as a man of limitations who started out with nothing and then, having reached great public standing, had little more independence than his forefathers in chains. Even the most unforgiving viewer of the hearings got a sense that Liston's choices coming out of jail were either to fight under the management of the mob or to face the job market as an illiterate black man in 1956. "I had to eat," he would say, and the mob was there to mete out the gruel.

During the course of his testimony, Liston was asked about a letter he allegedly wrote or dictated to the fighter Ike Williams. Liston claimed he didn't remember anything about such a letter, and on this point Senator Everett Dirksen, a hoary Republican from Illinois, began to press him in his uniquely orotund way. Liston's lawyer reminded the committee that his client did not read.

"You do make out figures, though, don't you?" Dirksen asked Liston. "You can tell figures? Suppose there is a dollar sign and '100.' Can you tell that means one hundred dollars?"

Liston allowed that he could.

"Or one thousand dollars?" Dirksen said. "Well, you can make out figures. I thought I saw your name signed here allegedly by you. Do you sign your name?"

"Yes, sir."

"Do you sign your address? Can you sign your address?"

"No, sir," Liston said.

"Your house number? Who does that for you?"

"Well, I can write '5785.' "

"You can write numbers?"

"Right."

"For instance, here is a signature that says, 'Charles Liston, 39 Chestnut.' Would you be able to write 'Chestnut'?"

"No, sir."

"You wouldn't. But you can write your name?"

"Yes, sir."

"And the number. Suppose your share of the purse, a fight purse, was twenty-five thousand dollars, and they handed you a check for it. Could you tell whether they were giving you a check for twenty-five thousand dollars?"

"Well," Liston said, "not exactly."

The level of condescension on the committee (and here the noxious Dirksen deserves special mention) was such that Liston was treated much like a curiosity in a circus sideshow: Sonny the Strongman. Watch him punch! Watch him speak! It seemed to be a matter of amusement to the senators that Liston—a black man, raised in the rural South during the Depression—was no scholar.

"How much education did you get?" Kefauver asked.

"I didn't get any," Liston said.

"You didn't go to school at all?"

"No, sir."

"You didn't have much opportunity, I guess."

"Too many kids."

"How many kids were there?"

"Well, my father had twenty-five."

"Twenty-five children?"

"Altogether."

"Twenty-five children altogether," Kefauver said. "Senator Dirksen has an observation."

Senator Dirksen did, indeed. "I was going to say your father is a champion in his own right." The committee and the audience in the Senate Office Building, Room 308, had a nice laugh at that.

CHARLES LISTON STARTED OUT WITH LESS THAN NOTHING. HE may have lied to the committee about his associations with the underworld, but he told the truth about his origins insofar as he knew the details. To the end of his life, Liston never really knew the exact year and place of his birth. He tended to insist on 1932 or 1933 and he was said to have been born in various Arkansas cotton farming towns west of Memphis and east of Little Rock: Forrest City, or, perhaps Sand Slough, part of the Morledge Plantation, where his father, Tobe Liston, worked. When Liston turned professional and needed the necessary documents for the licensing process, his managers cooked up a birth certificate that read May 8, 1932, though his early arrest records pegged the date, more realistically, at 1927 or 1928.

Later in Liston's career, when people would press him about his age (he always looked so much older than he said he was), his customary form of reply was intimidation. He would accuse the writer in question of calling his mother a liar, which was enough to end the conversation. In those rare moments when he was with someone he trusted, Liston would say that on the day he was born someone in the family commemorated the event by carving some names and dates on a tree.

"Trouble is," Liston said, "they cut down the tree."

The Liston family was enormous. Helen Baskin had eleven children with Tobe Liston before she gave birth to Charles. Tobe Liston had had a dozen children with another woman before he met Helen. The Listons were sharecroppers who had moved to Arkansas from Mississippi in 1916 when Tobe was fifty and Helen was sixteen. They rented land from a black farm operator named Pat Heron and grew cotton mainly, and also peanuts, corn, sorghum, and sweet potatoes. "The boss man," Helen Liston said, "got three-fourths of what you raised." The house was a flimsy and impossibly crowded shack that was cold in winter, broiling in summer.

Rather than send Sonny to school, Tobe Liston sent him out to the fields when he was eight. His credo was that if children were old enough to come to the dinner table, they were old enough to farm. Tobe was brutal to his children, not least to Sonny. He beat him so often that if he skipped a day, Sonny would ask, "How come you didn't whip me today?" The welts of childhood were easy to see on Sonny's back all his life.

"I can understand the reason for my failings," Sonny said years later. "When I was a kid I had nothing but a lot of brothers and sisters, a helpless mother, and a father who didn't care about a single one of us. We grew up like heathens. We hardly had enough food to keep from starving, no shoes, only a few clothes, and nobody to help us escape from the horrible life we lived."

During the war and for some time after, the harvest was poor in the farmlands of eastern Arkansas. Helen Liston went off to work in a shoe factory in St. Louis and took along a few of her children. She left her youngest son behind. But when Liston turned thirteen, he decided he could no longer stand all the cotton picking and the beatings, and he thought about joining his mother.

"One morning, I got up early, and thrashed the pecans off my brother-in-law's tree and carried the nuts to town and sold them," he told the sportswriter A. S. "Doc" Young. "That gave me enough money to buy a ticket to St. Louis. I figured the city would be like the country, and all I had to do was to ask somebody where my mother lived and they'd tell me she lived down the road a piece. But when I got to the city, there were too doggone many people there, and I just wandered around lost." Liston ended up sleeping at a police station for a few nights, where he was fed bologna sandwiches and taken good care of. "One morning I told my story to a wino and he says I favor this lady that lives down the street. He took me over to the house, and I knocked on the door and my brother Curtice opened the door. From then on I stayed with my mother."

At first, Sonny worked for an honest wage—if a pathetic one. "I sold coal. I sold ice. I sold wood. I got fifteen bucks a week in a chicken market cleaning chickens. . . . On the good days I ate. On the bad ones I told my stomach to forget it. And me and trouble was never far apart. If a colored kid's going to get by he's got to learn one thing fast—there ain't nobody going to look after him but him. I learned." Liston went to school for a short while, but he suffered from the embarrassment of his illiteracy and his size. His parents were small people—Tobe was five-six, Helen five-one—but he was not. In his early teens, Liston was already man-sized, with huge hands and a burly build from years of farmwork. "Other kids would see me coming out of such small kids' room and they would make fun of me and start laughing, and I started fighting," Liston said. "And then I started playing hooky, and from hooky I led to another thing, so I wound up in the wrong school—well, the house of detention."

By the time Liston was sixteen, he was over six feet tall and weighed more than two hundred pounds. He ran with some of the nastiest boys in his neighborhood, stealing from grocery stores and restaurants. "When I was a kid, I didn't have nothing going for me but my fists and my strength," Liston said. "I didn't have nothing to eat. I'd been eating a day here and a day there, but eating's a hard habit to get out of. Anyway, these kids come along and they had the bright idea of knocking over this store. All I could see at the end of it was a great plate of food, and if we had to take a gun along to get it that was okay, too." Sonny was a lousy criminal. He wore the same yellow-and-black-checked shirt so often that he became known to the police as the Yellow Shirt Bandit.

His first appearance on the St. Louis police docket came just after Christmas in 1949. Liston and two of his buddies held up a clerk near the Mississippi waterfront. On the wanted list, Liston became known as "#1 Negro." His arrest records show a mugging for six dollars; his gang beat a man in an alley for nine dollars in ones; there were petty robberies at gas stations, robberies at luncheonettes. One of Liston's criminal exploits netted him exactly five cents. He was finally arrested on January 14, 1950, after sticking up a place on Market Street called the Unique Cafe. The haul was thirty-seven dollars.

Twenty-five minutes after the robbery, a young patrolman named David Herleth arrested Liston when he saw him at one o'clock in the morning running from a barbecue place to his house. The only weapon Liston carried was a roll of nickels. He was, of course, wearing his yellow shirt.

Liston was convicted of two counts of robbery in the first degree and two counts of larceny. He was sentenced to five years in the Missouri State Penitentiary, a huge brick prison on the banks of the Missouri River in Jefferson City. He began his sentence in June 1950. According to Liston's accounting, he was twenty years old. The *St. Louis Globe-Democrat* said he was twenty-two.

EVEN AT HIS MOST SELF-DRAMATIZING, LISTON NEVER COMplained about prison. He always said that the food in the pen was the best he had ever eaten—a statement made all the more vivid when one is reminded that the prisoner riots at Missouri State in 1954 were over the quality of the food. Liston had not had the opportunity to cultivate much experience or expertise at table. When he was eventually paroled, a friend of his bought him a chicken dinner as a treat, but Liston stared down at the plate as if he were eyeing the impenetrable mysteries of the universe.

"Why don't you eat it?" his friend said.

"I don't know how," Liston said.

Except for a few fights in the yard, Liston was a fairly well-behaved prisoner. He worked in the laundry and as a messenger.

His singular stroke of fortune was to win the notice of the prison's chaplains, first the Rev. Edward Schlattmann and then Father Alois Stevens. At Missouri State Penitentiary the chaplain also carried the title of athletic director. Schlattmann brought Liston to the gym and introduced him to the sport of boxing, and then after he was transferred a few weeks later the job fell to Father Stevens. Stevens was immediately impressed by Liston's strength—Liston was knocking out men with his left jab alone—but he was worried that he would never be able to win him an early parole. Liston could hardly express himself, except with a baleful stare. He used an X to sign his name. "Sonny was just a big, ignorant, pretty nice kid," Stevens said. "I tried to teach him the alphabet, but it was hard to impress on him the importance of it. 'Surely you'll want to read the papers about yourself,' I'd tell him, but he wasn't too faithful. He was very penurious with his words."

Liston soon became the prison champion, heavyweight division. He got his training from Sam Eveland, a car thief and a Golden Gloves champion from St. Louis. "He was the real thing right away," Eveland told me. "You'd show him a punch or a technique and by the end of the day he had it down. But poor, poor Sonny. He could fight and that was it. He had the mind of an eleven-year-old, an overgrown kid. He could be the sweetest guy in the world, and then he'd just snap, go off. But there's no denying it—he could hit like a mule. Pretty soon there was no one left inside who would get in the ring with him."

Father Stevens saw potential in Liston, at least as an athlete, and he called the sports editor at the St. Louis Globe-Democrat, Bob Burnes, to get some advice on how to help train Liston as a fighter. Father Stevens was so naive about the greater world of prizefighting that he asked Burnes how he could arrange for Liston to fight the top heavyweight contender, Rocky Marciano. Burnes laughed and sent Stevens to two of his friends: Monroe Harrison, a former sparring partner for Joe Louis who was now working as a school janitor, and Frank Mitchell, the publisher of a black-oriented weekly called the St. Louis Argus. Harrison and Mitchell were interested enough to arrange a jailhouse sparring session, and they hired a well-regarded local heavyweight named Thurman Wilson and headed out to the penitentiary.

In the car, Wilson asked Mitchell, "How many rounds?"

"As many as you want," Mitchell said, "but we don't want to show the boy up."

At that point, Liston was not nearly the fighter he would be. He was all left hand. In the language of the game, he couldn't wipe his ass with his right. But the left was more than sufficient for Thurman Wilson; the jab was a bludgeon and the hook a deathblow. When Liston worked the heavy bag in the prison gym, he left behind a dent the size of a medicine ball. In the ring, he dented Wilson, landing the jab and the hook over and over again. After four rounds of battery, Wilson plodded back to his corner in terrible pain and told Mitchell, "You better get me out of this ring. He's going to kill me."

Harrison went to Burnes's office to thank him.

"You finally found me a live one," he said.

There was still the nagging problem of Liston's incarceration. After about a year of campaigning with the parole board, in October 1952 Father Stevens managed to arrange Liston's release from prison, with the proviso that he would look after him, along with Frank Mitchell and Monroe Harrison. This would eventually prove a dubious arrangement. Mitchell, it was well known in St. Louis, had a close relationship with the biggest mobster in town, John Vitale—and the more Liston attracted attention, the more he interested John Vitale and the mob.

Initially, Liston's closest working relationship was with Harrison, who was known as an honest and hardworking man. Harrison was eager to see Sonny on a righteous path. He set him up with a room at the Pine Street YMCA and a job at a local steel company. For a while, at least, this arrangement provided stability. At night, after work, Liston trained either at the local Masonic Temple or at the Ringside Gym on Olive Street. Right away he started working out to the sound of "Night Train," a sinuous favorite of strippers written and made popular by the St. Louis sax player Jimmy Forrest. (Later, Liston would convert to James Brown's "Night Train," a darker, more raucous version of the same tune.) With Harrison in his corner, Liston started to win fights—first in Golden Gloves competitions around the country and then, beginning in September 1953, against professional heavyweights. Eventually the papers started coming around. Liston was a prospect.

"Sonny's the type of person who needs understanding," Harrison told a reporter who visited him in his basement office at the Carr Lane Branch School in St. Louis. "He's vicious all the way. Youth, all his youth! He needs someone to help him control his emotions. He must be kept busy until all that youth and strength leaves him, like it leaves all of us. Right now he's like the leopard, that animal out there in the jungle. . . . He needs training. He needs love. The right people have to take an interest in the boy and treat him like a member of the family. You got to talk to him about what he talks about. Otherwise, he's got no conversation."

Harrison tried to keep Liston occupied and off the streets when he wasn't working or in the gym. They'd listen to the radio, play checkers. And every once in a while, Harrison would bring Liston down to the *Globe-Democrat* for an interview with Burnes.

"Tell Mr. Bob you been a good boy," Harrison would prompt Liston.

"You been a good boy?" Burnes would ask.

"Yes, Mr. Bob."

MONROE HARRISON HELPED MANAGE LISTON THROUGH EIGHT professional fights. Then Sonny met a clever boxer named Marty Marshall, a tough journeyman who broke Liston's jaw and beat him in a close eight-round decision. Liston would claim that Marshall had caught him with his mouth open—"I was laughing!" But for at least that moment, Liston's prospects dimmed. Harrison, for his part, had to take stock. His wife was extremely ill. He was broke. Liston was now no longer a sure thing—far from it. Harrison had no choice, really, but to sell his share in the future of Sonny Liston. Frank Mitchell bought him out for six hundred dollars.

A few years later, Mitchell would also appear before the Kefauver hearings, but he would not be quite as open about his past as Liston. For good reason. His record showed twenty-six arrests. He had a reputation as a gambler and, far worse, as a front for Vitale. Vitale, for his part, had been arrested fifty-eight times and convicted three times. When Mitchell was asked about his acquaintance with Vitale, he said it was all a matter of golf etiquette, a chance meeting on a public course, a fervent desire to be polite: "You see, there were twosomes. They started Vitale's twosome and then they added my twosome in. I couldn't afford to discriminate on a public golf course, me of all people." Certainly not.

The two main mob operations in St. Louis were run by the Syrians and the Sicilians. The Sicilian operation was John Vitale's realm. The center of mob control in the Midwest was Chicago— the province of Bernard Glickman and Glickman's ultimate boss, Sam Giancana—and Vitale, as the St. Louis boss, always made sure to pay tribute to Chicago. Vitale was ostensibly the president of the Anthony Novelty Company, a jukebox and pinball machine concern that he left to his underlings; he kept himself busy in the construction business and in the world of organized labor.

Through Frank Mitchell, Vitale soon met Liston, and he gave him a job at the Union Electric plant in South County unloading firebricks. Liston was not called upon to unload bricks very often. His true employment was otherwise. Working alongside a three-hundred-pound goon named Barney Baker, Liston was put in charge of keeping black workers in line. Baker was a New Yorker who kicked around various unions and mob organizations, including Meyer and Jake Lansky's operation in Washington, D.C.

"At any sign of trouble they'd send Sonny out and maybe he'd stare a guy down or just break his leg," said Sam Eveland, Liston's friend from prison. "In those days they didn't make much of a secret of those things." Liston had become, in the Teamsters parlance of the day, a head-breaker. Later, Liston admitted that yes, many of his new friends had been in jail or were headed there. "I never knew there were other kinds of people," he said. "I'd heard of Negro doctors and lawyers and outstanding businessmen, of course, but how was I going to get with them? They were educated, refined people. I wasn't educated and I knew I wasn't refined."

Officers of the St. Louis Police Department who testified at the Kefauver hearings were interested more in the assault than the sociology of the situation. "He whopped a few out in the country," said Sergeant Joseph Moose. "He didn't need to whop too many— just stared at them."

Liston also did odd jobs for an associate of Vitale, Raymond Sarkis. "Mostly I'd drive his car, a white Cadillac," said Liston. "I know they was jealous and they would even the score by pulling me in."

Captain John Doherty was a tough cop in charge of what was known in town as the "hoodlum squad," and it was not long before he identified Liston as precisely that, a hoodlum. He set out to cut off Liston's relations with Vitale's men and ordered his officers to carry out a policy of diligent harassment. "Every time we could jump Liston up, find him, we did," he said. "We wouldn't tolerate beating any citizens up, robbing them, which he was known for. I must have talked to Liston on twenty occasions. 'Where you coming from?' 'I don't know.' 'Where you going?' 'I don't know.' We tried to treat him pretty good. I told him he had great potentialities, but if you're going to associate with Vitale and them other hots, I said, you can't make a decent living. He never accepted my advice. He's dumb. He's got a vicious temper."

Liston said that not only was he picked up repeatedly and held overnight occasionally, his life was threatened. He said Captain Doherty finally told him to leave St. Louis, and if he didn't, "they are going to find you in the alley." The police denied that story in its particulars, but not in its general theme. James Chapman, the assistant chief, said, "Doherty got a bum rap on that. *I'm* the one that told him that."

While working in his union slot, Liston also beat men up in the ring. He could hardly wait to avenge his laughing loss to Marty Marshall. In fact, he avenged himself twice, both vicious knockouts. Years later, Marshall said, "Nobody should be hit like that. I think about it *now* and I hurt. . . . I've got two parts of me that remember Sonny Liston—that ear he hit and my stomach. He hit me in the stomach with a left hand in the sixth. That wasn't a knockdown. It couldn't be. I was paralyzed. I just couldn't move. I didn't move enough to fall down."

But for all his success, Liston continued to enrage the city police with his daytime employment. To anyone reading the local papers, it was obvious that the constant minor confrontations between Sonny and the police would escalate, and the police were not afraid to say so publicly. Sergeant James Reddick, a former Golden Gloves champion, said of Liston, "He hangs out with a bunch of dogs. I'd like to show him how bad he is. If he ever crossed me, I'd *baptize* his ass."

One of the few good things ever to happen to Liston came about in a rainstorm in 1956. A young local munitions factory worker named Geraldine was soaked through as she stood out on the sidewalk waiting for a bus. Liston was driving by and saw her. What happened next had to count, in Liston's book, as true chivalry: he threw the car into reverse, got out of the car, *picked up* Geraldine, put her in the front seat, and said, "You're a very attractive lady. You shouldn't have to stand out there and get wet." They married later in the year.

But 1956 was also a year of disaster. On the evening of May 5, the Listons went out to a party. The night would end with Sonny beating up a police officer, an offense that brought him the better part of a year in a state workhouse.

Both Liston and his antagonist, Patrolman Thomas Mellow, agreed in testimony that their dispute began in an alley and centered around a waiting taxi. Mellow said that when he saw the cab idling in the alley, he told the driver, a black man named Patterson, to move along or risk a summons. Liston appeared and told Mellow, "You can't give him no ticket."

"The hell I can't," Mellow said, and took out his ticket book.

According to Mellow, Liston then snatched him up in a bear hug and lifted him off the ground. "I didn't realize what was happening until he grabbed me. Kind of caught me off guard. After they got me in the dark part of the alley, Patterson says, 'Get his gun.' We struggled and all three of us fell. Liston got my gun out. Then Patterson says, 'Shoot that white son of a bitch.' Liston releases me and points the gun at my head. I'm pushing up on the barrel with both hands to keep from looking down the muzzle. They were walking all over me. I hollered, 'Don't shoot me.' Liston let up all of a sudden, hit me over the left eye with either the gun or his fist. It took seven stitches." Mellow's arm and knee were broken "either from the fall or somebody stomping me."

Liston's version of the story has him protesting Mellow's treatment of the cab driver and Mellow then turning to him and saying, "You're a smart nigger." "And when I say, 'I'm not smart,' he reaches for his gun and tries to take it out his holster, but I take it away from him," Liston said. "Later the cop said I was drunk. Now how could a drunk handle a sober cop trained to make arrests and to pull his gun?"

BY EARLY 1958, LISTON HAD FINISHED HIS STINT IN THE WORK-house and was fighting again. He was winning at a rate sufficient to attract the attention of mobsters bigger than the likes of Vitale and even Bernie Glickman. Liston acceded to a new ownership arrangement organized by New York–based mobsters (as if he had any choice) and moved to Philadelphia in order to be closer to the real action in boxing, which in the fifties meant New York and its ancillary cities.

The new contract meted out 52 percent to Frankie Carbo, the most powerful figure in boxing; 12 percent each to Vitale and Carbo's liege man, Frank "Blinky" Palermo; and 24 percent to Joseph "Pep" Barone, another Carbo "associate" who would act, for public purposes, as Liston's manager. According to an FBI investigator, William Roemer, the Midwest mobsters were outraged that they had lost a fighter of such enormous potential. A couple of years after the takeover, according to *Vanity Fair*, Sam Giancana flew from Chicago to Atlantic City for a meeting of the Commission, the ruling body of organized crime. Giancana appealed to Thomas "Three-Finger Brown" Lucchese and Carlo Gambino of New York, among others, but he was rebuffed. Carbo himself was a member of Lucchese's mob family. A potential heavyweight champion was too big a property to leave to St. Louis.

Liston was, in essence, the last in a long line, the last great champion to be delivered straight into the hands of the mob. It would take Cassius Clay, who was still finding his way as a contender, to break the grip of organized crime. For him, the Nation of Islam would form that sense of protection.

Long before the rise of Frankie Carbo, a generation of Prohibition-era gangsters ran fighters, promoted fights, fixed fights, and bet on fights, such men as Owney Madden, Frenchy DeMange, Bill Duffy, Frankie Yale, Al Capone, Lucky Luciano, Boo Boo Hoff, Kid Dropper, Frankie Marlow, Legs Diamond, and Dutch Schultz. The underworld liked boxing because boxers themselves are outsiders. The saying in boxing is that only a fool or a desperate man gets hit in the head to earn a living. And since boxers come into the game from the margins, they are approachable by men from the margins of business. They are not likely to complain too loudly, for their life presents them with so few choices. Boxers don't get scholarships; there is no alumni society waiting at the door, glad hand extended.

Paul John Carbo was born on New York's Lower East Side in 1904 and grew up mainly in the Bronx. He did a great deal of that growing up committing petty crimes. At eighteen, he was arrested for assault and grand larceny. When he was twenty, he was charged with shooting a butcher to death in a poolroom on East 160th Street. Carbo and the butcher, a man named Albert Weber, were arguing over possession of a stolen taxicab. At the time, Carbo was known variously on the street as Frankie Carbo, Frank Fortunato, Frank Martin, Jimmie the Wop, and Dago Frank. (His choice of monikers would expand with his power. By the fifties, his aliases would also include, according to his police wanted poster, Mr. Fury and Mr. Gray.)

To avoid arrest on the shooting charge, Carbo relocated to Philadelphia, but was soon arrested there after a holdup and sent back to New York to confront the consequences of Weber's demise. He was convicted of first-degree manslaughter and sent off to Sing Sing. No rehabilitation seems to have taken place. When Carbo was paroled in 1930, he became a full-fledged triggerman during the Prohibition wars, working most prominently for the Brooklyn division of Murder Incorporated.

In the ease with which he avoided prosecution, Carbo proved a man of uncanny talents. On April 12, 1933, Max Hassel and Max Greenberg, two henchmen aligned with the beer baron known as Waxie Gordon, were found shot dead at the Hotel Carteret in Elizabeth, New Jersey. Several witnesses fingered Carbo. The police questioned Carbo and charged him with the killing. He was released on ten thousand dollars bail and nothing came of that investigation, either.

Carbo's most notorious alleged homicide (and closest call) came on Thanksgiving Eve 1939 in Los Angeles. The victim was Harry "Big Greenie" Greenberg, himself late of Murder Inc. and Louis (Lepke) Buchalter's gang in Brooklyn. Big Greenie had been shot five times as he sat behind the wheel of his car on a quiet residential street. The grand jury handed down indictments against Carbo as the triggerman, Bugsy Siegel as the driver of the getaway car, and Emanuel "Mendy" Weiss and Louis Lepke, who was then in prison on a narcotics charge, as accomplices. The case seemed reasonably strong, especially against Carbo. Albert "Tick Tock"

Tannenbaum, a Lepke henchman, swore he saw Carbo shoot Big Greenie; another hood, Abe "Kid Twist" Reles, said he saw Carbo headed for the scene of the shooting and running away after. The first problem for the prosecution, however, came when Kid Twist, while under police guard at the Half Moon Hotel in Coney Island, sailed out his window and down five stories to his death. To this day, Kid Twist's defenestration remains a mystery, if only to the New York City Police Department. Carbo, in any case, was not claiming credit. The case went to trial in 1942 (by now Carbo was the sole defendant), and the jury members decided that as much as they doubted the innocent mewings of Frankie Carbo, they could not entirely trust Tick Tock Tannenbaum as a stalwart witness. After fifty-three hours of deliberation, Carbo was acquitted.

Finally, according to the famous Mafia snitch Jimmy Frattiano, Carbo was given the job of murdering Bugsy Siegel in 1947 after Siegel failed to pay his debts to the Italian mob. "Bugsy had built the Flamingo Hotel out in Las Vegas," Jack Bonomi told me, "but he made the mistake of welshing on his creditors. You're not supposed to do that. So they gave Meyer Lansky the contract to collect or kill Bugsy. Frank Carbo got the call."

BETWEEN COURT DATES, CARBO HAD BECOME THE MAJOR POWER in the boxing world. With the fall of Prohibition, boxing was fresh meat, an opportunity. In major cities like New York, Chicago, Boston, and Los Angeles, there were boxing cards nearly every night of the week, and with the advent of television, a sponsor like Gillette, selling razor blades, was as eager to secure fight night as it would be to secure pro football a generation later. The mobster Gabe Genovese had given Carbo his first real opportunity by taking him on as a partner in managing Babe Risko, the middleweight champion in 1936. Carbo did not invent the Mafia way of running fighters, but he did refine the details and established such dominance in the field that especially in the years after World War II until his arrest in 1959, he was known as the "underworld commissioner."

Carbo's most important business relationship was with James Norris, the head of the International Boxing Commission, which was originally formed to buy up the contracts of the leading heavyweight contenders after Joe Louis retired in 1949. Eventually, the IBC gained control of the top fighters in every division as well as the Madison Square Garden Corporation. On paper, at least, Norris, and his associate, Truman Gibson, was the lord of prizefighting. For Norris, running the IBC was a kind of hobby; from his father he had inherited grain and real estate fortunes running into the hundreds of millions. And yet Norris hardly made a match without Carbo's approval. When Norris was having trouble with fight managers who resisted his control of the game, he asked help from Carbo.

"Among other things, Jim Norris was a horseplayer," Truman Gibson told me. "He kept a stable called Spring Hill Farms and was around all the New York tracks and knew the various Italian bookmakers. He was an inveterate gambler. The horse world is where he met Frank Carbo. Slowly but surely, Jim got close with Carbo. The big mystery that no one can solve is why he got *that* close to Carbo."

"Actually there's no mystery, no matter what Truman Gibson thinks," said Jack Bonomi, the congressional counsel. "Norris and Carbo got close because Norris had Madison Square Garden and Chicago Stadium and all that money and Carbo had the fighters and the managers in his pocket. They needed each other, and together they had absolute power over boxing."

With violence and the threat of violence, Carbo muscled in on hundreds of fighters. He installed shadow managers (men like Herman "Hymie the Mink" Wallman, Willie "the Undertaker" Ketchum, Al "the Vest" Weill, Joseph "Pep" Barone) and then took his piece of the action. If a fighter refused to go along, he had a hard time finding fights, much less title fights. The penalty for noncompliance was savage and inevitable. Ray Arcel, a well-known fight manager in his eighties, refused to deal exclusively with Carbo and was rewarded with a lead-pipe thrashing that almost killed him. Carbo left nothing to chance. He personally offered to gouge out the eyes of one West Coast promoter who resisted him. If he did not control both fighters in a match, he would dispatch an underling to bribe a judge and then bet accordingly. Carbo single-handedly controlled the lightweight, welterweight, and middleweight titles for twenty years as he kept a grip on such champions as Joe Brown, Jimmy Carter, Virgil Akins, Johnny Saxton, Kid

Gavilan, and Carmen Basilio. Carbo also exercised varying degrees of control over many other fighters; his tentacles touched, and profited from, the likes of Sugar Ray Robinson, Jake LaMotta, and Rocky Marciano. Rather than add up the fighters he controlled, a better exercise would be to find the few he did not.

"Carbo had a house in Miami, but he lived out of his hat for the most part," Bonomi said. "He was constantly on the move, going from one city to the next, one hotel to the next. He would come into a town, get together with his friends and business acquaintances, see ten or fifteen people, then repair to whatever nightclub he liked." Carbo always wore a dark suit, white-on-white shirts, and elevator shoes, and, often, ties that hinted of the underworld: one of his favorites featured dice and five aces. He was five-eight and a ball of muscle. He loved to flash chubby rolls of hundred-dollar bills and threaten his dinner companions with assassination. "What do you want?" he'd say. "A hit in the head?"

Carbo exploited fighters as thoroughly as he could and then, when they were through, he abandoned them. On March 5, 1959, Johnny Saxton, a former world welterweight champion and one of Carbo's first big-name attractions, went before a judge in New York to face charges of breaking and entering, a crime that had yielded exactly five dollars and twenty cents. Saxton, who had earned in his time as a fighter more than a quarter of a million dollars in purses, was broke and owed sixteen thousand dollars to the IRS.

"Johnny, where did your money go?" the judge asked.

"I didn't get much of it," Saxton said.

"Why did you give up fighting?"

"They didn't need me no more."

Later, Saxton attempted suicide and was committed to Ancora State Hospital in New Jersey. He had gone mad. "I was supposed to have got the big money from fighting on TV but I never saw it," he told a reporter who visited him in Ancora. "No one ever gave me more than a couple of hundred dollars at a time. Now I'm here in the hospital. That's what boxing did for me."

BY THE TIME CARBO'S SHADOW MANAGERS TOOK CONTROL OF Sonny Liston in the late fifties, Carbo was in his late mannerist phase. He had been so powerful for so long that one might have wondered when the decline would come. "Sometimes it's not whether you really have the stick or not," Kefauver would say later about Carbo, "but whether a fellow *thinks* you might have it."

Carbo held court with all his managers and various flunkies at places like Goldie Ahearn's, a restaurant in Washington, D.C., that had been thoroughly infiltrated by undercover detectives sent by Frank Hogan, a New York district attorney who had pledged war on organized crime. At one dinner at Goldie Ahearn's in 1957, Carbo presided over a meeting attended by a range of managers: Tony Ferrante, the manager of middleweight champion Joey Giardello; Benny Magliano (aka Benny Trotter), a Baltimore promoter; Sam Margolis, Blinky Palermo's restaurant partner from Philadelphia; and a young manager named Angelo Dundee. Angelo Dundee was the brother of Chris Dundee, who had set himself up as the leading promoter in the Miami area. In a few years, Angelo would get the biggest fighter of his, or anyone's, life, Cassius Clay.

As undercover agents began to accumulate evidence on the IBC, Norris, and most of all Carbo, the entire organization showed signs of deterioration, slight at first. Cus D'Amato's principled refusal to deal with Carbo may have been shaded with hypocrisy—he was not above having a friendship with a convicted bookie named Charley Black—but it showed that Carbo was not entirely invulnerable. At one of the dinners of Carbo's guild of managers, Blinky Palermo announced in despair, "The trouble with boxing today is that legitimate businessmen are horning in on our game."

In July 1958, Hogan's office handed down indictments against Carbo charging him with the "undercover" management of fighters and illegal matchmaking. Considering Carbo's biography, the indictment, which centered on the illegal machinations surrounding a bout the previous March at Madison Square Garden between Virgil Akins and Isaac Logart, may have seemed insignificant. But according to Alfred J. Scotti, Hogan's chief assistant DA, the bout "unequivocally established Carbo as the most powerful figure in boxing. Not only did he assert control over both contenders, but he also determined where and under what terms the match was to take place."

Carbo must have recognized the danger of his situation, because he immediately went into hiding. Police floundered until they finally tracked him down in May 1959 in Haddon Township, New Jersey, near Trenton. Carbo was holed up in a house owned by a mobster. When plainclothes police arrived, Carbo, thinking the Mafia had come to kill him, tried to jump out the back window. He was captured and taken in manacles to the local police barracks. The officers called Jack Bonomi, from Hogan's office.

"I'm not gonna say anything about boxing," Carbo told Bonomi as soon as he arrived.

"I figured," said Bonomi. And so the two men talked baseball instead.

"The troopers were awestruck by Carbo," Bonomi recalled. "They asked if they could take him out to breakfast. I guess they thought they had this great celebrity on their hands. I had to tell them that not only would Carbo not be provided with full restaurant service, he would be handcuffed and kept under armed guard. He'd been on the lam for a year. All I kept thinking about was the famous picture of John Dillinger, just before he escaped, standing with that smiling prosecutor. I didn't need that kind of publicity."

After all these years of successful wriggling in the courts, Carbo now saw he had no chance for acquittal. He pleaded guilty to three counts of "undercover managing and matchmaking" and was sentenced to two years in prison. His trials were now only beginning. In November 1959, federal marshals put him in handcuffs and flew him to Los Angeles to face felony charges of attempting to extort, with force, a share of the purses of Don Jordan, the welterweight champion. Carbo and his associates Joe Sica and Louis Tom Dragna, top members of the Los Angeles mob, had threatened Jordan's manager, Donald Nesseth, and some promoters on the West Coast.

"I was like a slave to them," Jordan said years later about the mob. "When they disowned me, I said, 'You're no friends. You're dogs. Now you're my enemies.' They said, 'Talk and you die.'"

Carbo was sentenced to twenty-five years in prison; he would spend time in Alcatraz and McNeil Island Penitentiary off the coast of Seattle. Blinky Palermo was also sent to jail in the same blizzard of convictions. Palermo appears to have spent his time in prison happily. He managed the Leavenworth baseball team.

. . .

WITH FRANK CARBO IN PRISON, JACK BONOMI ACCEPTED ESTES Kefauver's invitation to take charge of a federal investigation of boxing. Bonomi started collecting evidence on all the usual suspects, especially those who were not yet in jail. He soon discovered that one of the most compromised corners of the boxing world was the boxing press.

Throughout the thirties, forties, and fifties, many boxing beat writers would line up at Madison Square Garden on Saturday mornings for a weekly envelope filled with cash—not a fortune, but just enough so that the promoter could be reasonably confident that the reporters would talk up and cover his bouts, just enough to keep them from asking the wrong questions. On some fight nights, the same beat writers might find an envelope on their assigned seats at ringside, too. The practice of organized graft was not limited to boxing, nor was it considered particularly wrong. It was just part of the business. Ball teams paid for writers to travel with them on the road; owners of racetracks and arenas sent around Christmas presents: televisions, washing machines, tea services. At big events, like a championship fight, publicists and promoters sometimes offered a selection of prostitutes: no charge for the columnists, discounts for reporters. Bonomi also heard that some of the bigger names in the press, columnists mainly, would accept free food and drink at nightspots like "21," Toots Shor's, and the Stork Club.

"I had a lot of information, but finally I decided not to press it," Bonomi said. "It was a prosecutor's choice. I figured that if I was going to get anywhere with the hearings, I needed the press on my side, and the press has a long memory. What they were doing was pocket change compared to the big guys. To focus on the press would have been a diversion and counterproductive."

Predictably, not all the voices in the press were convinced that full-scale congressional hearings were necessary. "Outside the routine business of running the country," Red Smith wrote in December 1959, "the United States Senate has nothing to worry about except the space race, atomic warfare, spiraling living costs, the world march of Communism, Fidel Castro, Bishop Pike's views on birth control, the national debt, unrest in steel, and the 1960 elections. In the circumstances, anybody can understand why Sen. Estes Kefauver, a restless spirit, deems it necessary to relieve his boredom by investigating fistfighting." Smith described Carbo as "the more or less benevolent despot of boxing's Invisible Empire."

Carbo himself tried to undermine the enterprise with similar condescension directed at Kefauver. At a hearing he rebuffed Kefauver's questions for nearly two hours simply by repeating the lyrics typed out on a sheet of paper for him by his lawyer, Abraham Brodsky:

"What is your occupation?" Kefauver began.

"I respectfully decline to answer the question on the grounds that I cannot be compelled to be a witness against myself," Carbo recited.

"Notwithstanding your answer, the chairman directs you to respond to the question."

"I respectfully decline to answer the question on the grounds that I cannot be compelled to be a witness against myself."

After some more of this, Kefauver looked up at his witness and said, "You look like an intelligent man. Are you understanding the questions I am asking?"

"I respectfully decline to answer the question on the grounds that I cannot be compelled to be a witness against myself," Carbo said.

Just before he was to be excused, Carbo broke from his script.

"There is only one thing I want to say, Mr. Senator," Carbo said.

"Yes?"

"I congratulate you on your reelection."

"That is very nice of you," Kefauver said. "I appreciate that, Mr. Carbo."

Then Carbo's lawyer, Brodsky, asked if his client, a diabetic, could have a glass of orange juice.

"Orange juice?" Kefauver said.

"I had no breakfast," said Carbo.

"All right. We are about to excuse you, Mr. Carbo."

"I mean I am trying to hold on as long as I can," Carbo said.

"Very well," the chairman said. "You look like a pleasant man, Mr. Carbo."

"Thank you," Carbo said.

·   ·   ·

KEFAUVER NEITHER EXPECTED NOR REQUIRED REVELATIONS from Frankie Carbo. He began the hearings with Jake LaMotta's admission that he took a dive in 1947 against Billy Fox. LaMotta testified that he had refused a hundred-thousand-dollar payment; he threw the fight, he said, because under the strictures of mob-run boxing it was the only way he could get a shot at the championship. And it was true. Once LaMotta fulfilled his part of the bargain, he was presented with Marcel Cerdan at Briggs Stadium in Detroit and won.

LaMotta, of course, had long since retired from boxing when he made his admission to the Kefauver panel. Sonny Liston, who was still on the way up, and was still owned and operated by the few underlings of the Carbo operation who had not been jailed or indicted, was not as forthcoming.

In the end, the federal government did not intend to do much with the committee's findings. Between 1958 and 1961, Frank Hogan's office, the U.S. attorney in Los Angeles, and the Kefauver committee succeeded in publicly describing the state of boxing and indicting every major figure in the scandal with the exception of the IBC's James Norris. In order to clean up the sport, Kefauver argued, the Justice Department would have to install federal controls backed up by the FBI. Robert Kennedy was attorney general at the time and met repeatedly with Kefauver and Bonomi, but he finally made it clear that neither his office nor his brother, the president, would get involved. Boxing was just too dirty; to take control would be to invite inevitable scandal.

Kefauver, therefore, had no way to deal with a case like Sonny Liston's other than to rely on his gift for moral suasion. After Liston finished his testimony before Kefauver, Dirksen, and the rest of the committee, Kefauver took the floor to give a paternal lecture, directing the heavyweight to get back in touch with his old prison mentor, Father Stevens, "or some good man of the clergy. . . . Tell him that you want to get a manager who is absolutely clean, no record, fully licensed; someone that you can trust without question, who will advise you correctly.

"You are going to have to shake off the Palermos, the Vitales, and some of these people who have leeched themselves on to you," Kefauver went on. "They have taken advantage of you and that has to stop if you are going to get a chance."

Later Liston joked about the hearings, saying, "I'm gonna have to get me a manager who's not so hot—someone like Estes Kefauver." Of course he never did. Through one false front or another, with a succession of ostensible managers, Liston never moved far from the shade of Frankie Carbo. The funny thing about it all, Geraldine Liston would say, was that if Sonny "was hooked up with the mob we sure were poor."

CHAPTER FOUR

Stripped

LISTON FLEW OUT TO THE DESERT TO TRAIN FOR THE SECOND Patterson fight. The bout had originally been scheduled for Florida but was moved to Las Vegas when Liston needed time to recover from a twisted knee he suffered while playing golf. Las Vegas in those days was still an "all-the-steamship-roast-you-can-eat" town: no Spago, no pyramids or sphinx, no Statue of Liberty or Brooklyn Bridge. There were no "food courts" or baby strollers. The hotels were the Dunes, the Tropicana, the Hilton, the Desert Inn, the Stardust, and the Thunderbird. Except for the cocktail waitresses and the dishwashers, the mob guys and the iguanas, who really lived there? The promoters saw an opportunity in Las Vegas precisely because it was so empty. Television was killing off all the small arenas: Laurel Gardens and the Meadowbrook Bowl in Newark, St. Nick's, Eastern Parkway, and Sunnyside Gardens in New York. The law, however, was that a fight had to be blacked out in the city where it was held until the arena was a guaranteed sellout. The networks were not quick to black out a market like New York or Chicago. If you held a fight in Vegas, whom were you blacking out? The armadillos? In exchange for some free publicity, the casinos were happy to provide discounted rooms, training facilities, a makeshift arena in a sunbaked parking lot. Las Vegas was a good deal.

Liston's latest manager, Jack Nilon (late of a Philadelphia food concessions business), wanted his fighter to train in isolation, per-

Sonny Liston.

haps at some quiet desert camp far from the city. Liston would have none of it. If there had been a time when he wanted to be a model champion, a well-behaved and well-trained gentleman like Joe Louis or Floyd Patterson, he had gotten over it. In Las Vegas, Liston came to know a gambler and bad boy named Irving "Ash" Resnik, the "athletic director" of the Thunderbird Hotel. Resnik had grown up in Brooklyn and was a basketball star. But he was the sort of basketball star who practiced *missing* foul shots, should the need ever arise to shave a point. According to one of his close friends, Resnik came out to Las Vegas largely because he owed more than seven thousand dollars to Albert Anastasia and was slow in paying up. The debt was now so old that Anastasia had put a contract out on his life. He was saved only when a friend in the meat business, Milton Berke, paid off the marker and another friend, Charlie "the Blade" White, a partner in the Capri in Havana, helped set him up with jobs in Las Vegas—first at El Rancho, later at the Thunderbird. The casinos, in those days, were almost all mob-run.

Resnik was a big guy, over 250 pounds, and he reacted to losing at the craps table by lifting up the table and pitching it over. "Ah, Ash was a great guy, but he was a guy with a temper," Lem Banker, a friend and a well-known Las Vegas handicapper, told me. For publicity and for his ego's sake, Resnik wanted Liston to stay and train at the Thunderbird, and he went about seducing him. At one of his first meetings with Liston, Resnik arranged to have one of his flunkies come over to him, interrupt, and say that his tailor was in his suite awaiting his presence.

"Oh, I forgot all about that," Resnik said to Liston. "Sonny, would you come with me? I gotta get fit for some suits. We can keep talking there."

Once they were in the room, Resnik invited Liston to look at the swatch book, feel the cashmeres and the silks, pick out some material for himself.

"Go ahead," Resnik said. "Have a few suits made. On me."

By then Liston was so disgusted with his treatment back home in Philadelphia and in the press that he accepted, taking it as his due as champion of the world.

When Resnik and Liston were finished with the tailor, they went back to the casino floor and found Geraldine, who was jumping up and down, screaming with delight.

"Charles! Charles! You won't believe what happened! I hit the jackpot! I hit *two* jackpots!"

One of Resnik's flunkies was standing next to Geraldine smiling knowingly.

Liston understood what was going on, but who else was making offers? When Nilon insisted they go off to the desert and begin training in ascetic isolation, Liston cut him off.

"Shut the fuck up," he told Nilon. "We're stayin' here."

And so it was that Sonny Liston accepted the hospitality of Ash Resnik. Having dispensed with Patterson last time in two minutes and six seconds, he did not betray a great deal of worry in training for the rematch. He went through his usual rituals in the gym— skipping rope to the tune of "Night Train," hitting the speed bags and the heavy bag—but he did not spar very much or very hard. If a boxer trains for every fight full out, he won't last long, and Liston, even though he had not yet defended his championship, was prepared to enjoy himself. Liston generally ate the same dinner every night: shrimp cocktail, at least one big steak, baked potato, and cheesecake. Liston loved cheesecake.

It would not be easy to arouse interest in the rematch. Jerry Izenberg, a thoughtful columnist for the Newark *Star-Ledger,* developed an unusually trusting relationship with Liston and dared to ask him the question that was on every reporter's mind.

"The guy didn't hit you in the first fight," Izenberg said. "Can this fight be any better?"

Liston paused a long time, a conversational tic, and then said, very distinctly, "Anybody who pays to see this fight is stupid. This fight will be worse than the first."

The more Liston hung around with Resnik, the less he seemed inclined to fulfill the resolutions he had made to the press and on the plane from Chicago to Philadelphia. He was even surlier with the press than before and he was cruel to the help. Robert H. Boyle, a reporter for *Sports Illustrated* sent to cover the fight, wrote: "Well, Liston has had the championship for almost a year now, and in that time he has become insufferable. He is giving back all the abuse he ever had to take. He looks upon good manners as a sign of weakness, if not cowardice, and he accepts gifts and favors with all the good humor of a sultan demanding tribute. Most of the time he is sullen. A contemptuous grunt passes for speech. He acts this way toward almost everyone. Of course, he can cop a plea with the press by claiming that he has been unfairly treated because of his past. What counts, however, is the way he deports himself with bootblacks, porters, maids, waitresses. As a onetime nonentity himself, he might be expected to know how they feel. Yet he has carried into his public life the bullying and cockiness that he uses to intimidate opponents in the ring." The reporter quoted an unnamed black busboy at the Thunderbird Hotel: "Sonny Liston is just too mean to be allowed around decent people. They ought to ship him back to Africa. No, make that Mississippi."

Liston did not even bow to the conventions of the old fight world. One night in New York when Liston was eating a steak at Toots Shor's, the public relations man Harold Conrad escorted Shor over to the champion's table. For decades, Shor had been host to all the major columnists and athletes: Jimmy Cannon and Joe DiMaggio, Earl Wilson and Joe Louis were all his close friends. What was more, before going into business for himself, Shor had started out at a speakeasy called the Five O'Clock Club, owned by the mobsters Owney Madden and George "Big Frenchy" LaMange. He and Liston surely shared a few interests. And yet Liston couldn't be bothered to look up from his meat.

"I don't shake hands while I'm eatin'," Liston said.

Shor stalked away in a fury. Here was the proprietor of Mecca rebuffed by an impudent pilgrim. Shor turned to Harold Conrad and said, "Don't you ever bring that bum in here again."

A FEW DAYS BEFORE THE FIGHT, CASSIUS CLAY FLEW OUT TO Las Vegas with his trainer, Angelo Dundee. It is the custom for past champions and contenders for the title to come to championship bouts. Clay, however, came not for the sake of tradition but in the spirit in which Jack Johnson pursued Tommy Burns to Australia. Johnson wanted to embarrass the reluctant champion, to shame him into fighting. Clay wanted to taunt Liston, to sell himself as the number one contender even if most of the press corps still considered him little more than a light-hitting loudmouth.

One afternoon, Liston's friend Jack McKinney was in the ring with one of the champion's own sparring partners, Leotis Martin.

Liston was standing near the ring apron watching McKinney when Clay walked in.

"Hey, Sonny," he shouted across the ring, "you couldn't even beat McKinney!"

"That was a real quiver to the heart for Liston," McKinney recalled. "Everyone was laughing their asses off and Sonny didn't like it one bit. He wasn't of the opinion that it was terribly funny."

A night or two later, Liston was shooting craps at one of the casinos. From across the casino floor, Clay spotted him and headed straight for the table. Liston was down four hundred dollars. Clay delighted in Liston's distress.

"Look at that big ugly bear, he can't even shoot craps," Clay announced to everyone and no one.

Liston glared. He rolled again. Craps again.

"Look at that big ugly bear! He can't do nothing right."

Liston threw down his dice and walked over to Clay.

"Listen, you nigger faggot," he said. "If you don't get out of here in ten seconds, I'm gonna pull that big tongue out of your mouth and stick it up your ass."

Some time later, Liston spotted Clay on the casino floor.

"Watch this," Liston told his friend McKinney.

The champion went up to Clay and slapped him hard across the face, a blow that did not so much hurt as stun.

Clay's eyes widened.

"What did you do that for?" Clay thought it had been a big game, a charade, an advertisement for future ticket sales. Liston did not.

"Why?" Liston said. "'Cause you too fucking fresh." And as he walked away he said, "I got the punk's heart." And it was true. Clay admitted it, to Dundee, to his friends. He had been scared.

It was a jailhouse moment, or at least it was to a con, a moment in which you do not back down and the other man does and you have the better of him and he is your chicken, your slave, you have his heart, you have his everything, all yours, for all time. So Liston believed.

THE SCENE ON THE CASINO FLOOR WAS DOUBTLESS MORE TRYing for the champion than the second fight with Patterson. Liston spent the first half minute or so of the fight waiting to see if Patterson had anything new to offer. Considering his training, his long *vacances au soleil*, he did not care to wait longer and so, thus convinced of the challenger's lack of inspiration, he battered him to the ground with a terrific uppercut to the jaw and a straight right.

In a calmer moment, Liston would wax theoretical on the power of his punch and the damage it could do. He kept in his mind an image of tender human physiognomy, its equilibrium, and the way in which it can be forever altered by the power of the fist: "See, the different parts of the brain set in little cups like this. When you get hit a terrible shot—*pop!*—the brain flops out of them cups and you're knocked out. Then the brain settles back in the cups and you come to. But after this happens enough times, or sometimes even once if the shot's hard enough, the brain don't settle back right in them cups, and that's when you start needin' other people to help you get around."

To judge by the blankness of Patterson's eyes, his brain had flopped out of its cups, and only at the count of nine did it settle back in. He got to his feet, barely escaping the fastest exit in the history of heavyweight championship fights.

Little more than a minute later, Liston began a barrage that left Patterson a heap on the ground. Liston had calculated just right. He didn't need to train much at all. The fight lasted four seconds longer than the first, though, to be fair, this time it included two counts of eight after knockdowns. Patterson had gone into the ring determined this time to listen to his trainers, to box, to get warm, to test Liston's endurance—and once more he forgot everything.

"It was the same as last time," said Cus D'Amato. "We would have said something to correct him in the corner between rounds but the guy knocked him out before we had a chance."

"I felt good until I got hit," Patterson said. But once he was hit, that last time, he'd temporarily lost his ability to tell fantasy from reality. Somehow the sensation of being knocked out, of concussion, made it seem to him that everyone in the arena was in the ring there with him, circled around him like family. "You feel lovable to all the people," he told Talese. "And you want to reach out and kiss everybody—men and women. . . ." After he had regained his bearings and walked back to the dressing room, Patterson said he loved boxing and, seeing as how he was just twenty-eight, he was going to start "at the bottom and start all over again." There was no point in challenging Sonny Liston anytime soon. Who would pay to see a third Liston-Patterson fight?

Patterson went through the rituals of defeat: the hugs from family and friends, the news conference. But he did not intend to stay around very long. Since losing the first fight to Liston, Patterson had taken up flying and bought himself a little Cessna. He drove out to the airport hoping to get home soon. But once Patterson and his copilot, a former crop duster named Ted Hanson, got up and out over the Nevada desert, the controls said they were overheating, they were carrying too much weight in the luggage hold. They flew back to the Las Vegas airport, and as Hanson looked around for a plane to rent, Patterson hid from the fight fans who were waiting to leave town. His fake beard was buried away somewhere in his luggage. Instead, he hid in the dark, as he had as a child, in the alleys of Bed-Stuy, in the shed at the High Street subway station.

On the long flight back to New York (with stops in New Mexico and Ohio), Patterson tried to focus on his flying, on the instruments in front of him, but time and again Hanson had to break him out of reverie. Patterson was thinking, "How could the same thing happen twice? . . . How? . . . Was I fooling these people all these years? . . . Was I ever champion?" And he remembered how after the fight he had locked himself in the bathroom for a few minutes, and the press was banging on the door and the cornermen were banging on the door, yelling, "C'mon out, Floyd, c'mon out," and all he could think was, "What happened?" All the months of running, of living away from your children, all the fighting in the gym, the anxiety, the pain, and then it's over in a flash.

"What happened?"

THE MOST MEMORABLE PERFORMANCE OF THE EVENING CAME before the fight and just after. Patterson, after all, had crumbled, and Liston had put on a performance rather like a grown man whipping a dog—convincing, but hard to enjoy.

Before the opening bell, when the various fighters from the past and future were invited out for a bow, the old ritual, Clay bounded into the ring wearing a sharp checked jacket. He shook hands with some reverence with Patterson, but when he reached Liston's corner he threw up his hands in mock terror. If he had been frightened after the incident in the casino, he made sure to show he was frightened no longer: his eyes were too wide now for his terror to be anything other than a gag. Liston stared. Patterson laughed as if he had just seen Chaplin slip on a peel.

Patterson was barely on his feet before Clay came bounding back into the ring at the end of the bout. He headed for the television mikes, for the radio mike held by Howard Cosell.

"The fight was a disgrace!" Clay was shouting. "Liston is a tramp! I'm the champ. I want that big ugly bear!"

When Clay started running for Liston's corner, three police officers held him back.

"I'll whup him in eight!" he cried, holding up eight fingers. "Don't make me wait! I'll whup him in eight!"

Clay had come to the fight with props. He pulled out a phony newspaper that had a banner headline reading "Clay Has a Very Big Lip That Sonny Will Sure Zip." Sonny Liston looked across the ring, his eyes narrow. He poked his trainer, Willie Reddish, and said, "Can you believe this guy? He's next." Afterward, when a reporter asked Liston how long it would take to beat Clay, he said, "Two rounds—one and a half to catch him, and a half round to lick him."

PART TWO

Cassius Clay, age twelve.

CHAPTER FIVE

The Bicycle Thief

As a fighter, as a performer, as a man of independence and American originality, Cassius Clay would transcend the worlds of Sonny Liston and Floyd Patterson. He began his life with an advantage, an economic one. Boxing has never been a sport of the middle class. It is a game for the poor, the lottery player, the all-or-nothing-at-all young men who risk their health for the infinitesimally small chance of riches and glory. All of Clay's most prominent opponents—Liston, Patterson, Joe Frazier, George Foreman—were born poor, born more often than not into large families with a father who was either out of work or out of sight. As boys, they were all part of what sociologists and headline writers would later call the underclass. One of the less entertaining components of the Ali act was the way he tried to "outblack" someone like Frazier, call him an Uncle Tom, an "honorary white," when in fact Frazier had grown up dirt poor in South Carolina. If Ali was joking, Frazier never found it funny.

Cassius Clay was born on January 17, 1942, and in the understanding of his place and time, of Louisville after the war and through the fifties, he was a child of the black middle class. "But *black* middle class, black *southern* middle class, which is not white middle class at all," says Toni Morrison, who, as a young editor, worked on his autobiography. True enough, but still Clay was born to better circumstances than his eventual rivals. His father, Cassius Clay, Sr., was a sign painter and an occasional artist who drew religious murals and landscapes. He always worked, for others or on his own. His mother, Odessa Clay, worked sometimes cleaning houses and cooking meals for upper-class whites in Louisville. ("We *adored* Odessa! She's like one of the family!") Mainly she was a housewife and mother. The Clays had two children—Cassius Marcellus and Rudolph, who was born in 1944. The Clays bought their house on Grand Avenue in the West End when they were still in their twenties for $4,500. The house was a boxy cottage with a small yard, in an all-black neighborhood, but it was also distant from Smoketown, the poorer black neighborhood in the southwestern part of town. (The white elite in Louisville lived in the East End, in the River Road area, in Indian Hills, or in Mockingbird Valley; the tiny black elite of ministers, merchants, and funeral directors generally lived in the East End.) In those days, some of the roads in the West End were not well paved and many of the houses were mere shacks, but while the Clays never knew even the suggestion of material luxury until their son became the champion of the world, they never wanted for the basics of life. The two Clay boys were well clothed, well fed. Once in a while Cassius and Rudy helped their father paint signs on weekends or after school, and they took a few other brief jobs to earn some extra money (Cassius swept the floors for the nuns at the Nazareth College library), but unlike Sonny Liston and Floyd Patterson they never suffered the terrible anxiety of watching their parents fail.

"He wasn't a kid who ever missed a meal," said Lamont Johnson, a schoolmate of Clay's. "In those days, there was no other way to think of his circumstances as anything other than black middle class."

When he became a Muslim, Ali would say that Clay was his slave name—and that, of course, was true. But it was also a name in which his family took a certain pride. Cassius Clay was named for an abolitionist, a nineteenth-century Kentucky farmer who inherited forty slaves and a plantation called White Hall in the town of Foxtown in Madison County, Kentucky. Clay was six-foot-six and commanded troops in the war with Mexico. When he returned home, he became an abolitionist and edited an antislavery newspaper in Lexington called *The True American*. He was one of the first men in the state to free the slaves on his plantation. Clay ignored death threats and gave speeches in Kentucky denouncing slavery. "For those who have respect for the laws of God, I have this argument," he said, theatrically laying down a leather-bound copy of the Holy Bible. "For those who believe in the laws of man, I have this argument." Now he laid down a copy of the state constitution. "And for those who believe neither in the laws of God nor of man, I have this argument," and he laid down two pistols and a Bowie knife. During one debate with a proslavery candidate for state office, Clay was stabbed in the chest; luckily he was carrying his Bowie knife and stabbed his assailant back. Abraham Lincoln sent Clay to Russia for the government, but after a year he returned home from St. Petersburg for more abolitionist activity. He maintained his physical courage to the end. When he was eighty-four, he married a fifteen-year-old girl.

Cassius Clay—the boy, the fighter—grew up hearing stories about his great-grandfather, who was brought up on the property of the abolitionist Clay. "My grandfather was with the old man, but not in a slave capacity, no sir!" Clay senior, the fighter's father, told Jack Olsen, who interviewed the fighter's parents extensively. (They died in the 1990s.)

On Odessa's side of the family, the blood was mixed, a fact that would cause Ali some uneasy moments after his conversion to the Nation of Islam. Ali would claim that any white blood in his family came through "rape and defilement." The reality was more complicated. One of Odessa Lee Grady Clay's grandfathers was Tom Moorehead, the son of a white man and a slave named Dinah. Her other grandfather was a white man—Abe Grady, an Irish immigrant from County Clare, who married a black woman; their son also married a black woman, and one of the daughters was Odessa.

Odessa Clay was a sweet, light-skinned, moon-faced woman who took her sons to church every Sunday and kept after them to keep clean, to work hard, to respect their elders. Clay called his mother Bird and she called him, after his first "words," Gee Gee. (In retrospect, his father took this name as an omen, a harbinger of the Golden Gloves championships his son would win.) The extended Clay family was a big one, and at family gatherings Cassius was the beautiful child, always gabbing, making jokes, demanding, and winning, everyone's attention.

"He was always a talker," Odessa Clay said. "He tried to talk so hard when he was a baby. He used to jabber so, you know? And people'd laugh and he'd shake his face and jabber so fast. I don't see how anybody could talk so fast, just like lightning. And he never sat still. He was in the bed with me at six months old and you know how babies stretch? And he had little muscle arms and he hit me in the mouth when he stretched and it loosened my front tooth and it affected my other front tooth and I had to have both of them pulled out. So I always say his first knockout punch was in my mouth."

"He loved to talk," said Clay's father. "I'd come home and he'd have about fifty boys on the porch—this was when he was about eight years old—and he's talking to all of 'em, addressing them, and I'd say, 'Why don't you go in and go to bed?' A whole neighborhood of boys and he'd be doing all the talking. He'd always find something to talk about."

Cassius Clay, Sr., was a cock of the walk, a braggart, a charmer, a performer, a man full of fantastical tales and hundred-proof blather. To all who would listen, including the reporters who trooped off to Louisville in later years, Clay senior talked of having been an Arabian sheik, a Hindu noble. Like Ralph Kramden, Jackie Gleason's bus driver with dreams, Clay senior talked up his schemes for the big hit, the marketing of this idea or that gadget that would vault the Clays, once and for all, out of Louisville and into some suburban nirvana. His great weakness, however, was for the bottle, and when he drank he often got violent. The Louisville police records show that he was arrested four times for reckless driving, twice for disorderly conduct, and twice for assault and battery; on three occasions, Odessa called the police complaining that her husband was beating her. "I like a few drinks now and then," Clay senior said. He often spent his nights moving from one bar to the next, picking up women whenever possible. (Many years later, Odessa finally grew so tired of her husband's womanizing that she insisted on a period of separation.) John "Junior Pal" Powell, who owned a liquor store in the West End, told a reporter for *Sports Illustrated* about a night when the old man came stumbling to his apartment, his shirt covered with blood. Some woman had stabbed him in the chest. When Powell offered to take him to the hospital, Clay senior refused, saying, "Hey, Junior Pal, the best thing you can do for me is do what the cowboys do. You know, give me a little drink and pour a little bit on the chest, and I'll be all right."

At an early age, Clay appears to have learned how to block these chaotic incidents out of his mind; even after he had become perhaps the most visible and press-friendly figure on earth, he avoided probing questions about his father. He would joke about his father having an eye for other women—"My daddy is a playboy. He's always wearing white shoes and pink pants and blue shirts and he says he'll never get old"—but he would not let the discussion get much deeper than that. "It always seemed to me that Ali suffered a great psychological wound when he was a kid because of his father and that as a result he really shut down," one of Ali's closest friends said. "In many ways, as brilliant and charming as he is, Muhammad is an arrested adolescent. There is a lot of pain there. And though he's always tried to put it behind him, shove it out of his mind, a lot of that pain comes from his father, the drinking, the occasional violence, the harangues."

CASSIUS'S FATHER DID WORK HARD TO EARN A LIVING FOR HIS family, and there was a time in Louisville when his signs were everywhere:

JOYCE'S BARBER SHOP

KING KARL'S THREE ROOMS OF FURNITURE

A. B. HARRIS, M.D.: DELIVERIES AND FEMALE DISORDERS

But Clay senior was a resentful artisan. His greatest frustration was that he could not earn his living painting murals and canvases. He was not exceptionally talented—his landscapes were garish, his religious paintings just a step above kitsch—but he had not had any training, either. Clay senior quit school in the ninth grade, a circumstance he blamed, with good reason, on the limited opportunities for blacks. He would often tell his children that the white man had kept him down, had prevented him from being a real artist, from expressing himself. He was never subtle about his distrust of whites. And while he would one day accuse the Nation of Islam of "brainwashing" and fleecing his sons, he often went on at the dinner table and in the bars about the need for black self-determination. He deeply admired Marcus Garvey, the leading black nationalist after World War I and one of the ideological forebears of Elijah Muhammad. He was never a member of a Garvey organization, but like many blacks in the twenties, he admired Garvey's calls for racial pride and black self-sufficiency, if not, perhaps, the idea of a return to Africa.

Like any black child of his generation, Cassius Clay learned quickly that if he strayed outside his neighborhood—to the white neighborhood of Portland, say—he would hear the calls of "nigger" and "nigger go home." It did not require his father's dinner-table speeches to make him race-conscious at an early age. Kentucky was, and remains, a complicated border state. It did not secede during the Civil War, though the majority sympathized with the Confederacy. Kentucky lived under Jim Crow, if not as severely as did Mississippi or Alabama. Downtown, blacks were limited to the stores on Walnut Street between Fifth and Tenth. Hotels were segregated. Schools were de facto segregated, though there were slight signs of mixing even before *Brown v. Board of Education.* There were "white stores" and "Negro stores," "white parks" and "Negro parks." At most of the big movie theaters in town, like the Savoy, whites sat in the orchestra and blacks in the balcony; the rest—Loew's, the Mary Anderson, the Brown, the Strand, the Kentucky—were for whites only; the Lyric was for blacks. On public transport, blacks sat in the back, whites in the front. Chickasaw Park was black, Shawnee Park was mixed, and the rest were white. "That was just the way we lived," said Beverly Edwards, another of Cassius's schoolmates. "Kentucky is known as the Gateway to the South, but we weren't too much different than the Deep South as far as race was concerned."

Blyden Jackson, a black writer from Louisville, was in his forties when Clay was a child. He wrote that under Jim Crow it was only "through a veil I could perceive the forbidden city, the Louisville where white folks lived. It was the Louisville of the downtown hotels, the lower floors of the big movie houses, the high schools I read about in the daily newspapers, the restricted haunts I sometimes passed, like the white restaurants and country clubs, the other side of windows in the banks, and, of course, the inner sanctums of offices where I could go only as a humble client or menial custodian. On my side of the veil everything was black: the homes, the people, the churches, the schools, the Negro park with Negro park police. . . . I knew that there were two Louisvilles and, in America, two Americas. I knew, also, which of the Americas was mine. I knew there were things I was not supposed to do, honors I was not supposed to seek, people to whom I was never supposed to speak, and even thoughts that I was never supposed to think. I was a Negro." So, yes, Cassius Clay had certain advantages that other black children did not, but those advantages were as to nothing compared to the liberties he was denied.

When he was four years old, Cassius asked his mother, "Mama, when you get on the bus, do people think you're a white lady or a colored lady?" When he was five he asked his father, "Daddy, I go to the grocery and the grocery man is white. I go to the drugstore and the drugstore man's white. The bus driver's white. What do the colored people do?" Cassius was wounded by the accumulated slights of mid-century American apartheid: the sight of his mother being turned away for a drink of water at a luncheonette downtown, whites cutting in front of them in lines at the Kentucky State Fair as if by divine right, the sense of shame when his mother went across town to clean floors and toilets for white families. The Clays' standing in the black middle class did nothing to save them from those indignities. Clay used to say that from the age of ten he would lie in bed at night and cry as he wondered why his race had to suffer so.

The racial incident that would mark Cassius most deeply was the murder of a fourteen-year-old boy named Emmett Till in the summer of 1955, an event that helped trigger the civil rights movement. Emmett Till lived in Chicago, but often spent summers with relatives in the small town of Money, Mississippi. The state was a center of reaction against the *Brown v. Board of Education* decision in 1954 and integration generally. Mississippi's two senators, James O. Eastland and John Stennis, were among the most virulent racists in Washington, and the governor, J. P. Coleman, declared that blacks were not fit to vote. More than five hundred blacks were lynched in Mississippi since officials began keeping records in 1882. Emmett's summer trips made his mother so nervous that she repeatedly instructed her son in the racial etiquette of the Jim Crow South, the need to answer whites with "yassuh" and "nawsuh." Purely out of fear, she tried to instill in him the entire lexicon of bowing and scraping that was disappearing among the new generation that had grown up in northern cities like Chicago.

In late August, Emmett Till arrived in Money. One day, outside a grocery store, he told some of his friends about his integrated school back home in Chicago and pulled a picture from his wallet of his white girlfriend. One of the local kids pointed out that there was a white cashier inside the store and dared Emmett to go inside and talk to her. Emmett did just that, and, as he was coming back out, said, "Bye, baby." A few days later, the cashier's husband, Roy Bryant, and his half brother, J. W. Milam, broke into the house of Till's great-uncle, Mose Wright, and dragged the boy out of his bed and into the night. They beat him terribly, pistol-whipping him, and demanded that he admit what he had done and beg forgiveness. Till refused and they shot him in the head. With a length of barbed wire, they tied a heavy cotton-gin fan around his neck, and then threw the body in the Tallahatchie River. The black press, including *Jet* and *The Chicago Defender*, ran pictures of Till's mutilated face, and the white media covered the trial as well. The presence of the press, however, did nothing to ensure justice. An all-white jury acquitted Bryant and Milam after deliberating for just sixty-seven minutes. "If we hadn't stopped to drink pop," one juror said, "it wouldn't have taken that long."

Like so many others, Clay senior was enraged by the incident. He told his sons about it and made sure they saw the photographs. Cassius absorbed the crime on a personal level: Till was just a year older than he. The murder helped reinforce in him the sense that a black boy from Louisville was going out into a world that would deny him, rebuff him, even hate him. Sometimes, especially early in his career, reporters would ask Clay why he became a fighter and the answer would come without hesitation. "I started boxing because I thought this was the fastest way for a black person to make it in this country," he said. "I was not that bright and quick in school, couldn't be a football or a basketball player 'cause you have to go to college and get all kinds of degrees and pass examinations. A boxer can just go into a gym, jump around, turn professional, win a fight, get a break, and he is in the ring. If he's good enough he makes more money than ballplayers make all their lives. . . ."

"I saw there was no future in getting a high school education or even a college education," he told another writer. "There was no future 'cause I knew too many that had 'em and were laying around on the corners. A boxer has something to do every day. Go to the gym, put on the gloves, and box. . . . There wasn't nothing to do in the streets. The kids would throw rocks and stand under the street-lights all night, running in and out of the juke joints and smoking and slipping off drinking, nothing to do. I tried it a little bit, used to try, wasn't nothing else to do till boxing."

IN THE EARLY SEVENTIES, ELIJAH MUHAMMAD'S LIEUTENANTS arranged a book deal. The time was right, they decided, for an auto-biography of Muhammad Ali, and so, led by Elijah Muhammad's son and Ali's manager, Herbert Muhammad, the Muslims sold the book to Random House for a quarter million dollars (world rights included). They selected as ghostwriter Richard Durham, the edi-tor of the Nation of Islam's newspaper, *Muhammad Speaks.* Durham was not himself a Muslim—his politics were, if anything, Marxist. Durham was a talented writer, but at the same time he was obliged to do for Ali what Parson Weems had done for George Washington. Just as Weems had described a mythical Washington chopping down cherry trees and hurling coins across the Potomac to highlight moral purity and awesome physicality, Durham made Ali out to be a champion fueled almost solely by anger and racial in-justice. Ali's early financial backers, the Louisville Sponsoring Group, were portrayed as a bloody-minded band of white business-men who regarded their charge as little more than a property to ex-ploit, a Churchill Downs thoroughbred with strong legs and good teeth. Most famously, the book, titled *The Greatest,* had Ali hurling his Olympic gold medal into the Ohio River after returning from Rome, so disgusted was he after being turned away at a restaurant and harassed by a white motorcycle gang.

There was, of course, a great deal of truth in the book. There was, however, never any white motorcycle gang incident, and Clay did not throw away his medal, he lost it. Nor was Clay much of an activist until years later. At the one civil rights demonstration he attended in Louisville in the late fifties, a white woman dumped a bucket of water on the marchers, soaking Clay completely. "That's the last one of these I'm coming to," he said, and, for a long while, kept his promise. Like the autobiographies of Joe Louis and Jack Johnson, *The Greatest* mixes fact and folklore—in this case folklore in the service of Elijah Muhammad's agenda.

In writing the Ali autobiography and myth, Durham had limited creative independence. This was a crucial document for the Nation of Islam. In the early days of the Nation, Elijah Muhammad had declared boxing to be an especially unworthy diversion, an ugly spectacle of white men watching black men beat themselves silly, but in Ali he had his shining prince, an outsized symbol of Muslim manhood, a living recruitment poster. Toni Morrison, who was an editor at Random House before she left the company to work full-time as a novelist, was stunned by the way Herbert Muhammad would constantly demand changes in the manuscript—especially changes that made it seem that the pivotal player in the rise of Ali was, invariably, Herbert Muhammad. Ali was never particularly given to cursing, but Herbert disallowed rough language entirely. All the locker-room stuff was forbidden. At one point, in an early draft, Ali's first wife, Sonji, tells Ali he has to be firmer with the Muslims and says, "You the *champ*, muthafucker!" Well, out that went, of course.

"My anxiety on the Ali project was always Herbert, who threatened at every moment to do something awful," Morrison said. "In the end, the book was more accurate than not. But it gathered to itself some disbelief because after a while Ali stopped doing publicity for it. He wanted to do signings in urban stores, but the stores were terrified that their places would be overrun by black barbarians. Imagine! They kept wanting Ali to go out to the suburbs and he didn't want to do that.

"As for the gold medal story, Ali came to deny it was true when the book came out. I think it was at a press conference where he was asked about the medal and he said, 'I don't remember where I put that.' He also said he hadn't read the book. So he, in a sense, discredited the book in a way that was unfair to the stories he had told Richard in the first place or to the stories Richard may have invented to make a point."

"The story about the Olympic medal wasn't true, but we had to take it on faith," said James Silberman, who was editor in chief at

Random House at the time. "After some time, as happens with people, Ali came to believe it. When he was young he took everything with a wink, even the facts of his own life."

Although *The Greatest* strained the limits of belief as it tried to create a kind of Paul Bunyan story for the Nation of Islam, there really is a creation myth in the boxing career of Cassius Clay. The myth also has the virtue of being true. It is the story of the stolen bicycle.

On an October afternoon in 1954, when Cassius was twelve years old, he and one of his friends rode their bicycles to the Columbia Auditorium, which was hosting its annual convention of the Louisville Service Club, a bazaar held by black merchants. The boys were interested mainly in the free popcorn and ice cream the merchants were handing out and a way to kill the day. Cassius was especially eager to show off his new bike, a sixty-dollar red-and-white Schwinn. The two boys wandered around the booths for a few hours, stuffed themselves, and then decided to head back home. It was getting late. But when they walked back to where they'd left their bikes, the new Schwinn was gone.

Cassius was in tears. Someone told him that there was a police officer in the basement of the building, where there was a boxing gym, the Columbia Gym. Cassius walked down to the basement, furious, wanting a statewide manhunt for his bike and threatening to beat all hell out of the kid who had stolen it.

The officer, a white-haired man named Joe Martin, smiled as Cassius made his threats. Martin waited him out. He had nowhere special to go. Martin was an easygoing man. His friends called him Sergeant as a joke: after twenty-five years on the job he had never felt like taking the sergeant's exam. He lived well, driving a Cadillac around town and taking an annual vacation in Florida. On the beat he emptied parking meters. In his spare time he ran the gym and produced a local amateur boxing program called *Tomorrow's Champions,* which was broadcast Saturday afternoons on the local NBC affiliate, WAVE-TV.

After listening a long while to Cassius's loud oaths of revenge, Martin said, "Well, do you know how to fight?"

"No," Cassius said, "but I'd fight anyway."

Martin said that perhaps the best thing to do would be to come around to the gym.

"Why don't you learn something about fighting before you go making any hasty challenges?"

Soon Cassius started coming to Martin's gym on South Fourth Street, and after six weeks of learning the rudiments of boxing, he fought his first bout. The opponent was another stripling, named Ronnie O'Keefe. Each boy weighed eighty-nine pounds. The bout lasted three rounds, each round a minute long. The boys wore big fourteen-ounce gloves and flailed away at each other until they both had headaches. Cassius got in a few more blows and was awarded a split decision. He greeted the announcement by shouting to all that he would soon be "the greatest of all time."

At first, Cassius "didn't know a left hook from a kick in the ass," Martin said later, but as he grew bigger and stronger, as he gained a sense of the ring, he began to develop the style of fighting that would infuriate purists. Much like Sugar Ray Robinson, Clay carried his hands low, snaked out his left jab, and circled the ring on his toes. His greatest defense was his quickness, his uncanny ability to gauge an opponent's punch and lean just far enough away from it to avoid getting hit—and then strike back. Clay had remarkable eyes. They seemed never to close, never to blink, never to tip off an opponent. They were eyes that took everything in. And the instant his eyes registered an opening, an opportunity for mayhem, his hands reacted in kind. This much was there almost from the start. Martin also saw that Clay was not merely quick, but brave, cool in a crisis. Even among professional fighters, danger often reduces a man to his most foolish instincts: danger caused Floyd Patterson to wade thoughtlessly into Sonny Liston's straight left hands; danger forced George Foreman to panic and flail away at Muhammad Ali until there was no strength left in his arms. A true fighter can think in a crisis, and this, too, was an ability that Clay showed very early on. "Cassius really knew how to fight when he was in trouble," Martin told Jack Olsen, author of *Black Is Best*. "He never panicked or forgot what I'd taught him. When he'd get hit he wouldn't get mad and wade in, the way some boys do. He'd take a good punch and then he'd go right back to boxing, box his way out of it, the way I taught him."

It would be stretching the story to say that Cassius showed unusual talent in his fight against Ronnie O'Keefe. But in the next year or two, he not only showed himself to be extraordinarily gifted, with quick feet and hands, supernatural reflexes that impressed even the earliest of his amateur opponents and judges, but also proved to be one of the hardest-working athletes anyone had ever seen in Louisville. From the moment Clay won that first fight, he would come home in the evening and tell his parents how he was going to become champion of the world, was going to buy them all new cars and a new place to live, and he said it all not with the sort of misty fatalism favored in sports biopics ("And that homerun will be for you, Ma!"), but with a kind of offhand humor. He didn't just talk about it. Cassius practically lived in the gym. He never smoked, never drank. A couple of times, with some friends, he sniffed the fumes from a gas tank—his sole experience with hallucinogens. He was a nutrition nut. He carried around a bottle of water with garlic in it—a solution, he said, that would keep his blood pressure down and his health perfect. For breakfast he favored his own nutritional concoction, a quart of milk with two raw eggs. He announced that soda pop was as lethal as cigarettes.

Clay's discipline, from the age of twelve on, convinced Martin that he had a future as a boxer. Cassius woke between four and five in the morning, ran several miles, and then worked out at the gym in the afternoon, staying long past the hour when his peers had gone home for dinner. "All he ever wanted to do was run and train and spar," said Jimmy Ellis, a contemporary at the Columbia Gym who won the WBA heavyweight championship when it was stripped from Ali in 1967 for his refusal to go to Vietnam. "As long as there was someone to box, he'd take them on."

"He used to talk about his body being pure, a temple, even when he was a kid," said his classmate Beverly Edwards. "Then in the cafeteria he had to use two trays to carry his lunch: six small bottles of milk, bunches of sandwiches, hot food from the steam table. Man, he could eat! But it was always wholesome—fuel for his boxing."

There was a real sweetness, a naiveté, about Cassius. Despite his strength and his local celebrity from his increasingly frequent appearances on *Tomorrow's Champions*, he never picked on anyone. He was no street fighter. The football coach was interested in him, but Cassius wasn't interested in football. "You can get hurt playing football!" he said. "And that would be bad for my boxing." And as handsome as he was, he was not especially advanced where girls were concerned. He would flirt, he would give one girl or an-other his Golden Gloves pin and talk about how they would get married and have children, but when it came to more elemental moments, he was lost. When he was a junior in high school, Cassius dated a girl named Areatha Swint, a smart and beautiful girl who had her hair cut just like Dorothy Dandridge's in *Carmen Jones*.

"Cassius usually wore a red-and-gray jacket with a Golden Gloves appliqué," she wrote in a memoir for the Louisville *Courier-Journal*. "Cassius didn't say whether he liked my hair. At that particular time he was more interested in Floyd Patterson. He had his moments, though, when he used to tell me I was the pret-tiest girl he ever saw. Trouble was, Cassius didn't see that many girls."

After three weeks of dating, he asked her for a kiss. "I was the first girl he ever kissed, and he didn't know how. So I had to teach him. When I did, he fainted. Really, he just did. He was always jok-ing, so I thought he was playing, but he fell so hard. I ran upstairs to get a cold cloth."

When Cassius came to, he said, "I'm fine, but no one will ever believe this."

Many of the most trying hours for Clay came in school. He en-tered the main black high school, Central High on West Chestnut Street, in 1957 for the tenth grade, and his grades were so poor he had to withdraw the next year and then come back. Despite his academic record, he won over Central's courtly principal, Atwood Wilson. Clay was not Wilson's idea of a model student. He was constantly skittering through the halls, shadowboxing, showing off, pronouncing himself the greatest of all times, then flying into the bathroom to box some more in front of the mirror. In class, he daydreamed, drawing when he should have been taking notes. But what impressed Wilson was Clay's precocious discipline, the way he was up before dawn, running through Chickasaw Park in his steel-tipped clodhoppers and a sweat suit, always bragging, but al-ways making good on his boasts. When he told his friends that he was going to go on *Tomorrow's Champions* and whup Charley Baker, the toughest kid in the West End, he did it, even though Baker outweighed him by more than twenty pounds. Clay was a gentle kid who never used his muscle except in the ring. And so

Wilson decided to encourage him. At school assemblies, he would embrace him and announce, "Here he is, ladies and gentlemen! Cassius Clay! The next heavyweight champion of the world. This guy is going to make a million dollars!" If there were reports of misbehavior in the classrooms, Wilson flipped on the school intercom and announced in a mock-grim voice, "Any acting up and I'm going to set Cassius Clay on you!"

As graduation time approached, some teachers thought that Clay should not get a diploma, that letting him finish would send the wrong signal to the coaches, who might then want their own failing student athletes to get special treatment. Finally, Wilson got up at a faculty meeting held in the school's music room and said, "One day our greatest claim to fame is going to be that we knew Cassius Clay or taught him. . . . Do you think I'm going to be the principal of a school that Cassius Clay didn't finish? Why, in one night, he'll make more money than the principal and all you teachers make in a year. If every teacher here fails him, he's still not going to fail. He's not going to fail in my school. I'm going to say, 'I taught him!' "

After Wilson finished what would become known in school legend as his "Claim to Fame" speech, the teachers reluctantly relented. When Clay finally finished Central in June 1960, he was ranked 376 out of 391 and was awarded the minimum rite of passage, a "certificate of attendance." Clay's graduation was an act of generosity, the traditional debt of gratitude a school pays to its star athlete. Atwood Wilson had few illusions about Clay. Decades later, in middle age, Ali would still have trouble reading. No athlete would be more written about in this century, and yet the athlete in question would ask his friends and cornermen to read the clippings to him. "But the truth is," Wilson said, "the only thing Cassius is going to have to read is his IRS form, and I'm willing to help him do it."

In fairness, Clay was training like a professional when he was still in his mid-teens. At eighteen, he had already compiled an amazing amateur record: one hundred wins and only eight losses, two national Golden Gloves championships, and two national Amateur Athletic Union titles.

Christine Martin, Joe Martin's wife, would drive Cassius and some of the other boys in the gym to tournaments in Chicago, Indianapolis, and Toledo in her Ford station wagon. "In those days, the black boys couldn't go in the restaurants, so I didn't take *any* of the boys in," she once told a Louisville reporter. "I'd just go in myself and get what they wanted, however many hamburgers per boy, and bring it back to the car. Cassius was a very easy-to-get-along-with fellow. Very easy to handle. Very polite. Whatever you asked him to do, that's what he'd do. His mother, that's why. She was a wonderful person. On trips, most of the boys were out looking around, seeing what they could get into, whistling at pretty girls. But Cassius didn't believe in that. He carried his Bible everywhere he went, and while the other boys were out looking around, he was sitting and reading his Bible."

Martin was helpful (and so was another local trainer, Fred Stoner), but no matter who was in his corner, Clay was his own person, his own strategist, even as a teenager. Long before he mystified the national press with his verse and his psychological assaults on one opponent after another, he had begun to invent himself. Clay's performances served a dual purpose: to throw his opponent into a funk and to stir interest in the activities of Cassius Clay. He would duck his head into the dressing room of an opponent and loudly announce he'd better be ready for a whupping. At a city tournament, when he was still twelve, he started sassing a fighter named George King, flicking jabs at the air and asking, over and over, "You think you could stop this jab?" King was twenty-one and married with a child. Who was this twelve-year-old boy? When he mouthed off at his bouts on local television, the crowds at the Louisville arenas rooted against him, shouting, "Button his lip!" "Bash his nose in!"

"I didn't care what they said long as they kept coming to see me fight," he said. "They paid their money, they were entitled to a little fun. You would have thought I was a well-known pro, ten years older than I was."

Clay was already spouting the doggerel that would become an Ali trademark years later.

> *This guy must be done.*
> *I'll stop him in one.*

So went one poem performed for a reporter for *The Courier-Journal*.

The world would be shocked by his hysterical antics at the weigh-in before he faced Sonny Liston for the first time, but he had rehearsed the act even before he became a professional. At a tournament in Chicago in March 1960, Clay went to his weigh-in with his opponent, Jimmy Jones, who was the defending heavyweight titleholder in the competition.

"Mr. Martin, are you in a hurry to get away from here tonight?" Clay said to his trainer in earshot of Jimmy Jones.

"Not really," Martin said. "Why?"

"This guy over here, I can get rid of him in one round if you're in a hurry," he said, gesturing to Jones. "Or, if you're in no hurry, if you want me to box, I can carry him for three rounds."

Martin said, "I'm in no hurry."

And so that night Clay took his time. He won in three rounds.

By the time Clay was fifteen years old, in 1957, he had a sure sense of his own destiny. That year the well-regarded light heavyweight Willie Pastrano came to Louisville from Miami with trainer Angelo Dundee to fight John Holman. One evening, Dundee was sitting in the hotel room with Pastrano when Clay called him from the lobby.

"I'd always stay in the same room with Willie to bird-dog him, make sure he didn't go floating around on me," Dundee recalled. "I wanted to keep tabs on him. Cassius said, word for word, 'I'm Cassius Marcellus Clay and I'm the Golden Gloves champion, I've won this and won that.' Then he told me he was gonna win the Olympics. I held my hand over the phone and asked Pastrano if he was game to meet the kid."

"What the hell," Pastrano said. "There's nothing on TV."

Cassius and his brother, Rudy, came upstairs and stayed for several hours talking with Dundee and Pastrano. Cassius asked question after question about training, about other fighters, about technique. Dundee was amused and impressed. "The kid was just so *alive* and committed." A couple of years later, Dundee and Pastrano came back to town for another fight, this time against Alonzo Johnson. Clay was seventeen, still an amateur, but now he didn't want to talk. He wanted to spar with Pastrano. Dundee was confident of his fighter, but he was not eager for trouble.

"I didn't want him to spar with Willie," Dundee said, "but he would be there waiting in the gym, bugging me every day, telling me, 'Why don't you let me work with your guy?' Well, I don't like amateurs to work with pros, and this was the week of Willie's fight. But this kid was so enthusiastic and I sort of caved in a little bit and let them go two rounds. I figured, what could happen? Well, Willie couldn't find this kid. Muhammad—Cassius then—was so quick. Bouncing. You think he looks quick when you see him in his later fights, but that's slow compared to what he was as a young man. Slap, slap, slap, and gone. And could he hit? Anybody can hit. Anybody a hundred and ninety pounds can hit. The key is hitting a guy when the other guy don't expect it. Willie came out of the ring, and I said, 'Whoa, Willie, you're stale, no more sparring for you.' Willie said, 'Bullshit, the kid beat the hell out of me.'"

CHAPTER SIX

Twentieth-Century Exuberance

IN THE SUMMER OF 1960, JUST BEFORE THE OLYMPICS IN Rome, a young journalist named Dick Schaap walked from his office on Madison Avenue in Manhattan to a midtown hotel to meet two of the best boxing prospects on the American team, Cassius Clay and a fighter from Toledo named Wilbert "Skeeter" McClure. Schaap was *Newsweek*'s sports editor, and while he would not be joining the press rush to Rome, he wanted to meet some of the more promising athletes on the American team, to get a better sense of how the magazine should cover the Games.

Schaap knew everyone and got around; athletes loved him. He offered to take Clay and McClure up to Harlem to meet his friend Sugar Ray Robinson, an idea that appealed especially to Clay. Clay had built his boxing style on the principle that a big man could borrow the tactics of a smaller man, a man like Robinson; he had also spun his dreams of luxury on visions of Sugar Ray's legendary Cadillacs: shocking pink this year, lavender the next. Clay idolized Robinson, but if he was nervous about meeting him, he did not show it on the ride uptown. Block after block, he described how he would destroy everyone in the light heavyweight division, and after that, it was on to the summary destruction of Floyd Patterson. He would become the heavyweight champion of the world, he said, before reaching legal voting age.

"I'll be the greatest of all time," Clay said.

Louisville, 1963.

"Don't mind him," McClure told Schaap as the taxi sped up Seventh Avenue. "That's just the way he is."

Schaap didn't mind at all. "Even at eighteen, Clay was the most vivid, the most alive figure I'd ever met," Schaap said. "It was like meeting a great actor or an electrifying statesman, some sort of figure that had a glow, an energy inside him, and you knew right away that you'd be hearing about him for years."

Clay, McClure, and Schaap stopped at Sugar Ray's bar on Seventh Avenue and 124th Street, but Robinson wasn't in yet. They decided to kill some time eating dinner and wandering around Harlem. A block from the bar they saw a young man, neatly dressed, standing on a wooden box preaching a doctrine of "buy black" and black self-help, a theme that Clay had heard from his father (via Marcus Garvey) and that would resonate in the speeches of Elijah Muhammad and Malcolm X. There was nothing especially radical about the speech—there were no calls for separatism, no suggestions of the white man as a "blue-eyed devil"— and yet Clay was astonished to find someone out on the street preaching without fear of police or white racists.

"Ain't he gonna get in trouble?" Clay asked.

Schaap said he would not. There had been speakers like this one in Harlem for a long time. Clay listened hard to the young preacher and nodded approvingly.

Robinson finally pulled up in that season's model—a purple Caddy. Schaap wondered how Clay would behave, whether he would try to get up in Robinson's face and put on the braggadocio. In fact, Clay was humble, even hesitant. Robinson gave him just a few moments. With a bored and superior air, Sugar Ray said hello and then strode on past them into his bar. Clay was goggle-eyed. "That Sugar Ray, he's something," he said. "Someday I'm gonna own *two* Cadillacs—and a Ford for just getting around in."

It was only later, when Clay looked back on the meeting, that he felt ignored by Robinson. "I was so *hurt*," he said years later. "If Sugar Ray only knew how much I loved him and how long I'd been following him, maybe he wouldn't have done that. . . . I said to myself right then, 'If I ever get great and famous and people want my autograph enough to wait all day to see me, I'm sure goin' to treat 'em different.' "

Clay's only obstacle as an Olympian was his fear of airplanes. He had made his way through the amateur ranks on trains and in the Martins' station wagon. Why couldn't he do the same on his trip to the heavyweight championship of the world? It took Joe Martin four hours of sitting and talking with Clay in Central Park in Louisville to convince him that he could not take a train to Rome. He could grip the armrests, he could take a pill, he could rant and rave, but he had to fly. "He finally agreed to fly," Martin's son, Joe junior, told the Louisville *Courier-Journal*. "But then he went to an army surplus store and bought a parachute and actually wore it on the plane. It was a pretty rough flight, and he was down in the aisle praying with his parachute on."

In Rome, he proceeded to delight himself, inside and outside the ring. As usual, he had some doggerel to recite, this time some lines celebrating Floyd Patterson's defeat of Ingemar Johansson:

> *You may talk about Sweden*
> *You may talk about Rome.*
> *But Rockville Centre's*
> *Floyd Patterson's home.*
> *A lot of people said*
> *That Floyd couldn't fight,*
> *But you should have seen him*
> *On that comeback night.*

Clay wandered through the Olympic Village meeting people from all over the world and charming them with predictions about his great future. Clay was so much at ease that he became known as the mayor of the Olympic Village. "His peers loved him," said Wilma Rudolph, who won three gold medals for the Americans in the sprints. "Everybody wanted to see him. Everybody wanted to be near him. Everybody wanted to talk to him. And he talked all the time. I always hung in the background, not knowing what he was going to say." Clay developed a crush on Rudolph, but she was engaged to a fellow sprinter. That was all right. When Clay saw McClure writing a love letter to a girlfriend back home, he asked him to take dictation for him: he would write a love letter to a girl in Louisville, if only for the fun of it.

Clay's experience in the ring was no less blissful. He marched easily through his first three bouts and then, in the finals against a stubby coffeehouse manager from Poland named Zbigniew

Pietrzykowski, he came back from a clumsy first round to win a unanimous decision and the gold medal. By the end of the bout, the Pole was bleeding all over Clay's white satin shorts.

In Rome, Clay had fulfilled his mission, but he had done it with a style that offended the sensibilities of some of the older writers. Big men were supposed to fight like Joe Louis and Rocky Marciano, they were supposed to wade in and flatten their opponent. A. J. Liebling's boxing memory encompassed Pierce Egan's eighteenth-century ring compendium *Boxiana* and the fourteenth-century Tunisian chronicler Ibn Khaldun, and he found Clay interesting but wanting, in the historical sense. Liebling wrote in *The New Yorker* that Clay, while amusing to watch, lacked the requisite menace of a true big man. Liebling was not offended by Clay's poetic pretensions—he was quick to remind his readers of Bob Gregson, the Lancashire Giant, who used to write such fistic couplets as "The British lads that's here/Quite strangers are to fear." It was Clay's boxing manner that left Liebling in doubt. "I watched Clay's performance in Rome and considered it attractive but not probative," he wrote. "Clay had a skittering style, like a pebble scaled over water. He was good to watch, but he seemed to make only glancing contact. It is true that the Pole finished the three-round bout helpless and out on his feet, but I thought he had just run out of puff chasing Clay, who had then cut him to pieces. . . . A boxer who uses his legs as much as Clay used his in Rome risks deceleration in a longer bout."

Whatever Liebling's reservations, Clay was awarded his gold medal with the word PUGILATO emblazoned across it. "I can still see him strutting around the Olympic Village with his gold medal on," Wilma Rudolph said. "He slept with it. He went to the cafeteria with it. He never took it off. No one else cherished it the way he did." He would wear the medal for weeks to come, even to bed. "First time in my life I ever slept on my back," Clay said. "Had to, or that medal would have cut my chest."

After the award ceremonies, a reporter from the Soviet Union asked Clay, in essence, how it felt to win glory for a country that did not give him the right to eat at Woolworth's in Louisville.

"Tell your readers we've got qualified people working on that problem, and I'm not worried about the outcome," Clay said. "To me, the U.S.A. is still the best country in the world, counting

yours. It may be hard to get something to eat sometimes, but anyhow I ain't fighting alligators and living in a mud hut." That remark
was printed in dozens of American papers as evidence of Clay's
good citizenship. More than a decade later, the author of *The
Greatest* made sure to tell the reader that it had been a mistake.
And yet Clay did say it; it was not so much a mistake as it was a reflection of his youth, of how far he would travel in the next few
years.

The next morning, as Clay wandered the Olympic Village, he noticed that the crowds were suddenly drifting from him to an older
man.

"Who's that?" Clay asked a friend.

"That's Floyd Patterson," the friend said. "Champion of the
world."

"Well, I wanna meet him."

Clay approached Patterson and introduced himself.

Afterward, Clay said he had been slighted. "Floyd congratulated
me with a milquetoast handshake," he said. "It hurt me. That cat
insulted me and someday he'll have to pay for it."

CLAY FLEW BACK TO NEW YORK, WHERE DICK SCHAAP WAS
waiting for him at Idlewild. Schaap had been thrilled by Clay's performance on television and was now more certain than ever that if
boxing had a future Clay was it. All night until early the next morning, Schaap and Clay went on a Manhattan hegira, beginning at a
Times Square arcade where they ordered up a fake newspaper with
the headline CASSIUS SIGNS FOR PATTERSON FIGHT.

"Back home they'll think it's real," Clay said. "They won't know
the difference."

They ate dinner at Jack Dempsey's restaurant, where Clay had a
roast beef sandwich and a piece of cheesecake and marveled at the
"huge" bill ($2.50). Then they walked across the street to drink at
Birdland—Clay's first drink: a Coke with a drop, literally one drop,
of whiskey. All the while, Clay was delighted whenever he was recognized and congratulated in the restaurant or on the street ("They
know me! They know me!"). He made sure they did by wearing his
official Olympic jacket and the gold medal around his neck. After
a postprandial run up to Harlem, the night ended at Clay's room at

the Waldorf-Astoria, where he was staying in a suite courtesy of a Louisville aluminum grandee named William ("Call me Billy") Reynolds. Reynolds was intent on putting together a package for Clay's career as a pro in which Joe Martin would be the trainer and Reynolds would provide financial backing and management. Toward the end of Clay's time in high school Reynolds had given him an easy summer job as a yardworker at his estate outside Louisville. Now, in New York, Reynolds gave him free accommodations and a roll of cash to spend at Tiffany's, where Clay was happy to buy watches for his mother, father, and brother. "You've never seen anyone in heaven the way Cassius Clay was in heaven after coming home with that medal around his neck," Schaap said. "He was so wired he could have stayed up a week straight." At around two in the morning, when Schaap was thinking hard about going home to bed, Clay insisted they go back to the Waldorf.

"C'mon," he said. "We can go up to my room and look through my scrapbook." And so they did.

CLAY FINALLY FLEW HOME TO LOUISVILLE AND A HERO'S WEL-come at Standiford Field Airport. This was the biggest boxing news in Louisville since 1905, when homeboy Marvin Hart beat Jack Root to win the heavyweight title. Mayor Bruce Hoblitzell, six cheerleaders, and three hundred fans cheered him on the tarmac, and the city provided a twenty-five-car motorcade. Clay provided poetry

> To make America the greatest is my goal.
> So I beat the Russian, and I beat the Pole
> And for the USA won the Medal of Gold.
> Italians said 'You're greater than the Cassius of old.' . . .

Terrible stuff, but no one much cared. A string of police cars escorted the caravan, which ended at Central High School. A band of cheerleaders greeted the homecoming hero with a huge banner, "Welcome Home Champ!" Atwood Wilson, the principal who had saved Cassius from embarrassment and failure so many times, stepped to the microphone and said, "When we consider all the efforts that are being made to undermine the prestige of America we can be grateful we had such a fine ambassador as Cassius to send over to Italy." Mayor Hoblitzell was no less enthusiastic. "You are a credit to Louisville and the profession," he said, and the crowd of more than a thousand students and teachers and townspeople cheered. "You are an inspiration to the young people of this city."

Back at the house on Grand Avenue, Clay senior sang "God Bless America" and showed off his newly decorated front steps: he had painted them red, white, and blue. Odessa Clay declared an early Thanksgiving and the family had roast turkey for supper.

For a while, life was a parade for Cassius. A few weeks after his homecoming, he took it upon himself to ride through the streets of the city once more. He stood up in the backseat of a pink Cadillac and declared, "I am Cassius Clay! I am the greatest!" Then he turned to Wilma Rudolph, who had come from Tennessee to visit, and proclaimed, "And this is Wilma Rudolph. She is the greatest!"

"Sit down," Rudolph said, cringing in her seat.

"Come on, Wilma. Stand up, Wilma!"

"No, I can't do that."

After Clay declared Rudolph the co-greatest a few more times, she warily got up, waved, and sat back down, but, of course, it was Cassius who enjoyed the attention.

The celebrations masked an underlying ambivalence about Clay in Louisville that would deepen with time. The Louisville Chamber of Commerce gave Clay a citation but declined to sponsor a dinner for him. "We just haven't time right now," executive secretary K. P. Vinsel explained. Later on, many Louisville residents—especially white residents—would scorn the fighter's decisions to convert to Islam and change his name, to refuse the draft, to speak out so fiercely and often on politics. In 1978, at the zenith of his fame, the city council approved a proposal to change the name of Walnut Street to Muhammad Ali Boulevard, but by the narrowest of margins, six to five.

Although he had sounded defensive about race for the benefit of the Soviet reporter in Rome, Clay was already mightily aware that his gold medal changed nothing about Louisville. The same old Jim Crow attitudes still prevailed. Not long after coming home, he walked into a luncheonette and ordered a glass of juice.

"Can't serve you," the boss said.

"But he's the Olympic champion!" one of the waiters told him.

"I don't give a damn who he is," the proprietor said. "Get him out of here!"

Inevitably, Clay declared himself ready to become a professional. What he needed was a manager and financial backing, and, having won the Olympic title and national publicity, he was a hot commercial property. A few years earlier, Clay would almost surely have landed in the soft palm of the Mafia; he would hardly have left Rome before one of Frankie Carbo's lieutenants had him out to dinner, making splendid offers. As it happened, the usual mob suspects were now in disarray, and for perhaps the first time since the early part of the century, a boxer as promising as Cassius Clay could choose who would manage him, who would back him. As a convict, Liston had been fairly delivered into the arms of the Cosa Nostra; from the start, Clay was blessed with more resources, internal and external.

The Clay family hired a lawyer from the West End named Alberta Jones and at first tried to put together a deal with William Reynolds's lawyer, Gordon Davidson. "Billy Reynolds had all the money he'd ever need and his real motivation was to have some fun and get behind this local kid," Davidson said. "We drew up a contract that included a salary for Cassius, which was unheard-of in those days, and a trust. Finally, we reached an agreement. But then Alberta called me to tell me the deal was off. I was absolutely stunned. I couldn't understand why."

The main obstacle was Clay's father, who objected to the presence of Joe Martin as chief cornerman in the deal. Ostensibly he rejected Martin because he had never trained a professional fighter before; but more important, Clay senior saw Martin as the embodiment of the police, the white Louisville police who had arrested him more than once. The entire deal quickly dissolved into bad feeling. Martin, for his part, thought that Clay senior was taking credit for his son where no credit was due. "All of a sudden you'd think the old man did all the work," Martin said bitterly. "The old man never did care about what the kid was doing until Clay got all of that publicity. He's something, he is. He's got all the brains God gives a goose—about a half a teaspoonful."

Soon everyone in Louisville knew that Martin was out of a job, and within a few days William Faversham, Jr., a former investment counselor, former actor, and son of an English-born matinee idol, filled the vacuum. (Reynolds, for his part, was loyal to Martin and was not prepared to woo Clay without Martin as part of the package.) Faversham was vice-president at one of the biggest businesses in the area, Brown-Forman Distillers (makers of Old Forester and Early Times), and he and a few of his friends in the Louisville business world invited the Clays to a meeting. Faversham offered to back Clay with a syndicate made up of eleven of the richest men in the state; the deal itself was almost an exact copy of the contract originally drawn up by William Reynolds.

The members of the syndicate were, in fact, the city's oligarchs: Patrick Calhoun, Jr., a horse breeder and a retired chairman of the American Commercial Barge Line, who admitted, "What I know about boxing you can put in your eye"; William Sol Cutchins, grandson of a Confederate soldier and president of Brown & Williamson Tobacco; Vertner DeGarmo Smith, former sales manager for Brown-Forman and a salesman of everything from bonds to fraternity pins, whiskey to table salt; William Lee Lyons Brown, chairman of the board of Brown-Forman and a near-caricature of the Southern gentleman ("Ah wonder if you realize that Cassius Clay's aunt cooks for my double first cousin?"); Elbert Gary Sutcliffe, a retired farmer with enormous interests in U.S. Steel; George Washington "Possum" Norton IV, a secretary-treasurer of WAVE-TV, the local NBC affiliate, which broadcast *Tomorrow's Champions*; Robert Worth Bingham, scion of the Bingham publishing and broadcasting empire, which then included the local CBS affiliate, *The Courier-Journal*, and the *Louisville Times*; J. D. Stetson Coleman, chairman of a Florida bus company, a Georgia drug firm, an Illinois candy company, and an Oklahoma oil company; James Ross Todd, the youngest of the group at twenty-six, and the descendant of an old-line Kentucky family that made its money, he said frankly, in "wheeling and dealing"; and Archibald McGhee Foster, senior vice-president of a New York–based advertising agency, Ted Bates, which handled the Brown & Williamson account. Faversham also hired Gordon Davidson to "dust off" the original Reynolds contract and use it for the new arrangement.

The Louisville Sponsoring Group was all-white, of course, and represented a group of old-line families who tended to send their boys off for polishing to boarding schools and Ivy League colleges before they came home to pick up where Daddy left off. In all, the members of the group represented the major businesses of the city: cigarettes, whiskey, transportation, banking. Most of them belonged to the all-white Pendennis Club on Walnut Street and played golf at all-white country clubs. (When Bill Cutchins brought Clay to the Pendennis Club he was rewarded with an official letter of reprimand.) These men lived in fine Louisville houses, wintered in Florida and Nassau, talked about business and horses, and rarely met the citizens of the West End except as employees, cooks, and domestics. In the majority, the Louisville Group was resistant to the civil rights movement. The Binghams, however, were the city's leading white liberals. They paid for their integrationist editorials with racist pickets and rocks hurled through their windows. As sportsmen, they were partial to golf and hunting. Boxing was not their element, generally speaking. Faversham had some slight acquaintance with boxing; when he was working on Broadway he kept in shape working out at Philadelphia Jack O'Brien's gym, where he sparred with another actor, Spencer Tracy. William Lee Lyons Brown fought at Annapolis as a heavyweight on the plebe team. But the rest knew very little or nothing at all of the prize ring. Their real asset, besides cash, was that in men like Possum Norton and Robert Bingham, they had access to the main avenues of publicity in Louisville.

For these men Cassius Clay was an amusement, a sign of social belonging, a minor investment, a lark. Each partner contributed $2,800—tax-deductible. The total cost of launching the fighter, in their estimate, would be $25,000 to $30,000. They really had nothing to lose. One of the less idealistic members of the Louisville Group, waxing candid, told a reporter for *Sports Illustrated* that the collective motivation for taking on Clay was, at best, part civic, part mercenary. "Let me give you the official line—we are behind Cassius Clay to improve the breed of boxing, to do something nice for a deserving, well-behaved Louisville boy, and finally to save him from the jaws of the hoodlum jackals," he said. "I think it's fifty percent true, but also fifty percent hokum. What I want to do, like a few others, is to make a bundle of money. Why, do you know a Clay-Liston fight might gross a winner's share of three million dollars? Split that up and it comes out one and a half million for Cassius and one and a half million for the syndicate. Best of all, it comes out a hundred and fifty thousand for me."

And yet no matter how cynical that surely was, it was nothing compared to the cynicism of the usual fight crowd. Next to the mobbed-up managers of Sonny Liston and hundreds of boxers before him, the Louisville Sponsoring Group was a missionary venture, an adventure in Jim Crow paternalism. In accepting the deal, Clay immediately received a $10,000 signing bonus (more than enough to buy a Cadillac for his parents), a guarantee of $4,800 for each of the first two years of the contract, and a $6,000 draw against earnings for the following four years until the contract expired in 1966. The syndicate and Clay agreed to split all gross earnings evenly, while the group underwrote training and travel expenses. Fifteen percent of Clay's profits would go into a pension fund, not to be touched until he was thirty-five. That final provision, which was meant to prevent Clay from becoming yet another fighter with nothing left at the end of his career except his injuries and his clouded memories, would sometimes prove irritating to him.

"I don't want money in no bank," Clay said later on. "I want it in real estate where I can point to a lot with an apartment on it and say, 'There, that's mine.' I want to be able to see it. The bank might burn down or something. I don't want to have to worry about no stocks, or have a lot of investments and have to spend all my time checkin' up on them." Considering the way he spent his money and his generosity toward family, friends, and hangers-on through the years, the pension plan was probably the most sensible part of the package.

For the first two years of the contract, losses ran ahead of earnings, and as promising as Clay may have seemed on some nights, the members of the Louisville Group did not think of their fighter as a potential champion, much less as the most celebrated man of his era. As late as 1963, Cutchins said, "If anyone had told me a year ago that Cassius would develop into an international figure, I would have said he was smoking marijuana." Gordon Davidson said, "There's no way to view the whole experience as a financial killing, or even a financial venture. These were millionaires who ended up investing, over six years, more than ten thousand dollars each—and a lot of that was deductible—and came out with twenty-five thousand, in dribs and drabs."

AND SO WITH HIS BACKING COMING INTO PLACE, CLAY BEGAN A professional career. On October 29, 1960, he beat up the police chief of Fayetteville, West Virginia, Tunney Hunsaker, in a six-round match at Freedom Hall in Louisville. To prepare for his debut, Clay had sparred mainly with his brother, Rudy; his trainer for the fight was Fred Stoner, a local boxing man with experience. Clay senior preferred Stoner to Martin mainly because he was black. And yet for an ambitious Olympic champion, neither Clay nor the Louisville Group thought Stoner was sufficient in the long run. Clay should have been able to knock Hunsaker out. He would not go far hammering out decisions against officers of West Virginia law enforcement.

One of the first telegrams Clay had received after winning in Rome was from Archie Moore, who still held the light heavyweight title and ran a training camp in the hills outside San Diego. Moore appealed to Clay as both a fighter and a personage. And he appealed to the Louisville Sponsoring Group because once Clay established California residence its contract with Clay would hold. Unlike other states, California had passed a law saying that minors with firm state residency could sign binding contracts and enlist the court to watch over their earnings until they reached a majority. (The law was written mainly to protect child actors.) Elsewhere, minors could ignore contracts at will; at the same time, their earnings were not protected from avaricious relatives or anyone else with legal authority. Both sides liked the California variant.

Moore had always been a clever fighter, but with age and the loss of strength, he had become the Euclid of the ring, a master of angles, of evading the aggression of the young and eager and landing a precise blow to end it. Moore also loved to talk. Clay's verbiage was borrowed from his father and the badinage of the playground—he was the first rapper, the precursor to Tupac Shakur and Puff Daddy—but Moore affected the fancy speech of the vaudeville Englishman, splashing the blood of his game on the lace of his syntax. (There was little mystery as to why Moore was a favorite of A. J. Liebling's. Moore's talk resembled Liebling's prose, and one could not help but wonder if, consciously or not, they had formed a symbiotic literary relationship.)

Clay had sought out Ray Robinson as a trainer, but Robinson, a more remote figure, demurred. And so, just days after dispatching Chief Hunsaker, he was off to Ramona, California, and the training camp that Moore had dubbed the Salt Mine. Clay loved the sight of the place. The gymnasium, known as the Bucket of Blood, was a big barn with a skull painted on the front door. Outside there were boulders strewn all around, monuments to great fighters of the past; the names of such men as Jack Johnson, Ray Robinson, and Joe Louis were painted on the rocks. Years later, when Ali had a camp of his own in Deer Lake, Pennsylvania, he set up similar monuments.

Moore was immediately impressed with Clay's seriousness. He marveled at how he ran up and down the steep hills surrounding the camp and stopped only when Moore demanded it. As an innovator himself, Moore saw nothing wrong with Clay's unorthodox ring style, the low-slung hands, the movement. He saw unlimited potential in Clay and wanted to keep him. "I loved that speedy style of his even though he wasn't nearly as fast then as he would be in a year or two," Moore said. "In the back of my mind, I thought to myself, here, finally, is someone who could have knocked out Joe Louis, 'cause, God knows, I couldn't have." But Moore lacked the psychological flexibility that Clay needed in a trainer. Moore still had the vanity of a fighter, and Clay's vanity offended his own. When Moore tried to suggest ways of winning early knockouts— "Slip the punch, go under, and put him out! Then move on!"—Clay would rebel, if only verbally, telling him he didn't want to be another Archie Moore, he wanted to be a heavyweight Sugar Ray.

The Salt Mine was a spartan camp with no support staff. The young fighters were expected to pitch in, help with the cleaning and the washing up, chop wood for the stove, do all sorts of chores around the property. But Clay, who had been spoiled at home by his mother, was in no mood for that. He wanted to train and spar.

"Archie, I didn't come here to be a dishwasher," he said. "I ain't gonna wash dishes like a woman."

Eventually, Cassius did his chores, but he made it plain he didn't much like it. The arrangement, in short, was doomed. Moore wanted to keep Clay around not merely for the training fees the Louisville Group was paying out, but for the sport of it—here was a fighter waiting for guidance, for a chance to win the title. But after a few weeks, Moore called Faversham in Louisville.

"I think I'm gonna have to ask you to take the boy home," Moore said. "My wife is crazy about him, my kids are crazy about him, and I'm crazy about him, but he just won't do what I tell him to do. He thinks I'm trying to change his style, but all I'm trying to do is add to it."

Faversham, the spokesman and chief operative for the Louisville fathers, declared that perhaps Clay needed nothing less than a "good spanking."

"He sure does," Moore said, "but I don't know who's gonna give him one. Including me."

IN PUBLIC, THE MEMBERS OF THE LOUISVILLE GROUP TRIED TO show they didn't mind that their fighter refused to behave. "Cassius is a really dedicated boy," said Faversham. "His garrulity is a little rich at times, but we don't discourage him. He has decided to create an image and he works at it."

After looking around at available trainers, Faversham persuaded Angelo Dundee to take on Clay. Dundee had good memories of meeting Clay when he came to town with Pastrano and other fighters like Ralph Dupas, Luis Rodriguez, and Joey Maxim.

"I wanted to put off Cassius for a couple of months, but have you ever heard him take no for an answer?" Dundee said.

Angelo Dundee was the fifth of seven children of illiterate immigrants from Calabria. The family name was originally Mirena, but when one of Angelo's brothers began fighting under the name Joe Dundee (the Fighting Ashman) as a tribute to an Italian featherweight champion of the twenties, Angelo and his brother Chris took on the name. During the war, Angelo worked as an airplane inspector and then went into the navy; in 1948, he went to New York to join Chris, who had set himself up as a manager. Chris Dundee was well connected in the shadowy boxing world of that era, and he was given the go-ahead to set up camp in Miami as a promoter. "I'm sure the Dundees, especially Chris, had some dubious acquaintances in those days," said Gordon Davidson, "but when we went looking for a trainer we knew there was no one that was simon-pure. That was boxing in those days. Compared to everyone else, Angelo Dundee was as good as it gets." Television was taking its toll on the small clubs of the Northeast, and the great minds of the sport figured that Miami Beach, with its big-money tourist trade, could turn into a boxing center. Chris Dundee began running boxing and wrestling shows at the Convention Hall and in other local arenas, and Angelo joined him in the early fifties. With years of New York experience behind him and his brother a local lord, Angelo picked up fighters quickly, especially refugees from Cuba and the rest of Latin America.

The Dundees operated from a rat-infested, termite-ridden walk-up on the corner of Washington Avenue and Fifth Street in Miami Beach called the Fifth Street Gym. To get there, you entered a door next to a pharmacy and navigated a rickety staircase to the second floor, where you were greeted, more often than not, by Em-mett "the Great" Sullivan, a stooped old man with baggy clothes and an unlit cigar shoved in his toothless maw. Admission was fifty cents, and if you dared try to avoid it, Sullivan would call you a "mud turtle" and withhold from you his priceless smile. Inside there were two filthy windows with a pair of boxing gloves and the words "Fifth Street Gym" painted on them. The plywood floor was rubbed smooth from thousands of shuffling boxing shoes. There was a ring, speed bags, a heavy bag, rubdown tables, a couple of bare lightbulbs, some fight posters, and Chris Dundee's desk in a corner of the room. The gym was home at the time to such fight-ers as Sugar Ramos, Mantequilla Napoles, and Luis Rodriguez, who were all champions, as well as such contenders as Florentino Fernandez, Baby Luis, and Robinson Garcia. Most afternoons, the regulars (the Pugilistic College of Cardinals, as they were known) would stand around the ring and pass judgment on the quality of a prospect's punch. They were, in the main, old fat guys, bad-cigar guys, guys with names like Sellout and Chicky and Evil Eye. "Them guys would all say the same things about Muhammad that the sportswriter guys would say, that he kept his hands too low, that he can't punch, that he was a headhunter, no body shots, the usual," Dundee said.

Dundee put Clay up at a hotel in the black ghetto, the Mary Elizabeth, a headquarters for pimps, prostitutes, hustlers, and winos. Cassius, well brought up as he was, never succumbed to the temptations of the Mary Elizabeth. In fact, after the local hustlers found out that he was a fighter, and after they had met him and were charmed by him, they would take him out to the big local nightclub, the Sir John, to hear the best music in town, and while they got loaded, Clay drank orange juice and went home early. His day began with a long run at around five on Biscayne Boulevard near Bay Point, and later he would run from the ghetto to Miami Beach to train with Dundee on Fifth Street.

"Remember, this was Miami, pre–civil rights and all that stuff, the Deep South, and Muhammad would run across the MacArthur Causeway to the gym, and I got calls from the police saying that there's some tall skinny black guy *running*—and did I know anything about it," Dundee said. "I said that's our guy, Cassius Clay. He was the easiest guy in the world. He ate his meals at the Famous Chef and signed for the food there. Never complained about nothing. All he wanted to do was train and fight, train and fight."

Like any wise handler, Dundee wanted to bring Clay along slowly, purposefully, exposing him, with each successive fight, to a new challenge, a new set of problems, physical and mental. From the start, Clay accepted what was put before him with serene confidence. Which offended the Pugilistic College of Cardinals. Before taking on one Herb Siler in his second fight, Clay told the crowd, "I'm gonna beat Floyd Patterson! I'm gonna be champion!" Read now, so many years after his rise and eclipse, those words have a certain logic to them, a sweet familiarity, like an old pop tune heard once more on the car radio. But back then, in 1960, Clay was a kid, eighteen years old, an undercard fighter with promise; it was as if an outfielder in the American Legion league had called the general manager of the San Francisco Giants and vowed to take center field away from Willie Mays.

Part of Dundee's initial appeal to Clay was that he never tried to mold him, never tried to quiet him down, make him fight in another style. Instead, Dundee encouraged Clay's showmanship, he thought it was harmless at worst, and, more likely, a commercial and psychological boon. That year, Clay fought four times in Miami Beach—against Siler, Tony Esperti, Jim Robinson, and Donnie Fleeman—and each time he drew more people who had heard about the new kid with the fast hands, the kid with the gold medal and the silver tongue.

"One of those fights, with Fleeman, was at the start of spring training, and so some of the heavyweights of the literary field—Shirley Povich, Doc Greene, Al Buck, Dick Young, Jimmy Cannon—were down here with time on their hands," Dundee said. "They were friends of mine and I wanted to show my fighter off. Well, Muhammad came out of the shower. He had won. But the writers weren't that sold on him as a fighter—they thought he bounced around too much and did everything wrong. They figured he was all mouth and no talent. This was still an era when fighters thought they needed nine guys to talk for them. Joe Louis used to say, 'My manager does my talking for me. I do my talking in the ring.' Marciano was somewhat like that, too. But Muhammad was different right off the bat, and I thought it was great. So Muhammad waited for them to take their pads out. 'Aren't you gonna talk to me? Aren't you gonna talk to me?' And so he wore them down. They started to listen."

One of the regulars at Fifth Street was Ferdie Pacheco, a doctor who ran clinics in the black and Hispanic ghettos. For kicks, for a release from the pressures of medicine, Pacheco worked with Dundee in the corner for various fighters. Even before Pacheco joined the Clay entourage, he watched the way Dundee gave his new fighter leeway, the way he put himself in the background and used subtle psychological tricks to get the most out of him.

"Angelo had the reputation, and Ali respected that a lot," Pacheco said. "He was also strong when he needed to be strong and weak when he needed to be weak. Angelo had a survivor's instinct that came from dealing with his brother Chris, who was a strong boxing guy. In order to work with Chris, you had to learn how to bend and when to fight. By the time Ali—Clay—rolled around, he had that act down pretty good. Mainly, Angelo was always, always, always subservient to the fighter. He was never egomaniacal like most of these managers who say 'I'm fighting so-and-so' or 'I'll knock him out.' That was especially true in those days. Angelo felt he was the second banana in the show. The real show is the fighter, even if the fighter is a moron. That sat well with Ali. Ali was not an egomaniac, but you didn't try to control him."

"Angelo Dundee, I like him cause he's half colored," Ali once said jokingly. "Got a lot of colored nigger blood in him. He's Italian and passes for white, but he's got a lot of nigger in him. I get along with him. He never bosses me, tells me when to run, how much to box. I do what I want to do. I'm free. I go where I want to go. And he's a nice fella. Everybody likes him. He's got the connection and the complexion to get me the right protection which leads to good affection."

Even in those first fights, Dundee did not see Clay as a reclamation project, his Frankenstein. The idea was to refine what was there, to make him smarter, to have him watch out for the tricks— but to teach it all indirectly, by inference. "Every fighter has things to be worked on," Dundee said. "At first I wanted to get a little of the bounce out of him. But you couldn't actually direct him to do something. You had to sort of mold him. He resented direct orders. He wanted to feel that he was always the innovator, and so I encouraged that. I learned this from one of the great teachers, Charlie Goldman, who used to say if a guy's a short guy make him shorter, if he's tall, make him taller."

Like any traditionalist of the craft, Dundee would have liked Clay to batter an opponent's body instead of pursuing the head all the time. "Body-punching is a capital investment," boxing people say. But Clay would have none of it. "Keep punching at a man's head," he said, "and it mixes his mind."

So Dundee saw he would get nowhere trying to retool his man, and he made the best of it. "I tried to make Muhammad feel like he innovated everything," he said. "For instance, he'd be in there sparring and when he came out I'd say, 'Gee, your jab is really coming along. You're getting your left knee into it and really stopping him in his tracks.' He may not have been getting his knee into it at all. The next time out he'd be concentrating on it. But mainly, it was all him. His quickness, the ability to get in and get out, was unbelievable from the start. He was a big advocate of roadwork. Luis Sarria, Muhammad's exercise guy and his masseur, put him through endless calisthenics, which is big in boxing. That's why his body grew so fast from a little kid's body to such an impressive body. He came in here at about a hundred and eighty-nine pounds and he was over two hundred like a snap. And all muscle. It was a transition that scared you, but it was natural. No weights. It was light bag, heavy bag, roadwork, usually three miles and more. He could run like a gazelle."

Clay's speed overshadowed his size and strength, which is partly why he remained an underrated fighter in the eyes of the sports-writers for so long. But Pacheco, who became Clay's physician as soon as he arrived in Miami, said, "In 1961, 1962, 1963, he was the most perfect physical specimen I had ever seen, from an artistic and an anatomical standpoint, even healthwise. You just couldn't improve on the guy. If someone came from another planet and said, 'Give us your best specimen,' you'd give him Ali. Perfectly proportioned, handsome, lightning reflexes, and a great mind for sports. Even when he got a cold it went away the next day."

THE MIAMI FIGHT CROWD, HOWEVER, DID NOT FALL OVER backward for Clay—or at least not until Ingemar Johansson came to town for a rematch with Patterson. The publicity man for the fight was Harold Conrad, a dashing roué possessed of an oily charm that made him a regular on the "21"–Stork Club–Toots Shor's circuit. Conrad was a link to the days of Damon Runyon and Walter Winchell, the old Broadway saloon crowd, though he preferred a joint to a martini. He was an all-star pothead before the invention of rock and roll. He also had a fantastic instinct for promotion. Conrad had heard about Clay—especially Clay's mouth—and he thought it might help sell some tickets for the Patterson fight if he had Clay spar publicly with Johansson. Johansson was short on sparring partners, so he was willing, and Clay, of course, was eager for attention. His immediate response was not a simple yes, but rather "I'll go dancin' with Johansson."

Johansson, who had destroyed Patterson in their first fight, suddenly discovered he could not touch a nineteen-year-old with just a few pro bouts to his credit. The Swede was never a graceful fighter, but now he was a marionette with a clipped string. He stumbled after Clay, trying to keep up, and all the while Clay kept flicking the left jab in his face and chanting, "I'm the one who should be fighting Patterson, not you! Come on, sucker, what's the matter? Can't you catch me?" The longer Clay kept flicking his jabs and his taunts, the more furious and frustrated Johansson became, until finally his trainer, the legendary Whitey Bimstein, brought it to an end after two exhausting rounds.

"I'd heard a little about Clay, but as I sat there watching this amazing exhibition, I thought, 'Jesus Christ! What have we here?'" said Gil Rogin, who wrote for *Sports Illustrated* at the time. "We were still a pretty young magazine—we started up in 1954—and what I was seeing was the most important story we would ever have. To a great degree it was the story that we built the magazine on."

For his homecoming as a professional, Clay took on Lamar Clark, a tough heavyweight with forty-five knockouts in a row. For the first time as a pro, Clay made a prediction: Clark would be gone in two. And so he was. Two rounds into the fight, Clay broke Clark's nose and dropped him to the canvas twice. The referee ended it there. "The more confident he became, the more his natural ebullience took over," Pacheco said. "Everything was such fun to him. Maybe it wouldn't have been so much fun if someone had knocked him lopsided, but no one did. No one shut him up. And so he just kept predicting and winning, predicting and winning. It was like Candide: he didn't think anything bad could happen in this best of all possible worlds."

Clay's next fight was in Las Vegas against a gigantic Hawaiian, Duke Sabedong. It was his first trying battle. Sabedong never really had a chance to beat Clay—the difference in their abilities was clear from the first minute of the fight—but he started hitting Clay with low blows and hoped for the best. Clay won a ten-round decision, his longest bout so far. What he learned beforehand, however, was even more instructive.

One of Clay's prefight promotional duties was to appear on a local radio show with Gorgeous George, the preeminent professional wrestler of the time. Gorgeous George (known to his mother as George Raymond Wagner) was the first wrestler of the television age to exploit the possibilities of theatrical narcissism and a flexible sexual identity—a Liberace in tights. His hair was long and blond, and when he entered the ring he wore curlers. In his corner, he would release the curlers and let one of his minions brush out the golden hair to his shoulders. He wore a robe of silver lamé and his fingernails were trimmed and polished. One lackey sprayed the ring mat with insecticide, another sprayed Gorgeous George with eau de cologne.

At the radio interview, Clay was not exactly silent. He was already known by various nicknames in the press (Gaseous Cassius, the Louisville Lip, Cash the Brash, Mighty Mouth, Claptrap Clay, et al.), and he was quick to predict an easy win over Duke Sabedong. But compared to Gorgeous George he was tongue-tied.

"I'll kill him!" Gorgeous ranted. "I'll tear his arm off! If this bum beats me I'll crawl across the ring and cut my hair off. But it's not gonna happen because I'm the greatest wrestler in the world!"

Gorgeous George was already forty-six—he had been retailing this shtick for years—but Clay was impressed, the more so when he saw Gorgeous George perform. Every seat in the arena was filled and nearly every fan was screaming for George's gilded scalp. But the point was, the arena was filled. "A lot of people will pay to see someone shut your mouth," he told Clay in the dressing room after the show. "So keep on bragging, keep on sassing, and always be outrageous."

Clay took direction well. "I saw fifteen thousand people coming to see this man get beat," he said. "And his talking did it. I said, this is a gooood idea!"

As the press paid more attention to Clay, first in Louisville and Miami and then in such national media as *Sports Illustrated,* the idea kept cropping up that no twenty-year-old could possibly have come up with this act, this bizarre combination of loose-limbed athleticism and blatant showmanship. All manner of theories were proposed, and would persist for years to come: the fighting style came straight from Ray Robinson by way of Billy Conn; the lip came from Cassius Clay, Sr.; the flamboyance came from Jack Johnson, from Archie Moore, from Gorgeous George. Clay, in fact, was the latest showman in the great American tradition of narcissistic self-promotion, a descendant of Davy Crockett and Buffalo Bill by way of the dozens. Clay gave credit to his predecessors when he was aware of them, but he was insistent on his originality—and rightly so.

"I know some guys in Louisville who used to give me a lift to the gym in their car when my motor scooter was broke down," he said. "Now they're trying to tell me they made me, and how not to forget them when I get rich. And my daddy, he tickles me. He says, 'Don't listen to the others, boy, I made you.' He says he made me because he fed me my vegetable soup and steak when I was a baby, going without shoes, he says, to pay the food bill, and arguing with my mother, who didn't want me eating them things so little. My daddy also says he made me because he saved me from working so I could box—I've never worked a day in my life—and he made me this and he made me that. . . . But listen here. When you want to talk about who made me, you talk to me. Who made me is *me*."

Through 1961 and 1962, Clay gained speed as both fighter and performer. He beat a succession of ranked heavyweights—Alonzo Johnson, Alex Miteff, Willie Besmanoff, Sonny Banks, Don Warner, George Logan, Billy Daniels, Alejandro Lavorante—and even at the most perilous moment, when he got too careless in the first round, too glib, and Banks knocked him down, he showed a new ability to take a punch, and he recovered to win easily in four. Afterward, Harry Wiley, Banks's cornerman and a legendary New York boxing fixture, described the phenomenon of fighting Clay: "Things just went sour gradually all at once. He'll pick you and peck you, peck you and pick you, until you don't know where you are."

Here, for once, was a young man energized by fantasies of his own power and gorgeousness and wit who had what it took to fulfill those fantasies. He was, first of all, a great fighter. "Watching Muhammad get up off the floor against Sonny Banks, kill out the rest of the round, and then recover to win—that was the night I fell in love with the kid," Dundee said. In between these various exams in the ring, Clay had a good time. For five hundred dollars, he took a bit part in *Requiem for a Heavyweight*, the story of a destroyed old fighter, played by Anthony Quinn, who is pushed into taking more bouts by Jackie Gleason. Clay, of course, played the role of the fresh-faced challenger.

In November 1962, Clay signed a contract for an episode right out of *Requiem*: he was scheduled to fight Archie Moore, who was now forty-seven (more or less) and the veteran of two hundred fights. "I wasn't a fool, I knew how old I was and I knew Clay from training him for a while," Moore told me decades later, "but I felt pretty good about Clay, and I thought if I could bear down, I could beat him. I had to outbox him or wait him out. He was so young, and you can never tell what a young man can do in boxing."

The truth was, Moore badly needed the purse. His only chance was that Clay's inexperience would yield an opening, a chance for a right hand and a knockout. That was unlikely, according to the oddsmakers. Clay was a three-to-one favorite, and his prediction was for a quick night: "When you come to the fight, don't block the aisle, and don't block the door. You will all go home after round four."

Clay and Moore sold out the arena in Los Angeles, not least because they kept up the verbal sparring at every venue possible, especially television. The two fighters even staged a half-hour mock debate.

"The only way I'll fall in four, Cassius, is by tripping over your prostrate form," Moore said.

"If I lose," said Clay (echoing Gorgeous George), "I'm going to crawl across the ring and kiss your feet. Then I'll leave the country."

"Don't humiliate yourself," the old man replied. "Our country's depending on its youth. Really, I don't see how you can stand yourself. I am a speaker, not a rabble-rouser. I'm a conversationalist, you're a shouter!"

Moore played the avuncular elder to the boorish wannabe. After the debate, he reflected on the young man at a certain professorial remove: "I view this young man with mixed emotions," he said. "Sometimes he sounds humorous, but sometimes he sounds like Ezra Pound's poetry. He's like a man who can write beautifully but doesn't know how to punctuate. He has this twentieth-century exuberance but there's bitterness in him somewhere. . . . He is certainly coming along at a time when a new face is needed on the boxing scene, on the fistic horizon. But in his anxiousness to be this person he may be overplaying his hand by belittling people. . . . I don't care what Cassius says. He can't make me mad. All I want to do is knock him out."

Once the two fighters were in the arena, stripped of their robes and their promotional poses, it was impossible to ignore the physical difference. Clay was sleek as an otter, beautiful, and not even at his peak of strength. Moore was middle-aged. His hair was going gray. Fat jiggled on his arms. He kept his trunks pulled up around his nipples.

In the first round, Clay conducted a survey. Moore had a reputation for speed (now gone) and as a sneak, the master of the quick, unseen punch. And as Clay flashed his jabs into Moore's face, he seemed to convince himself that there would be no answer coming. Each jab that Clay bounced off Moore's scalp assured the younger man of the cruelty of age—a soothing discovery to him, if not to Moore.

In the second, Moore actually caught Clay with a right hand. It shot up out of a crowd of tangled arms and gave Clay a start, but there was nothing much to it. By the third, Moore was already so exhausted from trying to keep up that his arms began to sink. His inclination to send any damage Clay's way was down to nothing. Moore crouched, lower and lower, as if to meld with the canvas, but Clay's reach was long and he leaned over to drill one left hook after another into Moore's bald spot. Years later, Moore would say that those punches, in their accumulation, made him dizzy: "They stirred the mind."

Clay was doing whatever he wanted. Every punch—the jabs, the hooks, the quick overhand rights—landed, and Moore was barely hanging on, squatting lower and lower. Midway through the third, Clay hit Moore square on the chin. Moore wobbled. Then he took a few running steps backward to the rope, found it, and hung on. Clay refused to follow up, more for aesthetic reasons, it seemed, than for lack of intent. He had predicted a fourth-round knockout and wanted to preserve his pure vision of the fight.

Clay came out flat-footed in the fourth, the better to leverage his punches, and after a few preliminary jabs to warm up the shoulders, he started looking for the knockout. Moore bent at the waist again, as if in prayer, but he could not bow low enough. Moore took a few wild swings to preserve his name, and Clay jabbed back, scolding him for the delay. Clay circled, circled, and then suddenly jumped in with an uppercut that straightened Moore out of his crouch, then a few more punches, all sharp and straight, like clean hammer raps to a nail, put him down. Clay stood over the prostrate lump to take his bow, shuffled his feet in a flash, and then retreated, reluctantly, to the neutral corner. He disdained this obligatory retreat; it meant leaving center stage.

Moore, meanwhile, roused himself and rolled onto his left side, an old man waking from a fitful sleep. Then he pridefully lifted himself to his feet just before "ten." With a look of annoyance (he'd thought it was over), Clay met Moore again in the center of the ring and started punching. Moore took one wild swing, as if to acquit himself of any lingering charges of resignation, and then slowly melted back to the floor as Clay hit him on top of the head. The time had come and Moore knew it. He stayed on his backside.

With the fight over, Clay hugged Moore sweetly, the way one would embrace a grandfather.

Later Moore responded with an endorsement. "He's definitely ready for Liston," he told the reporters gathered around him. "Sonny would be difficult for him and I would hesitate to say he could beat the champ, but I'll guarantee he would furnish him with an exceedingly interesting evening."

CHAPTER SEVEN

Secrets

BY 1962, CLAY WAS A TOP CONTENDER FOR THE HEAVYWEIGHT title, but by now his reputation was based as much on his persona as on his athletic abilities. "Word was getting around that I was something the world had never seen before," he said decades later. For all his dreaminess in the classroom, for all his trouble reading a book or a balance sheet, Clay may have been the most self-aware twenty-one-year-old in the country. Like the most intelligent of comedians or politicians or actors, he was in complete command of even the most outrageous performances. "Where do you think I'd be next week if I didn't know how to shout and holler and make the public take notice?" he said. "I'd be poor and I'd probably be down in my hometown, washing windows or running an elevator and saying 'yassuh' and 'nawsuh' and knowing my place."

Clay's references to the American racial divide in those days were frequent, but guarded. The truth was that Clay was holding on to a secret. Even before he went off to win the Olympic gold medal in Rome, he had become fascinated by a sect called the Nation of Islam, better known as the Black Muslims. Clay first heard about the group in 1959 when he traveled to Chicago for a Golden Gloves tournament. Chicago was home base for the Nation and its leader, Elijah Muhammad, and Clay ran into Muslims on the South Side. His aunt remembers him coming home to Louisville with a record album of Muhammad's sermons. Then, in the spring, before leaving for the Olympics, Clay read a copy of the Nation's

New York, 1964. With Elijah Muhammad.

official newspaper, *Muhammad Speaks*. He was clearly taken with what he was reading and hearing in the Muslim rhetoric of pride and separatism. "The Muslims were practically unknown in Louisville in those days," said Clay's high-school classmate Lamont Johnson. "They had a little outfit, a temple, run by a black guy with white spots on his skin, but no one paid it any mind. No one had heard about their bean pies, the way they lived, what they thought. It wasn't even big enough to be scary in 1959."

Clay stunned his English teacher at Central High when he told her he wanted to write his term paper on the Black Muslims. She refused to let him do it. He never let on that his interest in the group was more than a schoolboy's passing curiosity. Something had resonated in his mind, something about the discipline and bearing of the Muslims, their sense of hierarchy, manhood, and self-respect, the way they refused to smoke or drink or carouse, their racial pride.

After coming back from Rome, Clay attended meetings in various cities of the NAACP, of CORE, and of the Nation of Islam. Other athletes, like Curt Flood and Bill White of the St. Louis Cardinals, had stopped in to hear Muslim preachers, too, and left after listening for a few minutes to the rhetoric about "blue-eyed devils." But Clay was impressed by the Muslims in a way he was not by any other group or church. "The most concrete thing I found in churches was segregation," he said years later. "Well, now I have learned to accept my own and be myself. I know we are original man and that we are the greatest people on the planet Earth and our women the queens thereof."

In March 1961, after he had moved to Miami, Cassius met a man on the street who went by the name of Captain Sam—Sam Saxon, a poolroom guy, a street hustler, who had transformed himself in the mid-fifties after hearing Elijah Muhammad speak and joining the Nation. After a stint in Chicago, Captain Sam went to Miami to spread the word. The chief Muslim minister in town was Ishmael Sabakhan, and Saxon said that "the Messenger," Elijah Muhammad, wanted him to be Sabakhan's captain. When he wasn't recruiting new Muslims or selling *Muhammad Speaks* on the street, he was running concessions at the Miami racetracks: Hialeah, Gulfstream, Tropical Park. In the bathrooms he made tip money handing towels to white guys and offering shoe shines and Bromo-Seltzers.

Captain Sam and Clay started chatting about Elijah Muhammad. Saxon was surprised that the young man had heard of the group, knew something about it.

"Hey, you're into the teaching," he said.

"Well, I ain't been in the temple, but I know what you're talking about," Clay said. Cassius introduced himself and told Saxon (as he told almost everyone) that he was soon going to be heavyweight champion of the world. He invited Saxon back to his place to look at his scrapbook. Saxon went along, and in their talks he noticed how Clay talked about the Muslims. As untutored as Clay was, it was clear he had a great interest, and so Saxon invited him to a meeting at the local mosque.

The preacher, a man named Brother John, unspooled a sermon on black identity that would become, almost word for word, a set piece of Muhammad Ali's. "Why are we called Negroes?" Brother John preached. "It's the white man's way of taking away our identity. If you see a Chinaman coming, you know he's from China. If you see a Cuban coming, you know he comes from Cuba. If you see a Canadian coming, you know he comes from Canada. What country is called Negro?" Brother John then talked about the names of American blacks being slave names, names that gave no sense of ancestry, names that actively *erased* a black man's ancestry.

"That was plain to me," Ali told the writer Thomas Hauser many years later when they collaborated on an oral biography. "I could reach out and touch what Brother John was saying. It wasn't like church teaching, where I had to have faith that what the preacher was preaching was right. And I said to myself, 'Cassius Marcellus Clay. He was a Kentucky white man, who owned my great-granddaddy and named my great-granddaddy after him. And then my granddaddy got named and then my daddy and now it's me.' "

From then on, Clay started delving deeper and deeper into the Nation of Islam, reading *Muhammad Speaks*, listening to the record album called *A White Man's Heaven Is a Black Man's Hell*, and, most of all, hanging out with Muslims who saw him as a cherished recruit. Jeremiah Shabazz, the Nation's regional minister, based in Atlanta, traveled to Miami to meet Clay. He told him how in China Buddha looks Chinese, and the Europeans and Americans worship a white Christ. Why didn't black Americans worship a black god? Why did a black man like Cassius Clay, Sr., spend his time painting murals of a white Jesus? In fact, Shabazz told Clay, God was black, according to the Nation of Islam. He gave Clay oral lessons in the history of slavery, telling him that there could be no devil below ground worse than the devil on earth who oppressed the black man, put him in chains, made him build America while enslaving him, enslaving his children. He told Clay that the church he grew up in was a kind of slavery, too, a sophisticated form of pacification, a way of keeping the Negro singing and crying on Sundays instead of marching the streets and freeing himself. He told the young man how foolish the civil rights movement was, how foolish it was for black people to let themselves be gassed and beaten in the streets, bitten by dogs, knocked over by firehoses, all to impress white people; how foolish it was to *beg* for their liberties, for what was theirs by natural right. The preachers of the Nation called for uncompromising opposition, for opposition by any means necessary. "Anybody can sit," Elijah's disciple Malcolm X said, criticizing Martin Luther King's Freedom Riders and sit-in protesters. "An old woman can sit. A coward can sit. . . . It takes a man to stand." The Nation of Islam, Malcolm said, refused to sit and be beaten. He told white people, "You might see these Negroes who believe in nonviolence and mistake us for one of them and put your hands on us thinking that we're going to turn the other cheek—and we'll put you to death just like that."

These stark messages of strength resonated with Cassius Clay. He had grown up in segregated Louisville and now he was living in segregated Miami, where even Joe Louis couldn't get a room at the Fontainebleau Hotel. Clay was also a seeker, a man of drama, and the self-drama of the Muslims also resonated with him, the notion that the black man was the original man, that he had established great civilizations when the white man was still in caves. Cassius and his brother, Rudy, would go to the mosque or to Red's barbershop in Overtown to listen to the Muslims read from the Koran or recite the creation myth.

Gradually, Clay learned more about the Muslims and the strange and complicated man who proclaimed himself the Messenger. Elijah Muhammad was born in 1897 in rural Georgia. His name then was Elijah Poole, and he was the grandson of slaves. The Georgia of

Poole's youth made the Louisville of Clay's look benign. The poverty was hopeless, and lynchings of young black men were so common that they often went unnoticed by the local papers. In 1923, Poole joined the northward migration, settling in one of the poorest sections of downtown Detroit. The poverty in Detroit was in many ways worse than in Georgia—jobs in the automobile industry came and went, came and went, all with miserable wages—and Poole soon found himself on relief lines, drinking away his life.

Poole was a religious seeker, and like many other poor blacks in Detroit he began hearing about a preacher named W. D. Fard, a door-to-door salesman who had developed a theology, a history, and a worldview for the black man. Fard was a light-skinned man who said he was born near Mecca. In truth, he had never been to Mecca and had arrived in Detroit in 1930 by way of California and Chicago. Fard founded his sect, the Nation of Islam, with himself as its center, its light, the incarnation of Allah. He preached the recovery of the black man's ancient Islamic heritage and cultural superiority; he proposed an ethic of self-regard and self-help, of cleanliness and work. Fard was not an original. His thinking came from a variety of American sources and a rich history of black nationalism. The theme of self-help and upright moral behavior derived from Booker T. Washington and from countless sermons in the black churches. His version of Islam had roots in Noble Drew Ali's Moorish Science Temple of America, a popular sect among blacks in the 1910s and 1920s, which strictly forbade gambling, sports, drinking, and all manner of libertine activity. His emphasis on black pride derived from the back-to-Africa gospel of Marcus Garvey, who formed the Universal Negro Improvement Association in 1914 and came to the United States from Jamaica two years later to begin a spectacular career as the editor of the weekly *Negro World* and as a publicist for his nationalist ideas. Garvey was a spiritual descendant of nineteenth-century nationalists such as Edward Wilmont Blyden, Bishop Henry McNeal Turner (who claimed that God was black), Martin R. Delany (who explored the possibility of massive repatriation of black Americans to East Africa or even South America), and the utopians Isaiah Montgomery and Edward P. McCabe. But it was Garvey, the son of a Jamaica bricklayer, who truly popularized the essential questions that would fire Cassius Clay's consciousness:

"Where is the black man's government? Where is his king and his kingdom? Where is his president, his country, and his ambassador, his army, his navy, his men of big affairs?"

Like Blyden before him and the Muslims who came later, Garvey sought to instill pride in his people by arguing that while white men were still savages living in caves, "this race of ours boasted of a wonderful civilization on the Banks of the Nile." (Garvey is caricatured in Ralph Ellison's *Invisible Man* as the character Ras the Exhorter.) When Garvey won enormous popularity while based in New York in the twenties—one Garveyite rally was held in Carnegie Hall—the FBI pursued him endlessly and finally got a conviction on mail fraud. Garvey sat in prison for two years and was deported to Jamaica in 1927, never to return to the United States—except as a lingering influence on groups that most definitely included the Nation of Islam.

Elijah Poole was one of some eight thousand people who were following Fard by the middle and late thirties. (He had previously been a member of a Garvey organization in Chicago.) Poole's devotion to the sect was so intense, so disciplined, that Fard made him a top aide-de-camp. When they had known each other for a few years, Poole pressed Fard on the question of who he really was. Fard replied, "I am the one the world has been waiting for for the past two thousand years. I have come to guide you into the right path." Fard called himself a Muslim and the Koran his holy book, but he developed a cosmology far different from the Islam practiced in the world beyond Detroit. His religious universe was stitched out of bits of Islam, Christianity, the Book of Mormon, political need, and various other elements. For many poor blacks in Detroit, men and women whose grandparents were slaves and now found themselves in the most degrading circumstances, Fard's narrative offered hope, pride, and historical meaning.

According to Fard, and to lectures and books published by Elijah Muhammad in years to come, 76 trillion years ago, when the universe was lifeless and void, before the concept of time, a single atom began to spin, and out of that atom came the earth and then a man, a black man, the "Original Man" we now know as Allah. In turn, Allah created the known universe and then created the black race. The black man, therefore, had primacy in the universe and was divine. Life for him was a paradise of plenty and righteousness.

Fard declared that 6,600 years ago a black child named Mr. Yacub was born, a child with an unusually large cranium, known as "big head scientist." Mr. Yacub was a prodigy, a diabolical genius, who finished the university course of study by the time he was eighteen, but because he also began preaching dangerous theology, he and 59,999 of his followers were exiled to the island of Patmos in the Aegean. There Dr. Yacub proceeded to kill off his fellow black men and create a "devil race" born of lies, deception, and murder. Mr. Yacub knew that black men had a dominant black "germ" or gene and a weaker brown gene, but he was able to create lighter people by feeding the blacks to wild beasts (or sticking needles in their brains) and mating the lighter men and women. After two hundred years, Mr. Yacub was dead and there were no blacks left on Patmos. Six hundred years or so later, the men and women on Patmos had evolved from black to brown to yellow to white—whites with pale hair and blue eyes. Fard called them "white devils," a sickly people, with thin blood and weak bones, prone to disease and incapable of righteousness, if only because of their unusually skimpy six-ounce brains. The whites were rebuffed from returning east from exile by the Fruit of Islam and sent to Europe. For a long time, the whites degenerated into primitives, living like animals, even engaging in sexual congress with animals, until Moses was sent to civilize them. Eventually the whites came to be dominant, first in Europe, then in the New World, where they imported slaves from Africa and treated them brutally—force-feeding them swine and Christianity, making them lose touch with the radiant civilization of their ancestors, the Original Men.

That was the Nation of Islam's version of history. Its myth of redemption involves a wheel-shaped half-mile-wide spacecraft called the Mother Plane. The plane is piloted by the finest black men, who use their psychic powers to steer. Between eight and ten days before Allah's day of retribution, the Mother Plane will litter the planet with pamphlets written in Arabic and English telling all God-fearing righteous people where to hide from the imminent attack from the heavens. The attack will be brutal and complete: fifteen hundred planes will take off from the Mother Plane and unleash bomb after bomb and, as in the story of Noah and the ark, leave only the righteous alive. Borrowing from the rhetoric of the Book of Revelation, the story goes that America will burn in a lake of fire for 390 years and then will cool only after 610 years. Finally, the black man, the righteous man, will build a new civilization on the ashes of the old.

Clay imbibed these Muslim tales with fascination but with a notably casual grasp of the specifics. It was not surprising that when he described some of Fard's principles, noninitiates found them strange. One night, Ferdie Pacheco was driving around Miami in his vintage Cadillac convertible with Clay and two girls in the backseat. Clay leaned forward and tapped Pacheco on the shoulder.

"See that?" he said pointing at the sky. "It's the spaceship."

"What spaceship is that?" one of the girls asked.

Clay looked at her stunned.

"One day about seven thousand years ago, a bad, mad scientist named Dr. Yacub created the white race off the black. . . . The mad doctor made the whites superior, and pushed the blacks down into slavery. That period is coming to an end now."

"What's that got to do with a spaceship?"

"Well, a spaceship took off with twenty-six yellow families living on it, circling the globe. They called it the Mother Ship. The non-white races are being oppressed by the whites, and soon they will come down and wipe out the white race."

One of the girls smiled slyly.

"What they been waiting for, child?"

"Once a year," Clay went on, "they come down on the North Pole, put down a big plastic hose, and scoop up enough oxygen and ice to last them a year."

In the beginning, Clay did not discriminate much between what was and was not useful to him in Muslim ideology, but with time he did not talk much about these stories. What swept him up was the Muslims on earth, their sense of self, their upright military bearing, their pride. In Elijah Muhammad, he found a father substitute, a gnomish font of wisdom and magic who sat on plastic-covered couches and explained the world of black goodness and white evil. Elijah Muhammad, however, was deeply ambivalent about Clay at first; the Nation of Islam regarded boxing as no better than drinking, a worthless indulgence performed for the merriment of white men. By the time Clay came to know him in the early sixties, Elijah Muhammad had become an established leader, if little known among whites. In 1934, Fard had disappeared and Poole, now known as Elijah Muhammad, had taken over the Muslims as Fard's Messenger. After being arrested in Detroit for contributing to the delinquency of minors by not sending his children to accredited schools, he moved his family, and the sect, to Chicago. One of his legendary gestures was to refuse the draft and to accept a jail term instead.

"For Ali there was something in the notion of black superiority and the spaceship that was comforting and nourishing to him," said Robert Lipsyte, the *New York Times* reporter who knew him best in the early sixties. "After all, his father had spouted Marcus Garvey stuff. Ali moved away from his father, but he was influenced by him, felt white society was oppressive. Also, what would Ali have been without the Nation? It gave him a sense of self, a connection to something larger and more important at the time. It was the time of white anger at integration, and the Nation of Islam told a narrative of self-sufficiency."

"Ali was a searching guy, really young and filled with pain and curiosity and looking for specific answers," Ferdie Pacheco said. "He was looking for a teacher to tell him what to do, and the Muslim answer was definitive and sharp: don't trust anyone who is white. Black is best, black is beautiful, what do we need white people for. It hardly mattered that he had the Louisville Group and me and Angelo, all these white people around him. He's not a hater. But he's always marched to his own drummer. He sees things as he wants to. Whatever is best for him, whatever ideology is best for him, whatever program is best for the way he thinks his life should be. Ever since he went up to Detroit in '62 and met Elijah Muhammad he had a real fixation on him. He really conquered his mind. About the only one he felt he really had to listen to was the old man.

"Ali also understood strength. Just like Sonny Liston understood the Mafia, Ali understood that you did not fuck with the Muslims. He liked their strength. He turned his head away from the fact that, especially in the early days, the Nation was filled with a lot of ex-cons, violent people who would go after you if you crossed them."

By 1962, Clay had invited Captain Sam and a few other Muslims to the Fifth Street Gym to help with odd jobs and to provide spiritual support. Clay had accepted the dietary restrictions of Islam, and the Nation set him up with cooks. Some people at the gym, like Pacheco, knew that Cassius and his brother, Rudy, were spending much of their free time with members of the Nation, but Cassius was not eager to advertise his new loyalties. He was well aware that the few white people who did know something about the Nation of Islam saw it as a frightening sect, radical Muslims with a separatist agenda and a criminal membership. "I was afraid if they knew, I wouldn't be allowed to fight for the title," he said many years later.

When Clay went to a Muslim rally on the South Side of Chicago, some reporters asked him if he was a member. Clay, who usually welcomed reporters, now took their persistence as rudeness and turned defensive. Muslims, he said, are clean and hardworking, they don't cheat on their spouses, they don't drink or take drugs. Again they asked if he was a member.

"No I'm not, not now," he said. "But the way you keep pressing me I just might be. They're the cleanest people next to God."

CASSIUS CLAY EXPERTLY DIVIDED HIS DEVOTIONS. AS HIS CONcentration on the Nation of Islam increased, so did his attention to boxing. On January 24, 1963, he went to Pittsburgh to fight Charlie Powell, a former football player with a bad temper. Powell baited Clay at the weigh-in, and for the first time, Clay seemed to fight in anger. Clay fought without his usual sense of art-before-power, and Powell, lucky for him, was through in the third round. He spent the next hour vomiting blood in his dressing room.

As far as Clay was concerned, he had now dealt with enough top contenders and also-rans to win the notice of Sonny Liston. In fact, he had not really beaten anyone of moment. Archie Moore, the best-known of his opponents, came into the ring looking like a spent whale. Sonny Banks had floored Clay. The trick was to keep active and continue learning. Time was on Clay's side, after all; Liston had devastated Patterson twice, but had peaked as a fighter probably two or three years before that. Nor had his title done much for the living habits of the champion. Liston trained only sporadically, and while in the main he kept out of serious trouble, he drank, he stayed out all night. He had long since given up the notion of being a paragon of his sterling profession.

Clay signed to fight a clever boxer named Doug Jones at Madison Square Garden in March 1963. The event would be more notable for Clay's achievements in public relations than in the ring. As the fight approached, all the major newspapers in the city went on strike for 113 days. Clay, Jones, and the Garden were left to promote the fight through television and by whatever "alternative" media they could invent.

"This is unfair to the many boxing fans New York City has," Clay complained. "Now they won't be able to read about the great Cassius Clay."

Clay went on every television show that asked him, but his cleverest stroke was an appearance at the Bitter End, an outpost of Greenwich Village hip for folk singers, comedians, and other performers of the zeitgeist. The occasion was poetry night, and Clay appeared onstage with six women and another man, though it was obvious that he was the reason for the occasion. Robert Lowell, much less Allen Ginsberg, was not in the competition. The fix was in. The first poet was a bearded gentleman named Howard Ant, who recited his immortal "Sam, the Gambler, Talks to a Losing Horse." It became more obvious that the evening would be devoted to boxing when a woman called Doe Lindell recited her own "Poem for Cassius." Finally, Clay himself came to the microphone to recite an ode to himself:

> *Marcellus vanquished Carthage,*
> *Cassius laid Julius Caesar low,*
> *And Clay will flatten Doug Jones*
> *With a mighty, muscled blow.*
> *So when the gong rings*
> *and the referee sings out, 'The Winner,'*
> *Cassius Marcellus Clay*
> *Will be the noblest Roman of them all.*

Happily for poetry and for the art of self-promotion, the Bitter End performance was not televised. New York hungered for a big fight now that the championship bouts were starting to migrate to

Las Vegas, and the Garden (the *old* Garden, at Fiftieth Street) was sold out. By fight night, Clay had worn himself out trying to make up for the newspaper strike. He invited *Newsday*'s superb boxing writer, Bob Waters, up to his room at the Hotel Americana and told him, "It's all this running around that gets me. Last week or so it's been 'Cassius, will you be on my TV show?' 'Cassius, will you cut a tape for radio?' 'Cassius, will you pose for pictures?' Man, I'm tired. And all the time I gotta talk, you know. People expect it. Reporters say, 'We don't want to ask you questions, man. Just talk.' My mouth is tired."

The only thing that energized Clay before the fight was that he'd met a new friend, a mystical character with a long scar on his cheek named Drew Brown. Brown, who went by the nicknames Bundini and Fastblack, had spent seven years in Ray Robinson's entourage as a professional cheerleader and court jester. (At the height of Robinson's career, his entourage also included a voice coach, a drama instructor, a barber, a golf pro, a masseur, a secretary, and a dwarf mascot.) Bundini was a converted Jew married to a woman named Rhoda Palestine. He called God "Shorty" and believed deeply in Shorty's majesty. One day, Brown came up to Clay's hotel room and to Clay's surprise immediately went after him for predicting the ends of his fights.

"You gotta be fixin' 'em or else you couldn't tell Archie Moore when he was fallin'. You got to be a phony!" he said. "You either a phony or Shorty's in your corner. I been with Sugar Ray. I been with Johnny Bratton. I never heard of anybody predictin' weeks in advance the round they're gonna win in. Tell me the truth!"

"You know what the truth is?" Clay said toward the end of a long conversation. "The truth is, every time I go into the ring I'm scared to death."

Bundini, who wept easily, now wept buckets.

"I knew Shorty was with you," he said. "Shorty had to be with you. You mean you actually scared out there? Why?"

"I'm scared because after all that poppin' off, all that predicting, all those people wanting to see me get whipped, I know I'm in trouble. If I lose, they'll be ready to run me out of the country. I'm out on a limb and I know I gotta win. Now that's a fact that only you and me know."

"You, me, and Shorty," Bundini said.

From that moment on, Clay decided he had to have Bundini around as his own motivator-jester. Bundini was black, but he was an integrationist, a civil rights man. Clay didn't care. He *liked* Bundini, liked the way he could play off him verbally, the way Bundini could lift him up emotionally; he liked talking about spacemen and horror movies with Bundini, he liked playing the dozens with him, and he liked the fact that Bundini had been around, that he knew something of the world.

Drew Brown was born in 1929 and grew up poor in rural Florida. He said he started paying his own rent before he was ten and joined the navy as a messboy at thirteen. "I went through the Pacific and Atlantic campaigns and I know the mysteries of life," he once said with characteristic grandiloquence. "I know about men and women and love and death and the power and the glory." He left the navy after threatening an officer with a meat cleaver. After that he drifted, doing odd jobs, working for fighters. Over the years, Bundini would fall out of favor with Clay—not least when he sold his championship belt to a barber in Harlem for five hundred dollars—but the two men communicated on a level of magic and love that was quite different from the more orderly way that Dundee connected with the fighter. Bundini wept when Clay was hit, he cried tears of joy in victory. Years later, after he had worked the corner for many fights, he said, "I get sick before a fight. It makes me feel like a pregnant woman. I give the champ all my strength. He throw a punch, I throw a punch. He get hit, it hurts me. I can't explain it, but sometimes I know what he's gonna do before he even knows."

Clay would need whatever empathy Bundini could give him against Doug Jones. By fight time the odds were two to one in Clay's favor, but not only did he find it impossible to fulfill his predictions of a sixth-round knockout, he never really hurt Jones. In the end, all he could rely on was the aesthetic preferences of the judges and their good wishes for his future, for it turned out that Jones, weighing just 188 pounds, fourteen less than Clay, was elusive, sidewise, tricky. All night long, it was as if Clay had to box a sand crab.

Clay should have dominated the fight, or such was the feeling in the arena. But round after round, Jones slipped inside Clay's jab.

Jones's sole advantage was experience, and he used it to keep even, to counterpunch. With time, the crowd began to understand that Clay would fail to meet his deadline; in fact, he would be fortunate to win at all. The excitement in the crowd, the unending noise, had less to do with the quality of the boxing than with the expectation of an upset. "All the time that I was watching this quite ordinary fight—just good enough to watch at all," said Liebling, "my nineteen thousand fellow-viewers, to judge by the noise they made, were witnessing a vast allegorical struggle between the Modest Underdog and Mr. Swellhead Bigmouth Poet."

In the end two judges, Frank Forbes and Artie Aidello, scored it five to four (with one round even) for Clay, and the referee, inexplicably, scored it eight to one, one even, Clay. The crowd, which had turned antipoetical by the middle rounds, began booing the instant the decision was announced. The more ardent among them filled the air with crumpled beer cups, cigar stubs, and paper airplanes. Clay took off his gloves and picked up a few of the peanuts that had been hurled at him. He shelled them and, dramatically, ate them. He raised his hands in victory and defiance, but considering his usual level of exuberance, the gesture was ceremonial only. He knew he had failed. Afterward, Clay went up to Harlem for a victory party at Small's Paradise, but was so sick with exhaustion that he nearly collapsed on his victory cake. With the help of some hangers-on, he made it back to the hotel for a long sleep.

"I ain't Superman," he said uncharacteristically. "If the fans think I can do everything I say I can do, then they're crazier than I am."

When the newspapers went back to work, there were scores of columnists all too eager to lay their reviews on the young performer. Pete Hamill of the *New York Post,* a much younger and more liberal columnist than the better-known writers at the time, registered his impatience and distaste with the young sensation. "Cassius Clay is a young man with a lot of charm," he wrote, "who is in danger of becoming a dreadful bore."

IN HIS NEXT FIGHT, THREE MONTHS LATER, AGAINST HENRY Cooper at London's Wembley Stadium in June, Clay did not fare much better. Again he was favored and again his concentration drifted. Once more his prefight promotion was more than any promoter could have hoped for: he paraded around London in a bowler and carrying a cane and pronounced Buckingham Palace a "swell pad." But he carried his sense of play too far in the ring and risked his chance at a title bout.

Cooper was known as a one-punch fighter, the possessor of what his countrymen called "'Enry's 'ammer." But Clay showed no sign of caring. Cooper opened the fight by pushing Clay back on his heels. Clay was faster and his jabs kept bouncing off Cooper's forehead, but Cooper, performing in front of 55,000 Englishmen, was inspired and far slower to tire than an antique like Archie Moore. In the fourth round, Cooper had Clay against the ropes and lashed out with a terrific blow that spilled Clay to his backside. Clay's mouth made a little "O" of pain and surprise. Clay was up quickly and the round was over.

In the corner, Angelo Dundee noticed a slight tear in the seam of Clay's gloves. If his man had been clearly ahead, if he hadn't needed some extra time, Dundee might have ignored the flaw, but now he took advantage, sticking his finger in the hole and ripping the seam open even more. Then he called the referee over to show him the tear. During the time-out that followed, Dundee worked on Clay with cold wet sponges and smelling salts, and by the time the bell finally rang for round five, the mists had cleared from his eyes and he was ready. Since he had predicted a win in round five, he went in with a sense of mission, slashing Cooper with ripping jabs and hooks that suddenly turned Cooper's face into a river delta, so copious were the bloody streams on his brow and cheeks.

Finally, the referee, Tommy Little, turned to Cooper and held him back.

"The fight's over, chum," he said.

"We didn't do so bad for a 'bum' and a 'cripple,' did we?" Cooper said as he left.

Clay claimed that he had left himself open for Cooper's big punch in the fourth because he had glanced overlong at Elizabeth Taylor, who was sitting at ringside. The more skeptical among the fight press disagreed. The kid, they declared, was sometimes amusing, and he had potential, but he was not ready. Even Senator Kefauver, who now seemed to consider himself a professor of the fight game, solemnly told the press that it would be "many years" before Cassius Clay was mature enough to take on the champion.

Only the champion himself thought otherwise. He would not have to wait long. Liston had sent his manager, Jack Nilon, to London as his emissary, and, after the fight, Nilon went to Clay's dressing room to give him the news. "I've flown three thousand miles to tell you we're ready," Nilon said.

NILON, OF COURSE, WAS SURE HE WAS THE LION'S AMBASSADOR announcing to the lamb a willingness to engage. After the Jones fight, and now the uneven performance against Henry Cooper, Cassius Clay looked like nothing but easy money to the Liston camp. Liston took no fights after his second defeat of Patterson. His image as a destroyer was built on the two minutes it took him to win the title and the two minutes it took him to defend it. And now he was waiting for Clay. Despite the young man's flawed performances against Jones in New York and then Cooper in London, no other challenger on the scene would attract such a gate—and, in Liston's mind, few challengers would be easier to dispatch.

Clay knew that Liston thought he'd gotten the better of him at the craps table in Las Vegas. Now he had to change the psychological balance of power. And so before the two fighters even sat down to contract negotiations, Clay decided he had to goad the bear out of his hibernation and his lip-smacking self-satisfaction.

"I had been studying Liston, careful, all along, ever since he come up in the rankings, and Patterson was trying to duck him," Clay told Alex Haley in a *Playboy* interview. "His fighting style, his strength. His punch. Like that—but that was just a part of what I was looking at. Any fighter will study them things about somebody he wants to fight. The big thing for me was observing how Liston acted out of the ring. I read everything I could where he had been interviewed. I talked with people who had been around him, or had talked with him. I would lay in bed and put all of the things together and think about them, to try to get a good picture of how his mind worked. And that's how I first got the idea that if I would handle the thing right, I could use psychology on him—you know, needle him and work on his nerves so bad that I would have him beat before he ever got in the ring with me. And that's just what I did. . . . I set out to make him think what I wanted him thinking; that all I was was some clown, and that he never would have to give a second thought to me being able to put up a real fight when we got into the ring. The press, everybody—I didn't want nobody thinking nothing except that I was a joke."

As if running west from his arrest record in Philadelphia, Liston had since moved to Denver, declaring, "I'd rather be a lamppost in Denver than the mayor of Philadelphia." Clay decided to pay him a visit. Clay had bought a 1953 Flexible thirty-passenger bus the same colors as his childhood Schwinn, red and white. And like Toro Molino in *The Harder They Fall*, he turned the bus into his mobile camp and advertising vehicle. He painted a sign reading "World's Most Colorful Fighter: Liston Must Go in Eight." With one of his Muslim friends, Archie Robinson, and the man who would become his closest and most loyal friend, the photographer Howard Bingham, Clay set out for Denver to play with Sonny Liston's mind.

When they reached the Denver city limits at about two in the morning, Clay called the local papers and wire services and told them to gather around Liston's house in a little while for a good show. The bus pulled up to the house at around three, and the press was in place. Clay sent Howard Bingham to the door.

Liston answered wearing a silk robe and shortie pajamas.

"What you want, you black motherfucker?" the champion said by way of greeting.

On the curb, Clay and his friends were shouting, "Come on out of there! I'm going to whip you right now! Come on out of there and protect your home! If you don't come out of that door, I'm gonna break it down!"

Liston was reluctant to make a move. He was well aware that with his police record a fight in the middle of the street could lead to another arrest and another round of bad publicity in the papers.

"At first I couldn't get him really mad, because he had this idea fixed in his mind," Clay recalled. "But I kept right on working on him. A man with Liston's kind of mind is very funny. He ain't what you would call a fast thinker like I am. He's got one of them bull-dog kind of minds."

But before anything more could happen, neighbors called the police and the police sent Clay and his merry pranksters on their way. Liston closed the door and went back inside. According to his sparring partner Foneda Cox, he was furious and confused. Perfect. Clay went home happy, satisfied that he had accomplished what he had set out to do.

"While I was fighting Jones and Cooper," he said, "Liston was up to his neck in all of that rich, fat ritual of the champion. I'd nearly clap my hands every time I read or heard about him at some big function or ceremony, up half the night and drinking and all that. I was looking at Liston's age, too. . . . What made it even better for me was when Liston just half-trained for the Patterson rematch and Patterson looked worse yet—and Liston signed to fight me, not rating me even as good as he did Patterson. He felt like he was getting ready to start off on some bum-of-the-month club like Joe Louis did. He couldn't see nothing at all to me but mouth."

The truth was that almost no one could see much beyond that. The Liston people were sure of a knockout, and so, too, was the Louisville Sponsoring Group. "I have to be honest: until the last minute, I *knew* that Cassius couldn't possibly beat Sonny Liston, and when the time came to draw up contracts my entire orientation was that this was going to be his last fight," the group's lawyer, Gordon Davidson, said. "My only prayer was that Cassius wouldn't get hurt."

On November 5, 1963, Liston's representatives signed contracts in Denver to defend the title against Cassius Clay. The fight was scheduled for February 25, 1964, in Miami and would be shown live on closed circuit in theaters around the country.

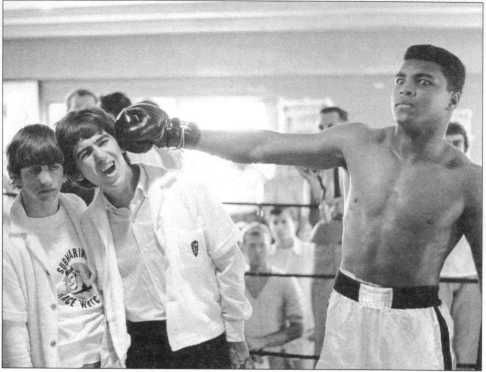

Miami, 1963. Playing with the Beatles.

CHAPTER EIGHT

Hype

THE PROMOTER OF THE LISTON-CLAY FIGHT WAS WILLIAM B. MacDonald, a former bus conductor who had made so great a fortune that he now got around in two Rolls-Royces and a fifty-foot cruiser named *Snoozie*. MacDonald was born in Butte in 1908, the descendant, he said, of generations of sheep thieves. There being few sheep to steal in Butte, he came to Miami and made his money in the parking business, then in laundry and dry cleaning, then in restaurant management, trucking, mobile homes, and a mortgage company based in San Juan. He married a Polish woman named Victoria and, just for fun, bought a stud farm in Delray Beach and a Class D baseball team called the Tampa Tarpons. MacDonald handed out gold cuff links like Chiclets. He lived in a quarter-million-dollar house in Bal Harbour and retained an assistant named Sugar Vallone, late of the bartending trade. His generosity as a father was unparalleled. He built his daughter a tree house with drapes and carpeting matching the main house, and for his daughter's eighth birthday he installed a jukebox in the tree. Bill MacDonald had a good time. He smoked his cigars and ate his steaks. He played golf and decorated his walls with the many marlin he had pulled out of the Atlantic. On the golf course, driving his cart, he held a Coke in his right hand and a root beer in his left, and steered with his forearms and his belly. He was very fat.

MacDonald had enjoyed his experience so far in the boxing business. He made some money, if not a lot, promoting the third Patterson-Johansson fight. When he first talked to Chris Dundee about a Liston-Clay title bout, it seemed a no-lose proposition. There was money to be made, what with all the big-money tourists and the winter crowds in Miami in February. How could it flop? Liston was already the most fearsome presence in boxing since Louis and Marciano, and Clay, with his mouth flapping, would sell as many tickets as the Miami fire laws would permit. No lose. And so MacDonald, who had $800,000 invested in the fight, serenely pegged the top ticket at an unprecedented $250.

MacDonald envisioned a great night, the ring surrounded by movie people and all the usual hustlers, the big-roll guys. He wanted all the big faces up close. "A guy calls me, for instance, wants to buy a hundred-dollar seat for Andy Williams," he told a reporter for *Sports Illustrated*. "I tell him Andy Williams's got to be up there with the big kids. I can't imagine him sitting back there with the little kids. He's got to be in there with the wheels, not the hubcaps."

Although MacDonald was not exactly expert in boxing, he was smart enough to tell the writers he was *acutely* aware of the possibility of surprise in the fight. "I figure Clay to win it," he said. "He'll take the title if he stays away, jabs and runs, but the little jerk is so egotistical—he's getting hysterical—he thinks he can punch Liston's nose sideways. It's liable to be a stinky fight to watch, but if Clay gets by seven or eight he's likely to win it." One could appreciate the sentiment if not the subtlety of MacDonald's maneuver. You don't sell tickets when David has no shot at Goliath.

MacDonald did not expect Liston to get into a verbal war with Clay before the fight. Liston had become so accustomed to hearing about himself as the indomitable champion, a seven-to-one favorite at the minimum, that he trained at the Surfside Civic Auditorium in North Miami Beach with a smug air of business as usual. In contrast to Clay's gloriously dismal surroundings at the Fifth Street Gym, Liston sparred with air-conditioning. An announcer would intone the next station of the cross—"The champion at the heavy bag"—and Liston would pound away for a short while. Then his cornermen, led by Willie Reddish, would rush to him and towel him off as if he were Cleopatra. Reddish would wing a medicine ball at Liston's gut a dozen times and then Liston would skip rope to "Night Train," as he had on *The Ed Sullivan Show.*

"Note that the champion's heels never touch the board," the master of ceremonies announced. "He does all this off his toes."

Liston trained the way Liberace played piano; it was a garish *representation* of a boxer at work. If Liston was taking Clay at all seriously, it was very hard to tell. He would not even deign to pretend to loathe his challenger. "I don't hate Cassius Clay," he said. "I love him so much I'm giving him twenty-two and a half percent of the gate. Clay means a lot to me. He's my baby, my million-dollar baby. I hope he keeps well and I sure hope he shows up." Liston's only health concern, he allowed, was for the destiny of his vaunted left fist: "It's gonna go so far down his throat, it'll take a week for me to pull it out again."

The columnists may not have liked Liston, but they respected him as a fighter. They figured him an easy winner over Clay. Lester Bromberg of the *New York World-Telegram* said the fight would "follow the pattern" of the two Liston-Patterson fights, the only difference being that this would last longer: "It will last almost the entire first round." Nearly all the columnists were middle-aged, raised on Joe Louis, and they were inclined to like Clay even less than Liston. Jim Murray of the *Los Angeles Times* predicted that the Liston-Clay matchup would be "the most popular fight since Hitler and Stalin—180 million Americans rooting for a double knockout. The only thing at which Clay can beat Liston is reading the dictionary. . . . His public utterances have all the modesty of a German ultimatum to Poland but his public performances run more to Mussolini's navy."

At the Fifth Street Gym, of course, Clay was exerting considerable energy in his post-training-session press conferences. Day after day he described how he would spend the first five rounds circling "the big ugly bear," tiring him out, and then tear him apart with hooks and uppercuts until finally Liston would drop to all fours in submission. "I'm gonna put that ugly bear on the floor, and after the fight I'm gonna build myself a pretty home and use him as a bearskin rug. Liston even smells like a bear. I'm gonna give him to the local zoo after I whup him. People think I'm joking. I'm not joking. I'm serious. This will be the easiest fight of my life." He told the visiting reporters that now was their chance to "jump on the bandwagon." He was taking names, he said, keeping track of all the naysayers, and when he won "I'm going to have a little ceremony and some *eating* is going on—eating of words." Day after day he would replay his homage to Gorgeous George when describing what he'd do in case of a Liston win: "You tell this to your camera, your newspaper, your TV man, your radio man, you tell this to the world: If Sonny Liston whups me, I'll kiss his feet in the ring, crawl out of the ring on my knees, tell him he's the greatest, and catch the next jet out of the country." Most spectacularly, he composed in honor of the occasion what was surely his best poem. Over the years, Clay would farm out some of his poetical work. "We all wrote lines here and there," Dundee said. But this one was all Clay. Ostensibly, it was a prophetic vision of the eighth round, and no poem, before or after, could beat it for narrative drive, precise scansion, and wit. It was his "Song of Myself":

> *Clay comes out to meet Liston*
> *And Liston starts to retreat*
> *If Liston goes back any further*
> *He'll end up in a ringside seat.*
> *Clay swings with a left,*
> *Clay swings with a right,*
> *Look at young Cassius*
> *Carry the fight.*
> *Liston keeps backing*
> *But there's not enough room*
> *It's a matter of time.*
> *There, Clay lowers the boom.*
> *Now Clay swings with a right,*
> *What a beautiful swing,*
> *And the punch raises the bear,*
> *Clear out of the ring.*
> *Liston is still rising*
> *And the ref wears a frown,*
> *For he can't start counting,*
> *Till Sonny comes down.*
> *Now Liston disappears from view.*
> *The crowd is getting frantic,*
> *But our radar stations have picked him up*
> *He's somewhere over the Atlantic.*
> *Who would have thought*

When they came to the fight
That they'd witness the launching
Of a human satellite?
Yes, the crowd did not dream
When they laid down their money
That they would see
A total eclipse of the Sonny!
I am the greatest!

Nearly all the writers regarded Clay's bombast, in prose and verse, as the ravings of a lunatic. But not only did Clay have a sense of how to fill a reporter's notebook and, thus, a promoter's arena, he had a sense of self. The truth (and it was a truth he shared with almost no one) was that Cassius Clay knew that for all his ability, for all his speed and cunning, he had never met a fighter like Sonny Liston. In Liston, he was up against a man who did not merely beat his opponents, but hurt them, damage them, shame them in humiliatingly fast knockouts. Liston could put a man away with his jab; he was not much for dancing, but then neither was Joe Louis. Liston was the prototype of what a heavyweight champion should be: he threw bomb after unforgiving bomb. When he hit a man in the solar plexus the glove seemed lost up to the cuff; he was too powerful to grab and clinch; nothing hurt him. Clay was too smart, he had watched too many films, not to know that. "That's why I always knew that all of Clay's bragging was a way to convince himself that he could do what he said he'd do," Floyd Patterson told me many years later. "I never liked all his bragging. It took me a long time to understand who Clay was talking to. Clay was talking to Clay."

Very few people would ever know how true that was and how much Clay feared Liston. One evening, just before signing the contracts for the fight, he visited *Sports Illustrated*'s offices on the twentieth floor of the Time-Life Building in midtown Manhattan. It was seven-thirty and Clay stood at the window looking out at the lights blinking along Sixth Avenue and beyond. He was quiet for a long time.

Finally, the writer Mort Sharnik said, "Cassius, all these things you're saying about Liston, do you really mean them? Do you really think you're going to beat this guy?"

"I'm Christopher Columbus," he said slowly. "I *believe* I'll win. I've never been in there with him, but I believe the world is round and they all believe the world is flat. Maybe I'll fall off the world at the horizon but I believe the world is round."

Clay had doubts, but he used those doubts the way a black belt in judo uses the weight of his assailant. Weeks before the fight, he approached Liston's manager, Jack Nilon, and said, "You know, I shot my mouth off to make this fight a success. My day of reckoning is about to come. If the worst happens I want to get out of there quick. I'd like to provision my bus and get out of there quick." Then he asked Jack Nilon for ten thousand dollars for the provisioning.

"No one could read this kid," Sharnik would say. "It was hard to know if he was the craziest kid you ever saw or the smartest."

BILL MACDONALD NEVER HOPED TO CONVINCE THE PUBLIC that Clay was a modest fellow in the Louis mold, but he had hoped that the writers would think he could fight. They did not. According to one poll, 93 percent of the writers accredited to cover the fight predicted Liston would win. What the poll did not register was the firmness of the predictions. Arthur Daley, the *New York Times* columnist, seemed to object morally to the fight, as if the bout were a terrible crime against children and puppies: "The loudmouth from Louisville is likely to have a lot of vainglorious boasts jammed down his throat by a hamlike fist belonging to Sonny Liston. . . ."

In the later acts of his career, Muhammad Ali would take his place in the television firmament and his Boswell would be Howard Cosell. But in the days preceding his fight with Sonny Liston in Miami, Cassius Clay was not yet Muhammad Ali and Howard Cosell was a bald, nasal guy on the radio who annoyed his colleagues with his portentous questions and his bulky tape recorder, which he was forever bashing into someone's giblets. Newspapers were still the dominant force in sports; columnists— *white* columnists—were the dominant voices; and Jimmy Cannon, late of the *New York Post* and, since 1959, of the *New York Journal-American*, was the king of the columnists. Cannon was the first thousand-dollar-a-week man, Hemingway's favorite, Joe DiMaggio's buddy, and Joe Louis's iconographer. Red Smith, who wrote for the *Herald Tribune,* employed an elegant restraint in his prose that put him ahead of the game with more high-minded readers, but Cannon was the popular favorite: a world-weary voice of the city. Cannon was king, and Cannon had no sympathy for Cassius Clay. He did not even think he could fight.

One afternoon shortly before the fight, Cannon was sitting with George Plimpton at the Fifth Street Gym watching Clay spar. Clay glided around the ring, a feather in the slipstream, and every so often he popped a jab into his sparring partner's face. Plimpton was completely taken with Clay's movement, his ease, but Cannon could not bear to watch.

"Look at that!" Cannon said. "I mean, that's terrible. He can't get away with that. Not possibly." It was just unthinkable that Clay could beat Liston by running, carrying his hands at his hips, and defending himself simply by leaning away.

"Perhaps his speed will make up for it," Plimpton put in hopefully.

"He's the fifth Beatle," Cannon said. "Except that's not right. The Beatles have no hokum to them."

"It's a good name," Plimpton said. "The fifth Beatle."

"Not accurate," Cannon said. "He's all pretense and gas, that fellow. . . . No honesty."

Clay offended Cannon's sense of rightness the way flying machines offended his father's generation. It threw his universe off kilter.

"In a way, Clay is a freak," he wrote before the fight. "He is a bantamweight who weighs more than two hundred pounds."

Cannon's objections went beyond the ring. His hero was Joe Louis, and for Joe Louis he composed the immortal line that he was a "credit to his race—the human race." He admired Louis's "barbaric majesty," his quiet in suffering, his silent satisfaction in victory. And when Louis finally went on too long and, way past his peak, fought Rocky Marciano, he eulogized the broken-down old fighter as the metaphysical poets would a slain mistress: "The heart, beating inside the body like a fierce bird, blinded and caged, seemed incapable of moving the cold blood through the arteries of Joe Louis's rebellious body. His thirty-seven years were a disease which paralyzed him."

Cannon was born in 1910 in what he called "the unfreaky part of Greenwich Village." His father was a minor, if kindly, servant of Tammany Hall. The family lived in cold-water flats in the Village, and Cannon got to know the neighborhood and its workmen, the icemen, the coal delivery boys. Cannon dropped out of school after the ninth grade and caught on as a copy boy at the *Daily News* and never left the newspaper business. As a young reporter he caught the eye of Damon Runyon when he wrote dispatches on the Lindbergh kidnapping trial for the International News Service.

"The best way to be a bum and earn a living is to write sports," Runyon told Cannon and then helped him get a job at a Hearst paper, *The New York American*. Like his heroes, Runyon and the Broadway columnist Mark Hellinger, Cannon gravitated to the world of the "delicatessen nobility," to the bookmakers and touts, the horse players and talent agents, who hung out at Toots Shor's and Lindy's, the Stork Club and El Morocco. When Cannon went off to Europe to write battle dispatches for *The Stars and Stripes*, he developed what would become his signature style: florid, sentimental prose with an underpinning of hard-bitten wisdom, an urban style that he had picked up in candy stores and nightclubs and from Runyon, Ben Hecht, and Westbrook Pegler. After having been attached to George Patton's Third Army, Cannon came home newly attached to the *Post*. His sports column, which would be the city's most popular for a quarter century, began in 1946 and was dubbed "Jimmy Cannon Says."

Cannon was an obsessive worker, a former boozer who drank more coffee than Balzac. He lived alone—first at the Edison Hotel, then on Central Park West, and finally on Fifty-fifth Street. He was a cranky egomaniac whose ego only grew with age. He sweated every column. When he wasn't at a ball game or at his desk, he was out all night, wandering from nightclub to nightclub, listening always for tips, for stray bits of talk that could make their way into his column. "His column is his whole life," said one of his colleagues, W. C. Heinz of the *New York Sun*. "He has no family, no games he plays, no other activities. When he writes it's the concentration of his whole being. He goes through the emotional wringer. I have no idea what Jimmy would do if he weren't writing that column, he'd be so lonesome."

For his time, Cannon was considered enlightened on the subject of race. That is to say that unlike many other columnists he did not make fun of the black athletes he covered, he did not transform their speech into *Amos 'n' Andy* routines. He gave them their due. As much as he adored DiMaggio, a fighter like Archie Moore captured his schmaltz-clogged heart just as easily:

"Someone should write a song about Archie Moore who in the Polo Grounds knocked out Bobo Olson in three rounds. I don't mean big composers such as Harold Arlen or Duke Ellington. It should be a song that comes out of the backroom of sloughed saloons on night-drowned streets in morning-worried parts of bad towns. The guy who writes this one must be a piano player who can be dignified when he picks a quarter out of the marsh of a sawdust floor. They're dead, most of those piano players, their mouths full of dust instead of songs. But I'll bet Archie could dig one up in any town he ever made."

Cannon was also a master of the barstool non sequitur. Very often he would title his column "Nobody Asked Me, But . . ." and then line up a few dozen choice thoughts:

"I have more faith in brusque doctors than oily-mannered ones."

"You're middle-aged if you remember Larry Semon, the comic."

"El Morocco is still the most exciting nightclub in the country."

"Doesn't Marty Glickman, the sports announcer, sound like an Atlantic City boardwalk auctioneer?"

"Guys who use other people's coffee saucers as ashtrays should be banned from public places. . . ."

He would begin other columns by putting the reader inside the skull and uniform of a ballplayer ("You're Eddie Stanky. You ran slower than the other guy . . ."), and elsewhere, in that voice of El Morocco at three in the morning, he would dispense wisdom on the subject he seemed to know the least about—women: "Any man is in difficulty if he falls in love with a woman he can't knock down with the first punch." Or, "You can tell when a broad starts in managing a fighter. What makes a dumb broad smart all of a sudden? They don't even let broads in a joint like Yale. But they're all wised up once a fighter starts making a few."

There are not many writers of any sort who do not date quickly, and journalistic writing, with rare exceptions, dates as quickly as the newsprint it's written on. Even some of Mencken dates, and

Cannon was no Mencken. The wised-up one-liners and the world-weary sentiment were of a time and a place, and as Cannon aged he gruffly resisted the new trends in sportswriting and athletic behavior. In the press box, he encountered a new generation of beat writers and columnists, men such as Maury Allen and Leonard Schecter on the *Post*. He didn't much like the sound of them. Cannon called the younger men "Chipmunks" because they were always chattering away in the press box. He hated their impudence, their irreverence, their striving to get outside the game and into the heads of the people they covered. Cannon had always said that his intention as a sportswriter was to bring the "world in over the bleacher wall," but he failed to see that this generation was trying to do much the same thing. He could not bear their lack of respect for the old verities. "They go up and challenge guys with rude questions," Cannon once said of the Chipmunks. "They think they're big if they walk up to an athlete and insult him with a question. They regard this as a sort of bravery."

Part of Cannon's anxiety was sheer competitiveness. There were seven newspapers in those days in New York, and there was terrific competition to stay on top, to be original, to get a scoop, an extra detail. But the Chipmunks knew they were in competition now not so much with one another as with the growing power of television. Unlike Cannon, who was almost entirely self-educated, these were young men (and they were all men) who had gone to college in the age of Freud. They became interested in the psychology of an athlete ("The Hidden Fears of Kenny Sears" was one of Milton Gross's longer pieces). In time, this, too, would no longer seem especially voguish—soon just about every schnook with a microphone would be asking the day's goat, "What were you *thinking* when you missed that ball?"—but for the moment, the Chipmunks were the coming wave and Cannon's purple sentences, once so pleasurable, were beginning to feel less vibrant, a little antique.

Part of Cannon's generational anxiety was that he wrote about ballplayers in an elegiac voice. He had plenty of scorn for the scoundrels of sport—Jim Norris, Frankie Carbo, Fat Tony Salerno—but you would never learn from Cannon that DiMaggio was perhaps the most imperious personality in sport or that Joe Louis, in retirement, was going slowly mad with drugs, that to guard himself against imagined predators from the IRS and the

CIA he clogged the air-conditioning vents with cotton and smeared his windows with Vaseline.

The new generation, men like Pete Hamill and Jack Newfield, Jerry Izenberg and Gay Talese, all admired Cannon's immediacy, but Cannon begrudged them their new outlook, their education, their youth. In the late fifties, Talese wrote countless elegant features for the *Times* and then, even more impressively, a series of profiles in the sixties for *Esquire* on Patterson, Louis, DiMaggio, Frank Sinatra, and the theater director Joshua Logan. None of the pieces were what writers would call "trash jobs"—they were filled with affection for the person and admiration for craft—but they also delved into Patterson's fears, Louis's terrible decline, DiMaggio's loneliness, Sinatra's nastiness, and Logan's mental breakdowns. Talese combined the techniques of reporting and fiction; he filled his notebooks with facts, interviews, and observations, but structured his pieces like short stories.

When Talese was still at the *Times* and writing about his favorite subjects, Patterson and Cus D'Amato, he was considered an eccentric. In the newsroom, Talese wore immaculate hand-tailored suits; he was, in the words of one colleague, "blindingly handsome." But for all his outward polish and youth, he approached his work like a reporter, seeking out ballplayers, getting to know them. In those days, this was un-*Times*-like for the sports department. Daley, who was the dominant columnist since the forties, derived his prestige from the paper itself; when he won the Pulitzer Prize, many of his colleagues grumbled and said that it should have gone to Red Smith at the *Herald Tribune* or Cannon at the *Post*. Daley's prose was flat, but it was the prose that the Pulitzer committee read, if they read sports at all. Most of the other sportswriters on the *Times* were no less imperial: they carried themselves as if they were *The New York Times*'s ambassador to the court of baseball or the court of basketball. When Allison Danzig covered the U.S. Open at Forest Hills he did not deign to seek out a tennis player for an interview; the player sought out Allison Danzig. Not a few of the deskmen and reporters were appalled by the unorthodox presence of Gay Talese, and they could never figure out why the managing editor, Turner Catledge, had set him loose on the sporting world.

When Talese left the paper in 1965 to write books and longer magazine articles, he had one inheritor in place, a reporter in his mid-twenties named Robert Lipsyte. Like Cannon, Lipsyte grew up in New York, but he was a middle-class Jew from the Rego Park neighborhood in Queens. He went from his junior year at Forest Hills High School straight to Columbia University, from which he graduated in 1957. After mulling over a career as a screenwriter or an English professor, Lipsyte applied for a job as a copy boy at the *Times* and, to his astonishment, got it. "They usually said they hired Rhodes scholars in those days," he said. As a copy boy, Lipsyte admired Talese for his sense of style and innovation, for his ability to squeeze a distinct voice onto the uniform pages of the *Times*. Lipsyte made the staff at twenty-one when he showed hustle: one day the hunting and fishing columnist failed to send in a column from Cuba, and so Lipsyte sat down and, on deadline, knocked out a strange and funny column on how fish and birds were striking back at anglers and hunters. Lipsyte wrote about high school basketball players like Connie Hawkins and Roger Brown. He helped cover the 1962 Mets with Louis Effrat, a Timesman who had lost the Dodgers beat when they moved out of Brooklyn. Effrat's admiration for his younger colleague was, to say the least, grudging: "Kid, they say in New York you can really write but you don't know what the fuck you're writing about."

If there was one subject that Lipsyte made it a point to learn about, it was race. In 1963, he met Dick Gregory, one of the funniest comics in the country and a constant presence in the civil rights movement. The two men became close friends, and eventually Lipsyte helped Gregory write *Nigger*, his autobiography. Even as a sports reporter, Lipsyte contrived ways to write about race. He wrote about the Blackstone Rangers gang, he got to know Malcolm X and Elijah Muhammad. He covered rallies at which black protesters expressed their outrage against a country that would celebrate blacks only when they carried a football or boxed in a twenty-foot ring.

In the winter of 1963–64, the *Times*'s regular boxing writer, Joe Nichols, declared that the Liston-Clay fight was a dog and that he was going off to spend the season covering racing at Hialeah. The assignment went to Lipsyte.

Unlike Jimmy Cannon and the other village elders, Lipsyte found himself entranced with Clay. Here was this funny, beautiful, skilled young man who could fill your notebook in fifteen minutes.

"Clay was unique, but it wasn't as if he were some sort of creature from outer space for me," Lipsyte said. "For Jimmy Cannon, he was, pardon the expression, an uppity nigger, and he could never handle that. The blacks he liked were the blacks of the thirties and the forties. They knew their place. Joe Louis called Jimmy Cannon 'Mr. Cannon' for a long time. He was a humble kid. Now here comes Cassius Clay popping off and abrasive and loud, and it was a jolt for a lot of sportswriters, like Cannon. That was a transition period. What Clay did was make guys stand up and decide which side of the fence they were on.

"Clay upset the natural order of things at two levels. The idea that he was a loud braggart brought disrespect to this noble sport. Or so the Cannon people said. Never mind that Rocky Marciano was a slob who would show up at events in a T-shirt so that the locals would buy him good clothes. They said that Clay 'lacked dignity.' Clay combined Little Richard and Gorgeous George. He was not the sort of sweet dumb pet that writers were accustomed to. Clay also did not need the sportswriters as a prism to find his way. He transcended the sports press. Jimmy Cannon, Red Smith, so many of them, were appalled. They didn't see the fun in it. And, above all, it was fun."

A WEEK BEFORE THE FIGHT, CLAY STRETCHED OUT ON A RUBbing table at the Fifth Street Gym and told the reporters who gathered around, "I'm making money, the popcorn man making money, and the beer man, and you got something to write about."

The next day, Lipsyte heard that the Beatles would be dropping by the Fifth Street Gym. The visit had been arranged, of course, by the eternally hip Harold Conrad, who was publicizing the fight for MacDonald. The Beatles were in Miami to do *The Ed Sullivan Show*. Liston had actually gone to their performance and was not much impressed. As the Beatles ripped through their latest single, the champion turned to Conrad and said, "Are these motherfuckers what all the people are screaming about? My *dog* plays drums better than that kid with the big nose." Conrad figured that Clay would understand a bit better.

Lipsyte was twenty-six, a card-carrying member of the rock and roll generation, and he saw that for all its phoniness, a meeting between the Beatles and Clay was a meeting of the New, two acts that would mark the sixties. The older columnists passed, but he saw a story.

The Beatles arrived. They were still in the mop-top phase, but they were also quite aware of their own appeal. Clay was not in evidence, and Ringo Starr was angry.

"Where the fuck's Clay?" he said.

To kill a few minutes, Ringo began introducing the members of the band to Lipsyte and a few other reporters, though he introduced George Harrison as Paul and Lennon as Harrison, and finally Lennon lost patience.

"Let's get the fuck out of here," he said. But two Florida state troopers blocked the door and somehow kept them in the gym just long enough for Clay to show up.

"Hello, there, Beatles," said Cassius Clay. "We oughta do some road shows together. We'll get rich."

The photographers lined up the Beatles in the ring and Clay faked a punch to knock them all to the canvas: the domino punch.

Now the future of music and the future of sports began talking about the money they were making and the money they were going to make.

"You're not as stupid as you look," Clay said.

"No," Lennon said, "but you are."

Clay checked to make sure Lennon was smiling, and he was.

The younger writers, like Lipsyte, really did see Clay as a fifth Beatle, parallel players in the great social and generational shift in American society. The country was in the midst of an enormous change, an earthquake, and this fighter from Louisville and this band from Liverpool were part of it, *leading* it, whether they knew it yet or not. The Beatles' blend of black R&B and Liverpool pop and Clay's blend of defiance and humor was changing the sound of the times, its temper; set alongside the march on Washington and the quagmire in Vietnam, they would, in their way, become essential pieces of the sixties phantasmagoria.

For most of the older columnists, however, this PR-inspired scene at the Fifth Street Gym was just more of all that was going wrong in the world, more noise, more disrespect, more impudence from young men whom they could not hope to comprehend. "Clay is part of the Beatle movement," Jimmy Cannon would write famously a few years later. "He fits in with the famous singers no one can hear and the punks riding motorcycles with iron crosses pinned to their leather jackets and Batman and the boys with their long dirty hair and the girls with the unwashed look and the college kids dancing naked at secret proms held in apartments and the revolt of students who get a check from Dad every first of the month and the painters who copy the labels off soup cans and the surf bums who refuse to work and the whole pampered style-making cult of the bored young."

PART THREE

New York, 1963. With Malcolm X.

CHAPTER NINE

The Cross and
the Crescent

CLAY UNDERSTOOD THAT TO ANNOUNCE HIS INTEREST IN THE
Nation of Islam might jeopardize his chance to fight Liston for the
title, but he could not quite restrain himself. Hiding, concealment,
lying: that was not his temperament. As a result, his new faith
began to leak out in the press, if not as an all-at-once revelation,
then step by step, article by article. On September 30, 1963, the
Philadelphia Daily News wrote that Clay had attended a Black
Muslim rally in town at which Elijah Muhammad delivered his
customary three-hour tirade against the civil rights movement and
the white race. "Although he said he was not a Muslim," the article read, "Clay said he thought Muhammad was 'great.' "

What the *Daily News* did not know was that while Elijah
Muhammad was still keeping his distance from Clay, his most elo-
quent and best-known minister, Malcolm X, was not. Like so many
of the Nation's recruits in the fifties, Malcolm had come to the
sect from urban poverty, crime, and prison. As "Detroit Red," Malcolm Little had been a bootlegger, a numbers runner, a dope
dealer; he'd danced in nightclubs as Rhythm Red; finally, he served
time in Charlestown Prison and the Concord Reformatory, where
he converted, in 1948, to the Nation of Islam. When Malcolm got
out of prison in 1952, he got to know Elijah Muhammad and
quickly rose through the ranks of Muslim ministers. None of
Muhammad's followers had ever shown such intelligence and
rhetorical confidence. At the annual Savior's Day rallies, Malcolm

often spoke before Elijah Muhammad, and the protégé usually stole the show from the savior himself. Because of his youth, because of his life on the streets and his eventual redemption, because of his discipline, wit, and clear, ringing language, Malcolm was a powerful lure to recruits. He became a symbol of uncompromising strength, authenticity, and virility. Malcolm also dared to challenge Muhammad (subtly at first), urging him to abandon the Nation's traditional insularity for a more direct engagement in political action. He was not, by any means, the first black nationalist—he had come after Hubert Harrison, Henry McNeal Turner, Martin Delany, and many others—but no one, not even Elijah Muhammad, would popularize the idea of the black American's African identity with the same power. "While black nationalist and separatist ideas coming from Elijah Muhammad seemed cranky, cultlike, backwaterish, and marginal," writes Gerald Early, "the same ideas coming from Malcolm seemed revolutionary, hip, and vibrant."

Elijah Muhammad recognized Malcolm X as a potential rival, but he also saw his value, as a speaker and as an organizer, as a recruiter and as a bridge to the media and the greater world. By the late fifties and early sixties, Malcolm, as the head of New York's Mosque No. 7, became a fixture in the press; despite the sect's positions on violence and "blue-eyed devils," he managed to charm countless white reporters, from Murray Kempton at the *New York Post* to Dick Schaap, who had moved from *Newsweek* to the *Herald Tribune*. "The oddest thing about Malcolm was that, sure, he made speeches calling the white man the devil, but he treated you, one-on-one, with respect and humor, and it never seemed dishonest," Schaap said. "Why did I like a man who thought I was the devil? I don't really know, but I did. Maybe some part of me sensed that he would change. And he did." Elijah Muhammad was more exotic and distant to the white media: with his fez and his long, obscure speeches about the Mother Plane and Muslim cosmology, Elijah did not have Malcolm's capacity for directness, he did not appeal as easily to the young. This was true for Clay. While Clay had learned his first Muslim lessons from the representatives in Miami and the regional center of Atlanta, he was now enraptured by Malcolm. Clay revered Elijah Muhammad as the divine presence of his new religion, but he connected with Malcolm, as a young man might with a revered older brother. Malcolm was now his spiritual adviser, his friend and mentor.

"Malcolm X and Ali were like very close brothers," said Ferdie Pacheco. "It was almost like they were in love with each other. Malcolm thought Ali was the greatest guy he'd ever met and Ali thought this was the smartest black man on the face of the earth, because everything he said made sense. Malcolm X was bright as hell, convincing, charismatic in the way that great leaders and martyrs are. It certainly rubbed off on Ali. The only trouble Ali had with all of this was the idea that all white people were evil. Look at all the white people around Ali: me, Angelo, Chris, Morty Rothstein, the lawyer, the white Louisville Group that put aside a bunch of money so that he had money when he needed it. There were no white devils that he could see. But, again, he took from the Muslims what he needed. The Muslims filled a deep need in him, especially Malcolm X."

The two men met for the first time in Detroit in 1962. Cassius and his brother, Rudy, were in town to attend a rally at the local mosque. Before it began, the Clays ran into Malcolm X at the Students' Luncheonette next door. Clay immediately stuck out his hand and said, "I'm Cassius Clay."

Malcolm had no idea who this handsome young man was. Malcolm had boxed as a kid—he had been interested in all kinds of sports—but in recent years he'd been far too busy to pay any notice to the sports page. Eventually it was explained to him that Cassius Clay was a leading contender for the heavyweight title. And despite Elijah Muhammad's condemnation of boxing, Malcolm took an interest in this self-assured young man who was showing up at rallies around the country. Malcolm sought Clay out and talked with him about Islam and race, and Clay started confiding in Malcolm—he even confided some of his professional secrets.

"Cassius was simply a likable, friendly, clean-cut, down-to-earth youngster," Malcolm told Alex Haley for his autobiography. "I noticed how alert he was even in little details. I suspected that there was a plan in his public clowning. I suspected, and he confirmed to me, that he was doing everything possible to con and to 'psyche' Sonny Liston into coming into the ring angry, poorly trained, and overconfident, expecting another of his vaunted one-round knockouts."

By early 1963, Malcolm X was becoming disillusioned with Elijah Muhammad. He saw that for all of Muhammad's pronouncements about moral rectitude and discipline, he had got at least two of his secretaries pregnant. By way of seduction, Elijah Muhammad told his secretaries that his wife was dead to him—just as the wife of the prophet Mohammad had become dead to him—and he was therefore divinely sanctioned to seek out virgins to spread his holy seed. Agents of the FBI's fierce counterintelligence operation against the Nation of Islam had known since 1959 about Elijah Muhammad's various children and had spread word of them through anonymous letters. But the Black Muslims were loyal to the Messenger, and the smear campaign had little effect. Malcolm, a determinedly abstemious man, also saw the financial corruption in the Nation, the amassing of real estate, jewelry, and luxury cars. Malcolm was having his doubts about Muhammad's declaration of Fard as the Savior Allah incarnate, a claim inconsistent with orthodox Islam; he was even starting to have doubts about the fiery denunciations of the white man as the devil. In time he would begin to talk less of supremacy and more of the need for brotherhood.

In mid-November 1963, Malcolm defied the Nation's ban on secular activism in the white world when he endorsed a boycott of store owners in Queens who refused to hire black laborers. The Nation's leadership now saw him as beyond their control; he had to be muffled. A few weeks later, after the assassination of John Kennedy, Elijah Muhammad sent out written orders to his principal ministers to avoid any direct comment on the event. He went out of his way to warn Malcolm by telephone. Elijah Muhammad was not ordinarily tactful about the white leaders of the United States, but he was acutely aware that at that moment, with the country in mourning, the wrong comment, the wrong accent, could damage the Nation of Islam.

A few days later, in Harlem, Malcolm gave a speech at the Manhattan Center describing how, as in the days of Noah and in the days of Lot, the modern white man could expect only calamity as punishment for his sins. After the formal address, a woman in the audience got up and asked a question about the Kennedy assassination. Now Malcolm let loose, saying that the killing represented "the chickens coming home to roost." White America, he said, had for years used all its resources to put down blacks at home and abroad, and now this was all coming back to haunt its leaders. The Harlem crowd cheered, and, as they did, Malcolm added that as a farm kid, "chickens coming home to roost never did make me sad. They've always made me glad."

The quotations appeared in *The New York Times* the next morning, and Elijah Muhammad immediately summoned Malcolm X to Chicago.

"Did you see the papers this morning?" Muhammad said.

"Yes, sir, I did."

"That was a very bad statement," he said. "The country loved this man. The whole country is in mourning. That was very illtimed. A statement like that can make it hard on Muslims in general. I'll have to silence you for the next ninety days—so that Muslims everywhere can be disassociated from the blunder."

"Sir, I agree with you, and I submit, one hundred percent."

Elijah Muhammad was even more determined to isolate Malcolm than he let on in their meeting. He immediately ordered the sect's newspaper, *Muhammad Speaks*, to run a front-page memorial photograph of Kennedy. "The nation still mourns the loss of our president," Muhammad told reporters. Muhammad also told his lieutenants to make sure that Malcolm not be permitted to preach at Mosque No. 7 in New York; should he attempt to preach, he should be blocked, physically, from doing so.

"I'm going to strip him of everything," Muhammad told his Boston minister, Louis X, who would later add the name Farrakhan.

Back in New York, Malcolm suffered his censure as if he had been attacked with a knife, a bludgeon. When he began hearing rumors that he was not merely out of favor with Muhammad but in real peril, that he could be murdered at any moment, he knew enough to take the rumors seriously. "My head felt like it was bleeding inside," he told Alex Haley. "I felt like my brain was damaged." His family doctor, Leona Turner, told him that he was suffering from tremendous strain and needed rest.

Malcolm was torn between his loyalty to Muhammad and his urge to criticize him. At once he apologized to two of Muhammad's key lieutenants, Louis X and Lonni X, and vowed to do better. Malcolm also recorded his apology for Elijah Muhammad, but when the Messenger listened to the tape he sensed the edge of accusa-tion in some of Malcolm's words. "Sometimes he speaks nice and good," Muhammad said, "and other times he is altogether differ-ent." Muhammad extended his ban on Malcolm indefinitely.

Despite the battle among the leaders of the Nation, Clay invited Malcolm and his wife, Betty, and their three daughters to come stay with him in Miami. He intended the invitation as a sixth wed-ding anniversary gift. It would be the first vacation Malcolm and Betty had enjoyed since they were married. Malcolm certainly needed the rest, and he figured it would be a good thing to keep away from Chicago or New York. He accepted with relief. On Jan-uary 14, Clay met Malcolm at the airport—an event duly reported to the FBI by an informant. But the local FBI office thought the report so strange, so unlikely, that they did not send it along to Washington until January 21, when the two men flew to New York.

For any other boxer, breaking camp with a month to go before the fight would have been a serious disruption of routine, but Clay told Dundee he needed a few days off from training, and Dundee barely shrugged. Clay had not really asked permission to go and provided no details of where he was going.

In New York, the two ate dinner together, and then Clay went off to a Black Muslim rally at the Rockland Palace Ballroom near the old Polo Grounds. Malcolm stayed away from the rally, to avoid arousing anyone's anger. Two days later, in a front-page story for the *Herald Tribune*, Clay's old friend Dick Schaap described how he had first met Clay in 1960 when he was eighteen and how in Harlem, to Clay's astonishment, they had met the soapbox preacher talking about black self-help and buying black; and now, Schaap wrote, here was Clay, a contender for the heavyweight title, among fifteen hundred people cheering Elijah Muhammad. Schaap wrote that Clay was now an ardent follower of the Nation of Islam, though Clay himself refused to confirm the story. (In fact, Clay refused to talk to Schaap for a while after the story ran.) Schaap did, however, manage to reach Sonny Liston, who said, "I heard 'bout Clay and the Muslims a month ago. Don't make no dif-ference to me. I don't mess with his personal affairs, he shouldn't mess with mine. But tell him I got it in the contract that the fight can't be shown in no theaters where they don't let Negroes in to see it."

When Clay and Malcolm returned to Miami, the news really began to break. On February 3, the Louisville *Courier-Journal*, Clay's hometown paper, published an interview in which he dropped all pretense of distance from the Muslims. "Sure I talked to the Muslims and I'm going back again," he said. "I like the Muslims. I'm not going to get killed trying to force myself on people who don't want me. I like my life. Integration is wrong. The white people don't want integration. I don't believe in forcing it, and the Muslims don't believe in it. So what's wrong with the Muslims?"

Then came the most decisive news break of all. Pat Putnam, *The Miami Herald*'s boxing writer, tracked down Cassius Clay, Sr., and interviewed him about the rumors of his son's conversion to the Nation of Islam—a conversion that would be announced right after the fight. In an article that ran on February 8, seventeen days before the fight, Clay senior angrily confirmed the rumors and went into a tirade about how his son had been ruined. He claimed the Muslims were stealing money from his son and exploiting his name.

The story was a scoop for Putnam, but as soon as it was published he got calls threatening him and his wife. "So after work one night," Putnam said, "I went out to the black section of town where Clay was living and told him about what was happening. I knew him very well by that time. And he said, 'Pat, don't worry about it. You'll never get another call.' And he was right. That was the end of that."

For a while, Clay, Malcolm, and Malcolm's family enjoyed their time together. Clay put Malcolm's family up at the Hampton House motel, and they saw each other nearly every day. Sometimes in the evening the two would go walking through the black neighborhoods of Miami. Malcolm kept a camera strung around his neck and took dozens of pictures of Clay. Clay joked with the people, talked about politics and boxing, and kissed babies, as if he were running for office. The three little girls romped around the fighter; Betty, who was pregnant, had some time to relax; and Malcolm avoided the telephone. But Malcolm could not avoid his own despair over his collapsed relations with the Nation. "I was in a state of emotional shock," he told Alex Haley. "I was like someone who for twelve years had had an inseparable, beautiful marriage— and then suddenly one morning at breakfast the marriage partner had thrust across the table some divorce papers. I felt as though something in *nature* had failed, like the sun, or the stars." Malcolm worried, at times, about the rumors of assassination, but even worse was his increasing sense of betrayal, his shock at the idea that the man he had always understood to be the Messenger, a man of integrity, had covered up his own corruption and weaknesses rather than confessing them.

Malcolm's faith in Elijah Muhammad was crumbling, but he remained convinced of the need for a strong black nationalist movement. Over breakfast, he showed Clay pictures of the white Catholic priests who had been close to both Floyd Patterson and Sonny Liston. He tried to instill in Clay the idea that the fight with Liston was a religious battle, not merely a sporting event.

"This fight is the truth," he said. "It's the Cross and the Crescent fighting in a prize ring—for the first time. It's a modern Crusades—a Christian and a Muslim facing each other with television to beam it off Telstar for the whole world to see what happens. Do you think Allah has brought about all this intending for you to leave the ring as anything but the champion?"

Malcolm's presence in Miami was an inspiration to the fighter—by the day of the weigh-in he would be shouting, "It is prophesied for me to be successful!"—but it was hurting the gate. The promoter, Bill MacDonald, had to gross $800,000 dollars to break even on the fight, and it was becoming increasingly clear that he was not coming close. The David-versus-Goliath fight he thought he was getting was fast losing its balance of moral forces, especially to white Floridians, who were not inclined to see a brash young black man, much less a Black Muslim, in the role of David. The Miami Convention Hall held 15,744 people, and it was no secret to MacDonald now that he would be lucky to fill half the house.

Finally, three days before the fight, MacDonald confronted Clay about the press reports and told him that the news was going to cost him his shot at the title. MacDonald said he was getting ready to call off the bout. Was it true? Was Cassius really a member of the Nation of Islam? MacDonald told Clay that if he had to cancel this fight, he might not get another chance at the heavyweight championship.

Clay knew MacDonald was right, but he stood up to him all the same. The championship was all he'd ever wanted since he was twelve years old, it was his destiny, but he refused to deny his ties to the Nation. If MacDonald wanted to call off the fight, then that was his business.

"My religion's more important to me than the fight," Clay recalled saying.

Then the fight was off, MacDonald said, and that was it. Clay went home to start packing his bags.

After that meeting, the publicist, Harold Conrad, immediately went to the Fifth Street Gym to tell the Dundees that the fight was off and that Clay had gone home to pack. Then Conrad went to MacDonald and told him it was impossible to cancel the fight: think of all the tickets that had been sold, the closed-circuit contracts around the country.

"The hell I can't call it off," MacDonald said, according to Conrad. "You're a Northerner. You don't understand. You don't realize that Miami is the Deep South and is just as segregated as any town in Mississippi. How can I promote a fight down here with a guy who thinks we're white devils?"

"You know what you're doing?" Conrad said. "In this country we have freedom of religion."

"Bullshit," MacDonald said. "And don't you go start hitting me with the Constitution."

"Bill, you don't realize what you're doing. You'll go down in history as a promoter who denied a man the right to fight for the title because of his religion."

"Jesus, what the hell you want me to do? It's that Malcolm X. He's responsible for all this trouble and he's practically running the kid's fight camp. That don't look good."

"Suppose Malcolm X got out of town right away?" Conrad proposed. "Would that change your mind?"

MacDonald allowed that it might.

Conrad tracked down Malcolm and said, "Look, the way things are now, the fight is off. Cassius will lose his chance to win the heavyweight championship, but you can save it for him."

How? Malcolm said.

"You have to get out of town now. You're the focal point. You're the guy the press knows."

Malcolm said he would go, and everyone agreed that he could return the night of the fight, when the media's attention would be on the ring itself. Malcolm was given a ringside seat, seat number seven, near Clay's corner.

When the meeting was over, Conrad extended his hand to Malcolm X.

Malcolm refused to shake it. Instead, he touched Conrad's wrist with his forefinger and went off to the airport.

CHAPTER TEN

Bear Hunting

FEBRUARY 25, 1964

CLAY WAS IN NO WISE DELUDED ABOUT LISTON'S PHYSICAL gifts. Sonny was a world-class slugger who could move, and yet Clay saw how easily his feelings could be hurt, how he could become confused and vulnerable. Liston was capable of a funny remark, he was certainly smarter than his scant school records would indicate, but he was vulnerable. He had shown over and over that he was sensitive about his age, that he resented being thought of as mobster's meat, a killer in trunks, boots, and gloves. Liston demanded respect, the solemnity due a king. And so respect was precisely what Clay would deny him. He would play the fool, at once enraging Liston and also leading him toward the danger zones of complacency.

Clay's strategy was in place from the moment Liston arrived in Miami to train. Clay met Liston's plane, and as the champion came down the steps toward the tarmac, Clay was there to meet him, shouting, "Chump! Big ugly bear! I'm gonna whup you right now!"

As Liston got closer to Clay, he said, "Look, this clowning, it's not cute, and I'm not joking."

"Joking?" Clay said. "Why you big chump, I'll whup you right here."

Liston looked Clay up and down. He could not have failed to notice that Clay, for all his featherweight speed, was a big man, taller than himself.

Miami, 1964.

Liston was accompanied by Jack Nilon, his manager, and Joe Louis, who was being paid walking-around money to be in the champion's corner and tell the press what a fine fellow he was. Liston, Louis, and Nilon climbed in a VIP car and took off for the house Liston had rented on the beach.

But Clay didn't let it go. He drove after Liston's car, chasing him as he left the airport.

Liston's car suddenly pulled over to the side of the road, and Liston, fuming, got out and headed for Clay.

"Listen, you little punk. I'll punch you in the mouth. This has gone too far!"

Clay started to take off his jacket, screaming, "Come on, chump, right here!"

The two men were separated before anything serious could happen, but Liston had been given a taste of the harassment he was about to endure. Clay and his entourage made sure to put out rumors that they were going to stage a "full-scale raid" on Liston as he trained at the Surfside Auditorium, and once in a while they did send over an emissary to make sure that Liston kept thinking about them. Another time Clay just drove to the estate where Liston was living and held court on his lawn, knowing that the champion could see him from the window. "Liston was humiliated," said Mort Sharnik, who was in Miami for *Sports Illustrated*. "He had difficulty getting that house to begin with because it was in a white neighborhood. At first, he used to sit out there on the lawn with his family like a wealthy planter. But after Clay came around bear-hunting, he didn't sit outside anymore. He was like a prisoner in his own luxurious surroundings. This soured Liston's sense of expansiveness and of being king." Liston, who had craved acceptance, was getting just the opposite from Clay. He was champion of the world and a twenty-two-year-old kid who had barely gotten by Doug Jones and Henry Cooper was out on his lawn, inside his training camp, on television, and in the papers, everywhere making a fool of him. The gall!

In the meantime, Clay trained harder than ever. What was more, after studying films of Liston's bouts with Cleveland Williams, Eddie Machen, Patterson, and other opponents, he came up with a well-planned strategy.

"You know, a fighter can condition his body to go hard certain rounds, then to coast certain rounds," Clay told *Playboy* afterward.

"Nobody can fight fifteen rounds. So I trained to fight the first two rounds, and to protect myself from getting hit by Liston. I knew that with the third, he'd start tiring, then he'd get worse every round. So I trained to coast the third, fourth, and fifth rounds. I had two reasons for that. One was that I wanted to prove that I had the ability to stand up to Liston. The second reason was that I wanted him to wear himself out and get desperate. He would be throwing wild punches, and missing. If I just did that as long as he lasted on his feet, I couldn't miss winning the fight on points. And so I conditioned myself to fight full-steam from the sixth through the ninth round, if it lasted that long. I never did think it would go past nine rounds. That's why I announced I'd take him in eight. I figured I'd be in command by the sixth. I'd be careful—not get hit—and I'd cut him up and shake him up until he would be like a bull, just blind, and missing punches until he was nearly crazy. And I planned that sometime in the eighth, when he had thrown some punch and left himself just right, I'd be all set, and I'd drop him. Listen here, man, I knew I was going to upset the world!"

Liston, on the other hand, was training for a quick knockout. He went through the usual motions: skipping rope and hitting the bags to the throbbing "Night Train." But he ran far less than he should have—maybe a mile or two a few times a week—and worked out against mediocre sparring partners. Ever since the first Patterson fight, he had allowed himself to believe that he could climb in the ring and take off his robe, and the other man would drop for the ten-count.

"I don't think Sonny was in the best shape," said Hank Kaplan, one of the regulars at the Fifth Street Gym. "I myself saw him eat hot dogs and popcorn and drink beer over in Surfside not too long before the fight."

Clay's recreation time was taken up with Malcolm X. Liston's fun was less high-minded, taking, as he did, his after-hours counsel from Ash Resnik, who had come in from Las Vegas for the fight. One of Liston's cornermen told Jack McKinney that Resnik fixed Liston up with a couple of prostitutes. "Nilon has a heavy responsibility for the destruction of Sonny Liston," McKinney said. "He was a gutless worm and didn't assert himself. He wanted to play the part of the prosperous businessman, a fight manager on the side, but he was a worthless character. . . . In Miami Beach,

Joe Pollino pointed out two obvious hookers that Resnik had fixed Sonny with—and that's no credit to Sonny—he was screwing around with these bimbos on Twenty-third and Collins. That's what Ash Resnik brought him in the way of intellectual and cultural enrichment. See, no matter who you're fighting, you need people around you constantly telling you that anything can happen. You have to train—even with the pushovers."

"Sonny never got serious until about a month before a fight," one of his sparring partners, Foneda Cox, said. "And when he went to Miami, he firmly believed that he would kill Clay. I mean it, really *kill* him. Why work too hard?"

When someone in his camp would question his training, Liston just shrugged it off. Harold Conrad told Liston he was worried: Clay was fit and very much the real thing. Liston just smiled.

"Don't worry, Hal," he said. "I'll put the evil eye on this faggot at the weigh-in and psych him right out of the fight."

THERE IS NO COMPELLING REASON TO WEIGH HEAVYWEIGHTS before a fight. Unlike other fighters in the lighter divisions, they are not required to "make weight," to stay under a given limit. Occasionally there is, at the moment a heavy strips off his robe, a flash of drama: "Oh dear! He looks fat!" Or, "Oh my! How fearsome!" But there is little of that. The reporters have usually seen the fighters train and they know pretty well the physical condition of the champion and his challenger. If there is a reason for a heavyweight weigh-in, it is to intensify the sense of ritual, as sumo wrestlers stomp their feet and toss handfuls of salt prior to battle. As in actual warfare, rituals matter. The solemnity of weights and measures, of large men posing in their underwear on a scale, is crucial. It may matter most of all for the journalists, who are eager to have first-edition stories and pictures to run on the day when the main event, the fight, begins as late as eleven at night. The weigh-in allows for an evaluation of the "baleful stare"; the reporter can judge the fighter "ready" or "nervous"; the TV man can say with conviction that "these two men plain don't like each other." The promoter will try to sell tickets and, if he is generous, put in a word for the fighters on the undercard.

The Liston-Clay weigh-in was scheduled for the morning of the

fight; it was to be held in a freight area of the Miami Beach Convention Hall. Clay arrived at the arena wearing a blue denim jacket
with the words "Bear Huntin'" embroidered on it in red. His entourage included Dundee, Sugar Ray Robinson, William Faversham of the Louisville Group, and Bundini. Hardly anyone was at
the arena yet, but Clay was already warming up: he and Bundini
shouted, "Float like a butterfly! Sting like a bee!" and Clay
pounded the floor with an African walking stick.

"I'm the champ! I'm ready to rumble! Tell Sonny I'm here! He
ain't no champ! Round eight to prove I'm great! Bring that big ugly
bear on!"

The team marched into a dressing room, and, as Clay changed
into a white terry-cloth robe, Robinson and Dundee tried to calm
him down.

"You gotta act right," Dundee said. "This is for the championship. There's gonna be press people here." That Clay might
make a scene at the weigh-in was no secret to anyone who had
watched his press conferences and interviews in Miami, and so a
distinguished elder of the Miami Beach Boxing Commission came
to the dressing room to counsel Clay on manners.

"Then we went out and Clay went crazy," Dundee said. "The
problem was we were too early. No one was there yet. So we ended
up doing the whole thing twice. It was amazing: we thought it was
a certain time and I figured we're gonna make a big entrance and
Muhammad is saying, 'I'm the prettiest fighter in the world!'
Screaming, yelling, the whole shebang. But we were an hour early.
So we ran back, messed around in Chris's office for a while, and
then we did it all over again an hour later.

"I just knew it was gonna be chaos. Muhammad had told me at
the gym, 'Angie, I'm gonna bring Drew Brown down there.' And I
said, 'What are you doing? Don't do that! That guy's nuts. What are
you doing to me?' But he loved Drew because he got kicks from the
guy. He liked those kind of guys. They charged his battery."

Clay and Bundini came out screaming and yelling at 11:09. They
were still screaming when Liston came out two minutes later.

"I'm ready to rumble now!" Clay shouted. "I can beat you any
time, chump! Somebody's gonna die at ringside tonight! You're
scared, chump! You ain't no giant! I'm gonna eat you alive!"

Clay lunged at Liston. Bundini grabbed the belt of his robe and

Faversham, Robinson, and Dundee held him back. Robinson tried to shove Clay against a wall, and Clay shoved back, shouting, "I am a great performer! I am a great performer!"

Years later, when this sort of hysteria was understood as a standing joke, like Emmett Kelly slipping on a banana peel or Don Rickles calling someone in the audience a hockey puck, the writers merely rolled their eyes. It was just Ali. But no one had ever seen anything like this before. Traditionally, anything but the most stoic behavior meant that a fighter was terrified, which was precisely what Clay wanted Liston to believe.

"Ali whispered in my ear, 'Hold me back,' and then he winked at me," Mort Sharnik, the *Sports Illustrated* writer, said. "Ali had the capacity almost of self-hypnosis or self-induced hysteria and he'd work himself up to this crazy pitch."

"Round eight to prove I'm great!" Clay shouted, holding up eight fingers. "Round eight!"

Liston smiled thinly and held up two fingers.

When it came time to weigh the fighters, Clay insisted that Bundini and Robinson be allowed up on the platform. He refused to budge until the boxing commission officials bent their rules.

"This is my show, this is my show," he said.

"I'll keep him quiet," Bundini told the cops. "I have to be up there to keep him quiet." Finally, the commissioners relented and the police waved all three up. Clay weighed 210 pounds.

Then Liston stepped up on the scale.

"Liston, two hundred and eighteen pounds," shouted Morris Klein, the Miami Beach boxing commissioner. Liston stepped down from the scale.

"Hey, sucker!" Clay yelled up at him. "You're a chump! You been tricked, chump!"

Liston looked down at Clay with a slight, fatherly smile.

"Don't let anybody know," he said. "Don't tell the world."

"You're too ugly!" Clay shouted. "You are a bear! I'm going to whup you so baaad. You're a chump, a chump, a chump . . ." Clay's voice was shrill, his eyes were bugging out, and he was lunging around like a mental patient.

"No man could have seen Clay that morning at the weigh-in and believed that he could stay on his feet three minutes that night," Murray Kempton wrote later in *The New Republic*.

"Suddenly almost everyone in the room hated Cassius Clay," Kempton went on. "Sonny Liston just looked at him. Liston used to be a hoodlum; now he was our cop; he was the big Negro we pay to keep sassy Negroes in line and he was just waiting until his boss told him it was time to throw this kid out. . . . Northern Italian journalists were comforted to see on Liston's face the look that mafiosi use to control peasants in Sicily; promoters and fight managers saw in Clay one of their animals utterly out of control and were glad to know that soon he would be not just back in line but out of the business. . . . Even Norman Mailer settled in this case for organized society. Suppose Clay won the heavyweight championship, he asked. It would mean that every loudmouth on a street corner could swagger and be believed."

Clay's performance seemed to be the sweaty ravings of a nut, the frightened rant of a kid who had been terrified ever since he confronted Liston in that Las Vegas casino more than a year before, but what no one saw was how deliberate and effective this performance was, how it unnerved Liston. "It convinced Liston to the end of his life that Ali was crazy," said Clay's cornerman, Ferdie Pacheco. "Ali became impossible for his opponents to gauge. Years later, when Ernie Shavers almost knocked him out in the Garden, Ali was falling back against the ropes but Shavers held back because he thought Ali was kidding. The same thing happened to Joe Frazier, in the third fight in Manila. He saw Ali start to fall, staggering back, and instead of rushing him, Frazier just stood there and looked, because he couldn't believe that Ali was hurt. George Foreman, too, didn't know when Ali was hurt or when he was kidding. People always thought he was crazy. His reputation was so huge that you imputed things to him that he wasn't really doing. And it all began in Miami, at the weigh-in with Liston."

As Clay kept barking away and ignoring warning after warning, Klein stepped in and shouted, "Cassius Clay is fined two thousand five hundred dollars for his behavior on the platform and the money will be withheld from Clay's purse."

The commission doctor, Alexander Robbins, took the pulse and blood pressure of both fighters. Liston's counts were slightly above normal. Considering all the commotion, there was no worry there. Robbins could barely get to Clay, who kept jumping and shouting as if he had been stuck with a cattle prod. Several times Robbins approached Clay with his stethoscope outstretched and then Clay would keep wriggling and Robbins would jump back, frightened, bewildered. Finally, the doctor was able to make his reading: Clay's pulse, which was normally fifty-four beats per minute, had shot up to 120, and his blood pressure was soaring, too, at two hundred over one hundred.

Jimmy Cannon, who carried himself with such authority that one might have believed him to be chief of surgery as well as the columnist from the *World-Telegram*, slid into a chair next to Dr. Robbins and said, "Could it be that the kid is scared to death, Doc?"

"Yes, yes, Mr. Cannon," the doctor said. "This fighter is scared to death, and if his blood pressure is the same at fight time, it's all off."

Both fighters finally cleared out and went to their makeshift dressing rooms. Clay was already calming down.

"What do you think?" he asked as he sat on a training table. "He was really shook up. He was little and he was short, and they're telling me he was so big. I think he was shook up."

As Clay left the arena, he ran into a ubiquitous Miami character named King Levinsky. Levinsky had been one of Joe Louis's "bums of the month," a heavyweight with one night in the spotlight to his credit, but his fighting career had left him poorer of mind and pocket. Levinsky now sold bad-looking ties out of a worse-looking cardboard suitcase. "King used to grab you around the head and say, 'Wanna buy a tie from King Levinsky?'" George Plimpton recalled. "He was everywhere, and after you'd bought a few ties, you started running."

Now, as Clay left the arena, Levinsky came running after him, not to sell ties, but to offer him a job.

"He's gonna take you, kid!" the King shouted. "Partners with me, kid. You can be *partners* with me!"

THE COMMISSION INSTRUCTED PACHECO TO KEEP A REGULAR watch on Clay's blood pressure and to report if the numbers were still too high. Clay went back to the dressing room and came back out in his "Bear Huntin'" jacket. He and his entourage drove back out to his house.

"It was the most amazing thing," Pacheco said. "An hour after all the commotion, I took his blood pressure and the pulse was at fifty-four, normal for him, and his blood pressure was one-twenty over eighty, perfect. It was all an act."

"Why did you do that?" Pacheco asked Clay. "Why did you act so nutty up there in front of all those people?"

Clay leaned forward and said, "Because Liston thinks I'm a nut. He is scared of no man, but he is scared of a nut. Now he doesn't know what I'm going to do."

The gamblers in town were equally sure that Clay had revealed himself as a frightened challenger. As a team, Sammy Davis, Jr., Joe Louis, and Ash Resnik placed a call to a friend in Las Vegas, the gambler Lem Banker. They told Banker to lay down a huge bet on Liston.

"They were sure Sonny was gonna win because they thought Clay was insane," Banker said. "But Sonny had done his pretraining in Vegas at the Thunderbird and I'd seen him sparring with Foneda Cox and Jesse Bowdry and he'd looked lousy to me. He never took the fight serious. There was a racetrack behind the Thunderbird, and he'd run around the track twice. Anyway, Ash, Louis, and Sammy Davis called for the price of the fight to bet, and I said there was no price because of the weigh-in. You could only bet on Clay. But I said there is a four-round proposition: will the fight go four rounds? Ash wanted to bet fifty thousand. But Ash was slow-paying and Sammy never paid his bills, so I moved ten thousand on a four-round 'do or don't.' I knew Sonny wasn't in shape. Sonny was my friend, but I had to like Clay."

By evening there were reports on the radio that Clay was so frightened that he was escaping, that he had been seen at the Miami airport buying a ticket to fly abroad.

On the way into the arena that night, Mort Sharnik bumped into Geraldine.

"Sonny thinks that boy is crazy!" Geraldine Liston said.

"Who?" Sharnik said.

"That boy Cassius. Crazy. Out of his mind."

"You mean he thinks Cassius is a madman?"

"Just out of his cotton-picking mind," she said. "And you never know what to expect from a man like that. You never know what to expect from a madman."

CHAPTER ELEVEN

"Eat Your Words!"

FEBRUARY 25, 1964

AFTER THE QUESTION OF CLAY'S SANITY HAD BEEN RESOLVED IN the affirmative, he took a nap. And while he slept, his doctor, Ferdie Pacheco, called the local boxing authorities to let them know that the challenger's systems had returned to normal and that the fight could certainly go on.

But then Pacheco thought about the night ahead, about what *could* happen. Unlike Geraldine Liston and Jack McKinney and a very few others who were close enough to see how complex Liston really was—the sulfurous brew of deprivation and rage, the constant ache to prove himself worthy—Pacheco saw Liston as forbidding, frightening. Pacheco had been hanging around gyms in Florida for years and he had never before seen anyone as ruthless or as strong, inside and outside the ring. Pacheco was a pretty good amateur painter—he painted scenes of historical Mexico, of the cigar rollers in his native Tampa—and when he thought about Liston the colors that came to mind were raw umber and Prussian blue. "It never seemed to me like there were any gray areas with Sonny," he said. Like so many others in Clay's camp, Pacheco was worried that the night would end not merely in defeat, but in serious injury.

Dundee was a man of a different spirit, always up, always an optimist; he really did believe that "styles make fights" and Clay had the style to beat Liston. "I thought he could outquick him and outthink him and wear him down in eleven, twelve rounds," Dundee

"Eat your words!" Cassius Clay vs. Sonny Liston, 1964.

said. But Pacheco had the feeling that Liston, a great champion, was now so angry at Clay for all the accumulated humiliations— the taunts in the press, the mocking verse, and now the antic weigh-in—that he would want not just to knock Clay out, but to work him over, to hurt him. And so Pacheco made sure everything was in order. He was particularly concerned about the fastest routes to the various local hospitals. Which was closest? Where was the best emergency room? Who was on duty? Did he know the doctors? He finally settled on Mount Sinai, where he'd been an intern in 1958.

In the late afternoon, Clay ate a steak and a salad and vegetables, and in the evening he dressed in a tuxedo and headed off to the arena with Dundee, Pacheco, masseur Luis Sarria, Bundini, and a few others. He went earlier than he needed to because he wanted to watch his brother, Rudy, who was fighting in a preliminary bout against Chip Johnson, a solid journeyman heavyweight.

The arena, which held 15,744, was nearly empty when Rudy entered the ring. At a championship fight it is considered low-rent to attend too many of the preliminaries, and so the empty seats were no shock. Unfortunately for the promoter, Bill MacDonald, the arena was going to stay that way. Only 8,297 tickets had been sold. The high-end seats were sold out, but the middle and upper reaches were desolate. Although Clay and his backers split $630,000 and Liston and his sponsors divided up $1.3 million, Mac-Donald lost more than $300,000. It was hard to say what hurt the gate more: the forbidding odds in Liston's favor, the rumors of Clay's conversion to the Nation of Islam, or the rainstorm that was now beating down on Miami. No matter how hard Harold Conrad tried, the promoters never succeeded in putting a white hat on Clay's head; they could not repeat the promotional dumb show of Patterson-Liston, the Good Negro versus the Bad Negro. For most Caucasian Floridians (and who else had the money to pay for a seat?) this was a matchup between a Muslim punk and a terrifying thug.

Clay stood in the aisle, way back from the ring, and watched his brother fight. Rudy was not a particularly good boxer, and he fumbled his way through the first round, barely surviving it. The writers who had bothered to attend Rudy's bout spent as much time watching Clay yell encouragement to his brother as they did watching the fight. In the end, Rudy hung on to win a decision, but he was not impressive. He had been beaten up pretty thoroughly, and matters promised to be worse against tougher competition. It hurt Clay to watch his brother being bruised in the ring.

"After tonight, Rudy," he said, "you won't have to fight no more."

Slowly, the crowd, or what there was of it, started streaming into the arena. Malcolm X, who had returned to Miami the previous day, settled into his seat. As always, he was dressed in a conservative dark suit, dark tie, white shirt. Despite all the commotion around him, the conflict with the Nation, the ugly dustup with Bill MacDonald, Malcolm was in a fine mood, chatting with the reporters who approached him. There was probably no one in the arena as confident of an upset. The night before the fight, Malcolm had met with Murray Kempton, who was then writing his column for the *New York World-Telegram*. Kempton said that he hoped Clay would not be too immobilized by fear when he went into the ring to face Liston.

"To be a Muslim," Malcolm instructed Kempton, "is to know no fear."

But Kempton, who was the keenest observer of character on press row, saw something else in Clay that night. As he watched Clay survey the arena, he thought Clay's eyes were "blank" and wandering. "There was a sudden horrid notion," Kempton wrote, "that just before the main event, when the distinguished visitors were announced, Cassius Clay in his dinner jacket might bounce into the ring, shout one more time that he was the greatest, and go down the steps and out of the arena and out of the sight of man forever. Bystanders yelled insults at him; his handlers pushed him toward his dressing room, stiff, his steps hesitant. One had thought him hysterical in the morning; now one thought him catatonic."

In the locker room, Clay dressed slowly. He waited while he got his hands taped and then he began to loosen up, jabbing the air. He'd thought it all out: go out moving and jabbing for two or three rounds, start to wear Liston down, then coast awhile, wait until Liston was exhausted, and then start moving in for the kill in the eighth or the ninth. Usually, Dundee had to be careful that Clay did not tire himself out in the dressing room before a fight; he was so full of energy, so eager to perform, that he would throw a blizzard of punches and dance himself into a lather of sweat. But now his movements were wary, serious. This was not a performance, but a *fight*.

"For all the joking and the clowning that morning," Dundee said, "he knew this was serious business. This was everything he'd ever dreamed of and a very tough customer stood in his way."

"He was very nervous, you could see it," Pacheco said. "I was with him against Joe Frazier, all three fights, against George Foreman in Zaire, I was there for all of them, and this was the only time I ever really saw him nervous. The first and last time. After that, well, it's like the other night: I was watching *The Benny Goodman Story* and there was this scene when someone says to Benny's mother, 'Benny has to play the Mozart clarinet concerto tonight— isn't he nervous?' And she says, 'What? Are you kidding? The clarinet is his life. You put the music in front of him and he can handle it. He's never nervous. It's the *rest* of life that can be a problem.' That's Ali. Boxing was what he did. He could handle anything in the ring. It was the rest of life that could be confusing. Except for the first Liston fight. He was just a kid, and that night he had no idea if he could really do what he had been saying he could do all along."

Clay was not only nervous about Liston and the prospect of hurt and shame, he was also shaken up by the rumors that had been whispered in his ear.

"Watch out," Captain Sam Saxon had told him. "The white power structure is out to get you."

"Watch out," some of the other Muslims had told him. "Dundee's Mafia. You can't trust him, you can't trust Pacheco, and the other white guys around you."

Now Clay sat in the locker room fidgeting. "The plan was to go in, lock the door, and not let anyone in," Pacheco said. "One of the craziest rumors going around was that the Mafia was going to poison our water. The whole thing was ridiculous, but Muhammad was worried. So what we did was fill a bottle of water and then tape it shut. Muhammad had the Muslims fill the water bottle, not us. We were in there for more than an hour. There was just Luis Sarria and Bundini, both black, Angelo and me, both white, and Rudy. And if we took our eyes off the water, Muhammad would say, 'Pour out all the water and put new water in.' That happened three or four times. Finally, I said, 'Who's gonna poison you, Angelo or me? I'm your doctor. If I was gonna poison you I would've done it with some shot.' And with Angelo, he never got over the fact that the Muslims kept telling him that Angelo was Italian, with ties to Frankie Carbo, the same people who were around Liston. You can build paranoia in a fighter faster than you can in anybody. Just with a hint. The fact was that everyone in boxing had had relations with Frankie Carbo in the forties and fifties. If you knew boxing, you knew at least that much. But the Muslims were just guys from Chicago who knew nothing about boxing. They didn't even think sports were any good, until Ali furnished them with a good living. So the water bottle got emptied again and again."

As the fight drew closer, Cassius and Rudy tried to figure out which direction was east, and when they did, they got on their knees and, together with Malcolm X, prayed to Allah. In years to come, as Muhammad Ali, he would pray in his corner before the opening bell, his head bowed, his gloves up near his face, but tonight he was still Cassius Clay and what little remained of his secret he tried to keep that way.

In Liston's dressing room, the feeling was of confidence, calm. "As much as Clay got under Sonny's skin, we all believed the night would turn out okay," said one of Liston's cornermen. Willie Reddish and Joe Pollino put on T-shirts advertising Ash Resnik's Thunderbird Hotel in Las Vegas. Liston pulled on a pair of white satin shorts with black trim and allowed his handlers to drape towels all over his shoulders and chest, wrapping him like a mummy. Then he put on his robe and pulled up the hood—the "executioner's robe," as Willie Reddish put it.

AT TEN O'CLOCK, THE FIGHTERS ENTERED THE RING: FIRST CLAY, then the champion. Clay bounced and jabbed in his corner and Liston stretched, waking slowly to the task. The referee, a squared-off man named Barney Felix, stood in a neutral corner, his stubby arms stretched out along the ropes. With a Q-Tip tucked above his ear, Dundee kept his back to Liston's corner and watched only Clay, all the while reminding him that when he went to the center of the ring to hear Felix's instructions he should stand up straight and tall.

"He's gonna be staring at you, looking to intimidate you," Dundee said. "Show him you're bigger than he is."

At ringside, Steve Ellis and Joe Louis began their national closed-circuit broadcast.

The ring announcer, Frank Waymon, drew the microphone down from the ceiling.

"Good evening, ladies and gentlemen! Welcome to Miami Beach, Florida! Miami Beach Convention Hall! While we're here, may I introduce you to a couple of boxers you have seen in the past and will probably see again in the . . . fyuuu-cha!" And out they came: Clay's old friends, the former welterweight champion Luis Rodriguez, and the light heavyweight champion—"the dancing master!"—Willie Pastrano. Then Sugar Ray Robinson, in a sharp check jacket. Clay bowed twice in the direction of his earthly mentor.

"And now . . . the challenger, from Louisville, Kentucky, wearing white trunks with red stripes, and weighing two hundred and ten and one half pounds, the former Olympic light heavyweight champion . . . Cassius Clay!"

The crowd, small as it was, whipped up an impressive chorus of booing and jeering. Clay was impassive, fiddling with his mouthpiece and bouncing, bouncing on the balls of his feet.

". . . And his opponent, from Denver, Colorado, weighing two hundred and eighteen pounds, wearing the white trunks with the black trim, the heavyweight champion of the world, Charles . . . Sonny . . . Liston!"

Barney Felix summoned the two fighters to the center of the ring for the ritual recitation of the "instructions." In a title fight the referee's restatement of the injunctions against hitting after the bell or attacking the groin is rather like telling the top lawyers in the country that they will now hear a review of the rules of evidence; the ritual is purely psychological. Liston fixed his stare on Clay, and no matter how lax Liston had been in training, it was clear now that he meant to do only harm. The stare could not be mistaken for anything but high seriousness. Clay's fear was still in him—"Tell you the truth, I was *scared!*"—but he betrayed nothing. He stared back and looked *down* on Liston. That was critical. He looked *down* on Liston and established a physical point of information: he was fast, but he was big, too. Just before the litany of instructions was finished ("Do you understand, gentlemen?"), Clay opened his mouth for the first time that night to Liston.

He said, "I've got you now, sucker!"

BACK IN THE CORNER, WILLIE REDDISH TOLD LISTON TO TAKE his time. *Don't rush the knockout. You'll catch him sooner or later.*

But if Liston knew one thing at that moment it was that he did not have unlimited time to get rid of Clay. He had to do it sooner, not later. He had trained for six, seven rounds, at the very most; after that, Liston would feel worse, he'd feel the heaviness in his legs and shoulders, he'd taste the acid bile in his throat, he'd feel, above all, his age—whatever it was.

The bell sounded for round one.

Clay went out intending to score points, but one point in particular. He wanted to show Liston that he could not be hit, or, at least, not easily. He wanted to show Liston right away just how long a night it would be. He wanted him to feel, in advance, a whisper of the fatigue to come.

Clay started moving clockwise around the ring, a kind of numbing canter that he interrupted periodically by stopping and then wagging his upper body side to side, a quick windshield-wiper move that complicated an opponent's attempt to ready an attack. Liston trudged after him and within moments had to have seen how much faster it all was up close, how hard it would be to hit him. Liston tried a right lead—maybe he could end it right now!— but Clay was gone before the punch had straightened out. Then Liston missed with a jab, then another. He was missing by a foot, two feet.

"I just kept running, watching his eyes," Clay said later. "Liston's eyes tip you when he is about to throw a heavy punch. Some kind of way, they just flicker."

Liston finally hit Clay with a decent body shot, a left to the meat under the rib cage. The glove seemed to disappear, a painful blow, and yet Liston could not follow up. Clay spun out of Liston's grasp and made him look awkward as no one else ever had. "Sonny was finding out just how amazing Clay's reflexes were," said Jack McKinney. "He was slipping Sonny and moving backwards, or sometimes his feet were in place but he'd lean back so the jab would be a millimeter short. Sonny had the most devastating jab in history, a rising jab that was like a shotgun—he lifted people off the ground with that jab—and Clay was avoiding it. Liston was a superb athlete with superb reflexes and great foot control, quick feet, but when you look at that first round you had to laugh and be amazed. Clay is retreating and Liston is shuffling in, delivering the jab— and each jab is just short of touching Clay." Liston had fought quick fighters before—Marty Marshall, Eddie Machen, Zora Folley—but who had ever seen anything like this?

Then, with about a minute left in the first, Clay began adding his own punches to the mix. He started flicking his left jab against Liston's brows—first one jab at a time, and then jabs in flurries, two, three, four at a clip, and then jabs followed up with an overhand right or a left hook. It was as if Clay were revealing one weapon at a time, the better to demoralize Liston gradually, to make him see that there was no end to Clay's arsenal and guile.

With about forty seconds left in the round, Liston found himself covering up, stunned as much by the idea that Clay was beating him to the punch as by the punches themselves. At the very end of the round, Clay hit Liston with eight consecutive jabs, and by the time Liston straightened out of his crouch looking for something to hit, Clay was gone.

The bell sounded, ending the first, but the two men continued to fight until, finally, Felix moved in to end it.

"I remember I came to my corner thinking, 'He was supposed to kill me. Well, I'm still alive,' " Clay told Alex Haley a few days after the fight. "Angelo Dundee was working over me, talking a mile a minute. I just watched Liston, so mad he didn't even sit down. I thought to myself, 'You gonna wish you had rested all you could when we get past this next round.' I could hear some radio or television expert, all excited, you know the way they chatter. The big news was that I hadn't been counted out yet."

At ringside, Joe Louis, who was in Liston's corner spiritually and financially, could barely believe what he had seen. His tendency was to discount a slow start for a champion and assume he would come on stronger with time, but Louis did not withhold his praise for Clay. He knew that something significant was happening in the ring, something he had never witnessed before, not as a fighter or as an announcer. "I think we've just seen one of the greatest rounds we've seen from anybody in a long time," he told the closed-circuit viewers. "I think Clay completely outclassed Sonny Liston in this round. . . ."

"Who won that round?" Clay asked his corner.

"You did!" Bundini shouted.

"You won the round," Dundee said, "and you're gonna win the whole thing."

The fear was lifting. Now Clay opened his mouth wide, improbably wide, a dark oval mug, and he looked down at the writers at ringside. *Shut my mouth? You can't!*

LISTON CAME OUT FOR THE SECOND WITH DESPERATION, throwing big punches, one at a time. He missed badly. He tried bullying Clay against the ropes, where he could cut off all the dizzying motion, take aim, and fire. For a moment, it seemed that the strategy might work, but then Clay, after absorbing a few blows, deflecting a few others off his gloves, danced off the ropes and kept up his circling, that clockwise canter that was beginning to disorient Liston. He was like a man with a six-pack in him trying to survive a trip on the Screamer, the Gut-Tumbler, the Cyclone, the biggest nausea-inducing ride the funpark has to offer. At one point, Liston missed so badly with a left hook that he ended up punching a rope instead. The rope bounced around, a jangling mockery, and Liston was embarrassed. What could he do? What were the odds that Clay, so young and fit, would slow down? What odds were there that Liston would get *better* as the rounds wore on?

Now Clay started to stick his left jab at the fleshy pads under Liston's eyes, and suddenly, to the shock of everyone close enough to see it, a welt began to rise under Liston's left eye. The swelling gave the champion an exaggerated look not of pain but of age, of weariness. Clay was not escaping every blow, but now it was clear that the first round had not been a freak, not the result of some coltish hyperdrive from a hopped-up challenger. "He hit me some, but I weaved and ducked away from most of his shots," Clay told *Playboy.* "I remember one time feeling his arm grazing the back of my neck and thinking—it was like I shouted to myself—'All I got to do is keep this up.' And I got out from under and I caught him with some lefts and rights. Then I saw that first cut, high up on his cheekbone. When a man's first cut, it usually looks a bright pink. Then I saw the blood, and I knew that eye was my target from then on. It was my concentrating on that cut that let me get caught with the hardest punch I took, that long left. It rocked me back. But he either didn't realize how good I was hit or he was already getting tired, and he didn't press his chance. I sure heard the bell *that* time. I needed to get to my corner to get my head clear."

"In the second," Dundee said, "Liston was trying to load up on shots, but my guy wasn't there to be loaded up on. I'm telling you that Liston would've beaten Tyson at his best. He was a big strong guy, he had shoulders that reached across the ring, he was faster than Tyson. But he was in there with an intricate guy. Muhammad was even outstronging him, pushing him around in the clinches, then he kept moving around, popping him."

"My doubts vanished in the first and second rounds when I watched how Ali handled Liston," Pacheco said. "*Bab bap* and he was gone. Liston had no solution. After the first it was obvious he went back to the corner thinking, 'Now what the fuck do I do?' Sonny was a one-two jab fighter, like Joe Louis. But Sonny had nothing to hit, he was hitting open air."

In Liston's corner, Joe Pollino worked on his man's bruise, but by the third round it was a full-fledged cut. Clay came out flat-footed, the better to leverage his harder punches, and within thirty seconds, like a sculptor attacking marble, he started working at the eye. Nearly every time he threw the jab he followed with a chopping right that bounced off the top of Liston's head—the same sort of punch that Archie Moore had said "clouded my thoughts." After one combination, Liston's knees wobbled and he very nearly went down. Liston managed to hold on, to grasp at the ropes and steady himself, but now there could not have been a soul inside the arena or watching in the theaters who did not allow himself to think that Clay was completely in control of the fight.

"Come on, you bum!" Clay shouted through the muffling mouthpiece.

The audacity! Seconds after the taunt, Liston went straight at Clay, but Clay caught every body punch on his elbows and gloves, just as he had trained himself to do against "Shotgun" Sheldon in the gym for weeks. The blood now came from Liston's nose as well as the cut under his eye.

"Starting in the third round, I saw his expression, how shook he was that we were still out there and he was the one cut and bleeding," Clay said later. "He didn't know what to do. But I wasn't about to get careless, like Conn did that time against Joe Louis. This was supposed to be one of my coasting, resting rounds, but I couldn't waste no time. I needed one more good shot, for some more insurance with that eye. So when the bell rang, I just tested him to see if he was tiring, and he was, and then I got him into the ropes. It didn't take but one good combination. My left was square on his right eye and a right under his left eye opened a deep gash. I knew it was deep, the way the blood spurted right out. I saw his face up close when he wiped his glove at that cut and saw the blood. At that moment, let me tell you, he looked like he's going to look twenty years from now."

The bell ending the third round sounded, and Liston plodded back to his corner. He walked like a man lost in a wilderness of snowdrifts. The blood trickled down his face. He was worn out, not just from trying to chase Clay, but from all the punches he had thrown, all the punches that had ended up going nowhere.

"The punches you miss are the ones that wear you out," Dundee said. "You miss enough and it begins to wear at your head and your body." Jack Nilon peeked through the ropes at Liston. Liston sat on his stool breathing so hard he could not say more than a couple of words at a time. His lungs were pumping like a bellows. He looked up into the lights. Joe Pollino went to work on him. The two men exchanged words. No one at ringside could hear them.

THERE ARE MANY WAYS TO GET AN EDGE IN A FIGHT, AND TRAINERS know them all. One of the great boxing myths, never proven, is that Jack Dempsey's corner had wrapped his hands in plaster of Paris and told him to form a fist; they soaked the hands in water, let them dry, and then put on the gloves. Thus equipped, Dempsey shattered half the bones in Jess Willard's face. Other trainers, in less extreme moods, try to push the padding of the glove down off the knuckles and toward the wrist, so that the punch will be all the harder.

As it happened, after the brutal and frustrating third round, Liston told his main cornerman, Pollino, to call on their own special advantage. The evidence is hearsay (Liston, Pollino, and Reddish are all dead) but as close to reliable as it gets in boxing. "It's very simple," said Jack McKinney, the *Philadelphia Daily News* reporter who was so close to Liston and Pollino. "Immediately after the fight, Joe, who was very close to me, unburdened himself to me. He told me that Sonny had told him to juice the gloves, and he went ahead and did it. Not only that, he said that they *always* were ready to do that in case of danger, and that they'd done it in fights against Eddie Machen and Cleveland Williams." Pollino never told McKinney what substance he rubbed on Liston's gloves—a linimentlike oil of wintergreen, or ferric chloride, which was used to seal cuts—but he did say it was a stinging solution that was intended to blind Clay long enough for Liston to find his range and knock him out. "Pollino told me that he put the stuff on the gloves at Sonny's express instructions and then threw the stuff under the ring apron as far as he could," McKinney said. "Joe himself felt so conflicted over this. He'd been sucked into it, but he knew if he ever came clean he would never work again."

In the fourth round, Clay went back to his original plan. He coasted. He moved around the ring, but more slowly, easily, just enough to force Liston to keep moving and missing. He did not do much damage in the round, but he did enough to keep Liston on the run, to wear him down still further. What he had in mind was to keep tiring him out until it was time, once more, to go on the attack. But toward the very end of the round, Clay's eyes began to sting, and by the time the round was over and he was on his stool, it felt as if there were needles in his eyes. Clay had been hit before in the ring—Banks and Cooper had knocked him down, Jones had confused him—but this was a pain he could not identify. And suddenly, as the pain grew worse, Clay was almost blind. He was pawing at his face, trying to shake the pain out of his eyes. He was in a panic.

"I can't see! Cut 'em off!" Clay shouted into the void, into the noise of the crowd. "I can't see! Cut off the gloves!"

This would be the most important single minute of Dundee's two decades with Clay. Without this one minute, without Dundee's instinctive reactions, there might never have been a Muhammad Ali. Sonny Liston would not likely have given a rematch to someone who had humbled him, forced him to juice his gloves; nor would the public have gone out of its way to demand boxing justice for a member of a religious sect that professed hatred of white America.

While Dundee's fighter screamed at him, demanding he let him quit, Dundee was cool. "I'd had this problem before," he said. "Isn't experience wonderful? I've only been doing this for forty-eight years. You can't get to where you're hysterical and lose your cool. Then you're no good to the fighter." Dundee had an inkling of how painful the substance was. He had dipped his pinkie into the corner of Clay's eyes and then put the finger in his own eye. It burned like mad. But he would not relent.

"This is the big one, daddy!" Dundee shouted in Clay's ear. "Cut the bullshit! We're not quitting now."

With his sponge, Dundee tried to get as much clean water flowing into Clay's eyes as possible. He had no idea how this had happened—to this day he discounts the idea that Liston's corner juiced the gloves; he is almost too nice to believe it—and he cared less. He cared about the fight, about getting through the next round.

"You gotta go out there and run!"

In those tense seconds, Dundee also had to deal with the Black Muslims who were sitting behind the corner. Dundee's brother ran over to him and told him that the Muslims were now convinced that Angelo himself had blinded Clay on behalf of the Italian gangsters backing Liston.

Pacheco and Dundee could hear the Muslims shouting, "That white man is trying to blind Clay! It's a conspiracy! It's a conspiracy!"

Dundee thought the only way to prove he was clean was to take the sponge and rub the water in his own eye.

Barney Felix noticed the commotion in Clay's corner and started walking over. Dundee didn't want Felix to hear Clay's complaints, and so he positioned himself to cut the referee off from the fighter.

The bell sounded for round five.

"Now go out there and you run!" Dundee shouted.

"Yardstick 'im, champ!" Bundini shouted. "Yardstick 'im!"

The idea was that Clay would keep moving and measuring Liston with his left jab long enough for the solution to wash out of his eyes. Clay got to his feet, straightened himself, and walked in slowly.

"That was one time Angelo really earned his money," Pacheco said. "He said, 'You go out there and you run.' It was dangerous, but by the time the bell sounded it wasn't like he was completely blind. You don't need two eyes to stay away from Sonny Liston. You need one eye and a good pair of legs. Sonny had shot his bolt already."

Easy for Pacheco to say. Clay went into the fifth round blinking madly, his eyes on fire. He could see only the blurred outline of his opponent. Liston charged in after Clay right away. As tired as he was, he knew well that this was his chance. Clay's only hope was to keep moving and use the "yardstick"—he extended his long left and tried to keep it in Liston's face as both a measuring stick and a distraction.

"I was praying he wouldn't guess what was the matter," Clay told Alex Haley. "But he had to see me blinking, and then he shook me with that left to the head and a lot of shots to the body." In the early part of the round, Liston especially attacked Clay's body with big, loaded-up hooks to the ribs and belly, and many of them landed. "I was just trying to keep alive, hoping the tears would wash out my eyes. I could open them just enough to get a good glimpse of Liston, and then it hurt so bad I blinked them closed again. Liston was snorting like a horse. He was trying to hit me square, and I was just moving every which way, because I knew if he connected right, it could be all over right there."

Liston was hitting Clay and he was certainly winning the round, but he was just too worn out, and Clay was too skillful—Liston could not land a decisive shot. Months later, Clay looked back on the painful fifth and explained what it is like to be hit by a heavyweight:

"Take a stiff tree branch in your hand and hit it against the floor and you'll feel your hand go *boinggg*. Well, getting tagged is the same kind of jar on your whole body, and you need at least ten or twenty seconds to make that go away. You get hit again before that, you got another *boinggg*. . . . You're just numb and you don't know where you're at. There's no *pain*, just that jarring feeling. But I automatically know what to do when that happens to me, sort of like a sprinkler system going off when a fire starts up. When I get stunned I'm not really conscious of exactly where I'm at or what's happening, but I always tell myself to dance, run, tie my man up, or hold my head way down."

Clay did just that. He kept moving, yardsticking, and when Liston connected, Clay threw out his big arms and wrapped them around Liston in such a way that he could no longer throw an effective blow. The strategy would not work for long—Liston was just too powerful—but it bought Clay the two or three minutes he needed. With about a half minute left in the round, Clay's eyes came clear. This was the decisive moment in the fight, the moment at which Liston realized he had lost the opportunity of the challenger's blindness. Liston was a bully. In the ring, and even as an enforcer for the mob, he had always relied on intimidation, on backing other men down. Clay never backed down. And what happens with bullies, fighters who expect nothing from their opponents except capitulation, is that they quit in the face of resistance. Many years later, in the ring with Sugar Ray Leonard, Roberto Duran would stop in the middle of the fight and say, "No más," rather than go on with humiliation.

In the sixth, Clay came out with clear vision, and a second wind. He dispensed with choreography, and, flat-footed nearly the entire round, he went to work on Liston, doubling up on his jabs, throwing combinations, left hooks, right uppercuts in the clinch—and everything landed. Liston had nothing left. He was paying now for every hot dog and whiskey, every afternoon with the prostitutes on Collins Avenue, every run cut short out of arrogance. He knew now that even cheating was useless. Clay had thought it would take eight rounds or so to get Liston this tired, this beaten up, but now he knew he did not have to hold back.

At one point, Clay recalled, "I hit him with eight punches in a row, until he doubled up. I remember thinking something like 'Yeah, you old sucker! You try to be so big and bad!' He was gone. He knew he couldn't last. . . . I missed a right that might have dropped him. But I jabbed and jabbed at that cut under his eye, until it was wide open and bleeding worse than before. I knew he wasn't due to last much longer." Just before the end of the round, Clay slammed two left hooks into Liston's head, and it was a wonder that the champion did not go down.

"By now even the most inveterate Clay doubter had to know that something special was happening," Robert Lipsyte said. "Sonny's face was a mess and he couldn't do a thing to stop this terrible thing that was happening to him."

The bell sounded, ending the sixth. Liston walked back to his corner, blank-eyed.

"That's it," he said as he sat down.

For the first time that night, Pollino and Reddish felt a rush of encouragement. *That's it.* Now Sonny would finally throw himself into the fight, they thought. Now he would teach this kid not to play with him. Finally, he was angry enough to win. Both men started working on Liston. He had complained of sore shoulders, and so they massaged his shoulders and back, and they gave him water and smeared Vaseline on his brows. Then Pollino put Liston's mouthpiece in.

Liston spit it back out.

"I . . . said . . . *that's it!*"

Pollino and Reddish now understood what Liston really meant. He had quit. They argued with him, telling him that he couldn't give up the championship sitting on a stool, that he had to go out and fight Clay, take the fight back and win. Quitting was unthinkable, especially in a heavyweight title fight. Liston had not been knocked down once, and now he was quitting? The last time a heavyweight surrendered his crown had been on July 4, 1919, in Toledo, when Willard failed to answer the bell for the fourth round against Dempsey. Willard, however, did not have a sore shoulder and a couple of cuts; his jaw was broken, his ribs were cracked, and two of his teeth were on the canvas.

Liston did not appear to care. He stared straight ahead, right through his cornermen.

"That's it."

Reddish let out a long breath and sighed. "Well," he said, "maybe another day."

Reddish held out his hand and waved. Barney Felix immediately understood the signal.

As he sat on his stool waiting for the seventh round, Clay could hear the reporters buzzing. He could make out scraps of talk, the idea that he, this preposterous kid, was beating the hell out of Sonny Liston, and could you believe it? Clay twisted around and leaned down and shouted, "I'm gonna upset the world!"

"I never will forget how their faces was looking up at me like they couldn't believe it," he told Haley later. "I happened to be looking right at Liston when that warning buzzer sounded, and I didn't believe it when he spat out his mouthpiece. I just couldn't believe it—but there it was laying there. And then something just told me he wasn't coming out! I give a whoop and come off that stool like it was red hot. It's a funny thing, but I wasn't even thinking about Liston—I was thinking about nothing but that hypocrite press. All of them down there had wrote so much about me bound to get killed by the big fists."

Now Clay was on his feet, his hands thrust over his head. He knew immediately what Reddish's wave meant.

"I am the king!" he shouted. "I am the king! King of the world! Eat your words! Eat! Eat your words!"

Eat your words.

Clay's hysteria in the morning had been manufactured, but his exuberance now could not have been more real. Steve Ellis, for television, and Howard Cosell, for radio, were sticking microphones in his face, and Clay was shouting nonstop: "Almighty God was with me! I want everybody to bear witness! I am the greatest! I shook up the world! I am the greatest thing that ever lived! I don't have a mark on my face, and I upset Sonny Liston, and I just turned twenty-two years old. I must be the greatest! I showed the world! I talk to God every day! I'm the king of the world!"

At ringside, Red Smith of the *Herald Tribune*, who had written column after column doubting and mocking young Clay, could hear the new champion's taunt clearly. *Eat your words.* And after Smith heard it, he started writing: "Nobody ever had a better right. In a mouth still dry from the excitement of the most astounding upset in many roaring years, the words don't taste good, but they taste better than they read. The words, written here and practically everywhere else until the impossible became the unbelievable truth, said Sonny Liston would squash Cassius Clay like a bug. . . ."

Smith scored the fight overwhelmingly in Clay's favor, giving him the first, third, fourth, and sixth. He thought the second was debatable, and, of course, Clay had been practically blind in the fifth.

But some of Clay's other detractors could barely bring themselves to admit that they had been so wrong about him. Dick Young's column for the *Daily News* seethed with resentment, as if the outcome had been a conspiracy designed specifically to offend him. "If Cassius wants me to say he's the greatest, all right, I'll say it," Young groused in print, "but I'll also say he scored the greatest retreating victory since the Russians suckered Napoleon into a snowbank. I never saw Joe Louis run away and win, or Rocky Marciano, and I'm sure my father never saw Jack Dempsey run away and win, and my grandfather never saw John L. Sullivan run away and win. So, if Cassius wants to be rated, he'd better stand still long enough."

Clay was not about to stand still for anyone. He bounded all around the ring with Bundini and Dundee at his side. He never stopped shouting and pointing. The ecstasy! "Electric bulbs seemed to light up behind the great lagoons of his eyes, the way moonglow spangles water," Jimmy Cannon wrote.

Rocky Marciano, sitting next to Cannon, slapped his forehead with his palm and said, "What the hell is this?" Cannon used the phrase as the headline for his next day's column. Cannon allowed that Clay had fought with a "dignity" he clearly had not expected, but the real emotion in his copy was disappointment, contempt. Liston had let him down, and, in doing so, had ushered in something foreign and strange. When Liston's corner announced that he had quit because his shoulder had given out, Cannon, among others, was not accepting the excuse: "The old hoodlum, who had contemptuously ridiculed Clay as a big talking doll, explained he had dislocated his left shoulder in the first round of a fight which must be measured peculiar even by the standards of the mean racket."

In theaters around the country, the crowds could accept the victory of an underdog, but not the sight of a champion, a champion revered as the toughest man on the planet, giving up on his stool. At the Jefferson City prison, where Liston had learned to fight, the warden had set up a series of televisions and paid to have the fight piped in. When the prisoners saw that Liston was giving up his title sitting down, the shouts of derision were so loud you could hear them beyond the walls, ringing in the cold darkness. Liston's shoulders were undoubtedly sore. ("A man that strong can't swing and miss that often and *not* be sore," McKinney said.) But while Nilon, Pollino, and the other cornermen used the shoulder as an excuse, they were telling a story they knew was only partially true.

Liston wept as Pollino walked with him from the dressing room to a car. His left arm was in a sling and there was a bandage under his eye. On the way out, Liston said that losing made him feel the way he did when Kennedy was shot, but then he said that it was just "one of those little things that happens to you." Uncharacteristically, he thanked the reporters and was gone.

"Nasty as Sonny was, he was always a pussycat when he lost," Robert Lipsyte recalled.

Liston was taken to St. Francis Hospital. Mort Sharnik was the only reporter to catch up with him there. "At the hospital Sonny was laying on a table looking like an instant middle-aged man," Sharnik said. "He looked like a middle-aged truck driver who had driven into an abutment. He was swollen all over: his eyes, his whole face, his body. He just lay there with Nilon patting him on the shoulder and saying, 'We'll get him again.' While the doctors worked on Liston, Nilon said something about giving Sonny a job at Nilon Brothers, a food services company that sold hot dogs at ball games. Sonny looked like a lump of clay there. He was just swollen all over."

Dr. Alexander Robbins, the commission doctor, announced that Liston had injured his left shoulder, torn a tendon, but the question that would run through all the press coverage was whether the shoulder injury was the decisive one. It wasn't. "It was all bullshit," one of Liston's cornermen, who is still alive, admitted. "We had a return-bout clause with Clay, and if you say your guy just quit, who's gonna get a return bout? We cooked that shoulder thing up on the spot." The shoulder was indeed injured, as a half-dozen more doctors later confirmed, but Liston had endured worse physical pain; what he could not endure in Miami was more humiliation.

As Liston sat on his hospital bed, he turned to Nilon and Sharnik and, in a low, rumbling voice that they could barely make out, he said, "That wasn't the guy I was supposed to fight. That guy could hit."

They were all silent for a while, then Nilon said, "What are we going to do with Sonny?"

Anyone who knew Liston worried that he would soon revert to his worst and most self-destructive habits. Anything he had ever worked for, any semblance of pride he had ever achieved, he had left behind in Miami.

In the early morning, when Jimmy Cannon finished writing his column, he went back to the Fontainebleau and ran into the great lightweight Beau Jack, who had a job shining shoes at the hotel.

"Sonny's better off dead," Beau Jack told Cannon. "How can a man look at himself, and what's he tell his children and his wife?"

CLAY CARRIED HIS OBSESSION WITH THE PRESS FROM THE RING to the interview room:

". . . Whatcha gonna say now? It won't last one round? He'll be out in two? How many heart attacks were there? Oh, I am pretty. I beat him bad and that's so gooood. The bear couldn't touch me, couldn't even get a good lick of me. . . ."

The rant went on and on until finally Clay said he wanted justice from the reporters gathered around him.

"I'm gonna show you how great reporters are," he said. "Who's the greatest?"

There was no reply.

"No justice. I don't get no justice. No one's gonna give me justice. I'll give you one more chance. Who's the greatest?"

There was a pause. Then a few reporters muttered, "You are."

Jackie Gleason, who was playing reporter by filing columns for the *New York Post,* was probably the only truly contrite member of the press. In his column the next morning, he said, "So here I am munching on crow, which isn't the best meal in the world, particularly the feathers. It's not so much the $600 I dropped (when I back a man, I back him), it's the side bet . . . where I promised to down five belts of Old Overshoe for every round Blabber Mouth was still on his feet. Well, I don't think I have to explain the exact shape I was in when the end came. Ole Cassius got his revenge on me without doing a thing."

As Clay got ready to leave the arena, Gordon Davidson, the lawyer for the Louisville Sponsoring Group, who had only hoped

that his fighter would *survive* the fight, was in the position of trying to improvise the unforeseen victory party. "We'd never even
thought about it," he said, "so all of a sudden we were on the
phone to the Roney Plaza at around midnight, with the kitchen
closed, trying to get them to put together some food and champagne and the rest. Lots of people headed over there—our group,
some reporters, Budd Schulberg, George Plimpton, Norman
Mailer, and so on—but Cassius decided not to join us."

Clay drove out to the Hampton House motel and hung out for a
while with Malcolm X and Jim Brown, the great running back for
the Cleveland Browns, and ate a huge dish of vanilla ice cream.
Clay took a nap on Malcolm's bed and then finally went home. He
was planning for a change, he told his friends. "I made the noise I
had to make while I was campaigning for election," he said. "Well,
the vote is in now, and I won. I'm going to play it cool for a while."

CHAPTER TWELVE

The Changeling

CLAY ARRIVED FOR HIS MORNING PRESS CONFERENCE AT THE Veterans Room of Convention Hall. He answered all the traditional questions about how he felt, about which fighter he might take on next, about whether Liston was tougher than expected, less tough than expected, or *precisely* as tough as expected. The session was, by Clay's standards, remarkably subdued: no verse, no monologues, no taunts. "All I want now is to be a nice, clean gentleman," he said. "I've proved my point. Now I'm going to set an example for all the nice boys and girls. I'm through talking."

Loud, ironic applause greeted that declaration, and even Clay had to smile. But the thing about Clay was that he never really lied to the press; he believed what he was saying at the moment he was saying it. And at this moment he saw his career as a limited venture.

"I only fight to make a living, and when I have enough money I won't fight anymore," he went on. "I don't like to fight. I don't like to get hurt. I don't like to hurt anybody. . . . I feel sorry for Liston. He's all beat up." Clay said he would be a people's champion and would go back home to Louisville and "roam the streets, talk to the poor folk and the drunks and the bums. I just want to make people happy."

Finally, a reporter interrupted with a barbed question. Wasn't it true, he wanted to know, that Clay was a "card-carrying member of the Black Muslims?"

Egypt, 1964.

Clay recoiled not so much from the idea of breaking news—he had assumed by now that everyone knew he was a convert to the Nation of Islam—but rather from the terminology. "Card-carrying" had the ring of McCarthyism, and "Black Muslim" was a term repugnant to members of the Nation.

" 'Card-carrying.' What does that mean?" Clay said. "I believe in Allah and in peace. I don't try to move into white neighborhoods. I don't want to marry a white woman. I was baptized when I was twelve, but I didn't know what I was doing. I'm not a Christian anymore. I know where I'm going and I know the truth, and I don't have to be what you want me to be. I'm free to be what I want."

That was enough to confirm all the stories that had been in the press: Clay was a member of the Nation of Islam. But whether the press understood it or not, he had quietly forsaken the image of the unthreatening black fighter established by Joe Louis and then imitated by Jersey Joe Walcott and Floyd Patterson and dozens of others. Clay was declaring that he would not fit any stereotypes, he would not follow any set standard of behavior. And while Liston had also declared his independence from convention (through sheer don't-give-a-shit truculence), Clay's message was political. He, and not Jimmy Cannon or the NAACP, would define his blackness, his religion, his history. He was a vocal member of an American fringe group and America would soon be learning about it.

The sporting press, which knew barely a thing about the Nation of Islam, required more details, and so the next morning some reporters descended on Clay and Malcolm X as they were eating breakfast at the Hampton House motel. If any of the reporters thought Clay would back off from his previous day's statements, they were mistaken. Now he made the news plainer.

"A rooster crows only when it sees the light," Clay said. "Put him in the dark and he'll never crow. I have seen the light and I'm crowing."

Malcolm declared, "Clay is the finest Negro athlete I have ever known, the man who will mean more to his people than any athlete before him. He is more than Jackie Robinson was, because Robinson is the white man's hero. The white press wanted him to lose. They wanted him to lose because he is a Muslim. You notice nobody cares about the religion of other athletes. But their prejudice against Clay blinded them to his ability."

For the rest of the day, Clay was quick to fill everyone's notebooks. As the reporters stood around him, Clay felt himself in an instructive mood.

" 'Black Muslims' is a press word," he said. "It's not a legitimate name. The real name is 'Islam.' That means peace. Islam is a religion and there are seven hundred and fifty million people all over the world who believe in it, and I'm one of them. I ain't no Christian. I can't be, when I see all the colored people fighting for forced integration getting blowed up. They get hit by stones and chewed by dogs, and they blow up a Negro church and don't find the killers. I get telephone calls every day. They want me to carry signs. They want me to picket. They tell me it would be a wonderful thing if I married a white woman because this would be good for brotherhood. I don't want to be blown up. I don't want to be washed down sewers. I just want to be happy with my own kind.

"I'm the heavyweight champion, but right now there are some neighborhoods I can't move into. I know how to dodge booby traps and dogs. I dodge them by staying in my own neighborhood. I'm no troublemaker. I don't believe in forced integration. I know where I belong. I'm not going to force myself into anybody's house. . . .

"People brand us a hate group. They say we want to take over the country. They say we're Communists. That is not true. Followers of Allah are the sweetest people in the world. They don't carry knives. They don't tote weapons. They pray five times a day. The women wear dresses that come all the way to the floor and they don't commit adultery. All they want to do is live in peace.

"I'm a good boy. I never had done anything wrong. I have never been to jail. . . . I love white people. I like my own people. They can live together without infringing on each other. You can't condemn a man for wanting peace. If you do, you condemn peace itself. . . ."

On the day Clay announced his conversion, at a Savior's Day event at the Chicago Coliseum, Elijah Muhammad ended his public ambivalence about Clay and welcomed him to the fold. Until then, Muhammad had kept his distance, thinking Clay would lose and disgrace the Nation, but now, in victory, he was all good grace, all welcome. Indeed, Elijah Muhammad declared that Clay had won his fight thanks to Allah and his Messenger. And by coming out as Clay's friend and spiritual light, Elijah Muhammad had also stepped up his struggle with Malcolm X.

JUST ABOUT THE ONLY PEOPLE TO REACT TO THE NEWS OF Clay's conversion with a shrug were the men in his corner. "What's in a name?" Dundee said by way of Shakespeare. "To me he's still the same individual, same guy. Actually, I didn't know what Muslim was, really, because I thought it was a piece of cloth." Probably no other trainer would have been so foolish as to alienate his new champion—there was too much money to be had. But Dundee really didn't care what religion his fighter belonged to as long as he showed up at the gym. "I learned that much when I was a kid," Dundee said years later. "One thing you don't mess with in a fighter is his religion. And his love life. You don't mess with that either. How to throw the left—you're better off sticking with that stuff."

But outside of that small circle of handlers, Clay's conversion was a shock, not least to his family. His father, though never exactly a devout Christian, made clear his wrath in person and in the press. Clay senior told reporters that his son had been "conned" by the avaricious Muslims. "I'm not changing no name," he said. "If he wants to do it, fine. But not me. In fact, I'm gonna make good use of the name Cassius Clay. I'm gonna make money out of my own name. I'll capitalize on it." The relationship between father and son deteriorated to such a degree that the next time Clay went home to Louisville, he stayed in a hotel downtown. "He came out to visit us," his mother, Odessa, said, "but he only stayed twenty-five minutes and kept a cab waiting outside in the driveway. He's been told to stay away from his father because of the religious thing, and I imagine they've told him to stay away from me, too. Muslims don't like me because I'm too fair-complected."

The leading columnists reacted with almost as much outrage as Cassius Clay, Sr.

"The fight racket, since its rotten beginnings, has been the red-light district of sports. But this is the first time it has been turned into an instrument of hate," Jimmy Cannon wrote. "It has maimed the bodies of numerous men and ruined their minds but now, as one of Elijah Muhammad's missionaries, Clay is using it as a weapon of wickedness in an attack on the spirit. I pity Clay and abhor what he represents. In the years of hunger during the Depression, the Communists used famous people the way the Black Muslims are exploiting Clay. This is a sect that deforms the beautiful purpose of religion." Cannon's point of racial orientation would always be Joe Louis. Clay's association with the Nation of Islam, Cannon declared, was a "more pernicious hate symbol than Schmeling and Nazism."

Lipsyte's coverage in the *Times* was of a different order, partly because the paper's news columns did not allow for much opinion, but also because he was of a different generation and possessed of a far different set of experiences, not least his close friendship with Dick Gregory. "It's true that I wasn't freaked out about the conversion the way Cannon or Smith were," he said, "but you have to remember how scary Malcolm X was to some people, and not just white people. *The New York Times,* for one, never really knew how many people he could put on the street for a revolution."

Malcolm appreciated the depth and restraint of Lipsyte's coverage and told him so. Back at the newsroom on West Forty-third Street, Lipsyte recounted the compliment to one of his editors.

"Well, that's great," the editor said. "Maybe we should put huge ads on the side of all our trucks saying, 'Malcolm X Likes Bob Lipsyte!' "

The World Boxing Association suspended the new champion for "conduct detrimental to the best interests of boxing." However, the suspension had no real force to it after the key state commissions in New York, California, and Pennsylvania made it clear they would ignore it. Members of the Louisville Sponsoring Group reacted first with visceral shock. They realized, quite rightly, that Clay's conversion would cost him, and them, hundreds of thousands of dollars. What was more, they realized rather quickly that Clay would not likely renew his contract with them once it expired in 1966. "We guessed that the Muslims would want to control things on their own," said Gordon Davidson. "And it was a pretty good guess."

Just about the only white politician to speak out in support of the new heavyweight champion was Richard Russell, senator from Georgia and a segregationist. Russell thought it was splendid that the Nation of Islam's goal of separating the races coincided with his own. (In fact, in 1961, Elijah Muhammad had initiated contact with the Ku Klux Klan leadership, the idea being that both groups favored the separation of black and white.)

The most complicated reactions came from black commentators and political actors. Black-run newspapers were deeply involved in and supportive of the civil rights movement, and most were suspicious of the Nation of Islam. It was February 1964, and the country had already witnessed a decade of civil rights landmarks: the murder of Emmett Till in 1955, the Montgomery bus boycott in 1955–56, the Little Rock schools crisis in 1957–58, the student sitins in Nashville in 1960, the Freedom Rides of 1961, James Meredith's integration of Ole Miss in 1962, the Birmingham struggle and the Sixteenth Street Church bombing in 1963, the march on Washington. Many middle-class blacks, especially, privately admired certain aspects of the Nation—the way it rehabilitated men coming out of jails, the way it represented a certain upright morality in the home and safety on the street—but worried that such a vehement rhetoric of confrontation and a religious style so alien to mainstream America would jeopardize the movement.

In Clay's hometown paper, the black-run *Louisville Defender*, Frank Stanley wrote, rather delicately, "Our difference is not with Clay's choice of a religious group, although we have our reservations about the motives of this particular sect. We are dismayed at the Louisville youth's disassociation from the desegregation movement." King himself, who was now at the zenith of his power and appeal in the movement, indulged no such delicacies. "When Cassius Clay joined the Black Muslims and started calling himself Cassius X he became a champion of racial segregation and that is what we are fighting against," he said. "I think perhaps Cassius should spend more time proving his boxing skill and do less talking." Eventually King called Clay to congratulate him on his boxing triumphs—a phone call that was overheard by the FBI. According to the bureau's wiretap log of King's conversations, Clay assured King that he was "keeping up with MLK, that MLK is his brother, and [Clay is] with him 100 [percent] but can't take any chances." Clay told King to "take care of himself" and "watch out for them whities."

A month after the fight, Jackie Robinson wrote a piece for *The*

Chicago Defender, the most prominent of all black-run papers, in which he insisted on the magnitude of the new champion's victory in the ring and a cool acceptance of his conversion to the Nation of Islam. While Robinson's putative admirers among the white columnists brayed with anger and confusion about this self-assertive new champion, Robinson himself, who did not require their fatherly acceptance, saw some virtue in this young man's decision, even if he did not share it.

"I don't think Negroes en masse will embrace Black Muslimism any more than they have embraced Communism," Robinson wrote. "Young and old, Negroes by the tens of thousands went into the streets in America and proved their willingness to suffer, fight, and even die for freedom. These people want more democracy—not less. They want to be integrated into the mainstream of American life, not invited to live in some small cubicle of this land in splendid isolation. If Negroes ever turn to the Black Muslim movement, in any numbers, it will not be because of Cassius or even Malcolm X. It will be because white America has refused to recognize the responsible leadership of the Negro people and to grant to us the same rights that any other citizen enjoys in this land."

In the late sixties, when he was making his stand against the draft and went into exile, many voices, radical and not, celebrated Ali as a figure of defiance and courage. Eldridge Cleaver described him as a "genuine revolutionary" and the "first 'free' black champion ever to confront white America." Athletes like Lew Alcindor would be radicalized to the point of conversion. Even Red Smith would come around. But at the time, in 1964, very few people, black or white, openly celebrated Clay's transformation. "I remember in the early sixties how we felt at home about Ali," said the writer Jill Nelson, who grew up in Harlem and on the Upper West Side. "We weren't about to join the Nation, but we loved Ali for that supreme act of defiance. It was the defiance against having to be the good Negro, the good Christian waiting to be rewarded by the righteous white provider. We loved Ali because he was so beautiful and powerful and because he talked a lot of lip. But he also epitomized a lot of black people's emotions at the time, our anger, our sense of entitlement, the need to be better just to get to the median, the sense of standing up against the furies."

.   .   .

CLAY DROVE NORTH TO NEW YORK AND SETTLED IN AT THE
Hotel Theresa in Harlem. He arrived in a chauffeur-driven Cadil-
lac but quickly described for reporters how he was barred from var-
ious restaurants on his two-day trip from Miami. ("Man it was
really a letdown drag/For all those miles I had to eat out of a bag.")
The Theresa, a Harlem landmark, was far more welcoming. Joe
Louis used to stay there, as did dozens of other black celebrities
when they were visiting Manhattan. Fidel Castro stayed there.
Nearly every demonstration held in Harlem began outside the
Hotel Theresa.

For the first few days in March, Clay held court at the hotel and
went everywhere with Malcolm X—for walks around Harlem,
around Times Square, and to the United Nations for a tour and a
press conference. One reporter wrote that the boxer and the political leader had caused the greatest commotion at the UN since
Nikita Khrushchev came to bang his shoe on the desk. Malcolm,
who was eager to win Clay over to whatever new coalitions he was
forming, even brought him out to Long Island with the idea of per-
suading him to buy a house near his own in Queens. But Clay
could not straddle his loyalties for long. The rift between Elijah
Muhammad and Malcolm X was severe; the Nation leadership was
not likely to permit Clay to enjoy both membership and a friendship with their enemy. Even while he continued in public to vow
loyalty to Muhammad, Malcolm had already said that he would try
to form a new, independent group—a group that the Nation would
immediately view as a threat.

On March 6, Elijah Muhammad gave a radio address in which
he declared that the name Cassius Clay lacked a "divine meaning"
and must be replaced with a Muslim name. " 'Muhammad Ali' is
what I will give to him, as long as he believes in Allah and follows
me." In the past, the fighter had always admired the history and
the euphony of his own name. "Makes you think of the Colosseum
and those Roman gladiators. Cassius Marcellus Clay. Say it to
yourself. It's a beautiful name." But now he had been instructed
otherwise: "Muhammad" meant one worthy of praise and "Ali" was
the name of a cousin of the prophet. Most members of the Nation
used X as a last name; Elijah Muhammad gave "completed" Islamic holy names mainly as a great honor to longtime leading Muslims who had been with the movement for decades. Elijah needed

Clay not only as a cash cow and as a recruitment vehicle, but as a weapon in the war with Malcolm X.

Malcolm was listening to the speech on his car radio and was outraged. "That's a political move!" he said. "He did it to prevent him from coming with me."

Of course, Malcolm was right about that. Emissaries from Chicago arrived at the Hotel Theresa to make their appeals to the new champion, to Muhammad Ali. They appealed to Ali's loyalty and faith, telling him to remember who was the real "Messenger" and who was merely a pretender. They even promised Ali a wife, one of Elijah Muhammad's granddaughters if he wanted.

A few days later, Alex Haley came to the hotel on assignment for *Playboy* magazine. He was already very close to Malcolm; once or twice a week, Malcolm would visit Haley at his apartment to be interviewed extensively for the book that would become his autobiography. Haley discovered very quickly that Ali had made his choice.

"You don't just buck Mr. Muhammad and get away with it," Ali said. "I don't want to talk about him no more."

It is hard to exaggerate the sharpness with which Ali cut off Malcolm X. In May, Ali left for a month-long tour of Egypt, Nigeria, and Ghana with his close friend the photographer Howard Bingham and two friends from the Nation of Islam, Osman Karreim (formerly Archie Robinson) and Herbert Muhammad (the third of Elijah's six sons and Ali's future manager). In the years to come, the emotion of the trip to Africa—the demonstrations of affection, the chants of "Ali! Ali!" in the remotest villages—would all be repeated many times and in many countries. But this trip was the first of its kind, and Ali was thrilled. It thrilled him to be among Africans, "my true people," as he put it; it thrilled him to meet such world leaders as Kwame Nkrumah; and it thrilled him to be recognized in places that would never have known, or cared about, Joe Louis, much less Rocky Marciano. This was, in short, his first taste of what it would be like to be Muhammad Ali, international symbol, a fighter bigger than the heavyweight championship, the most famous person in the world. This was the start of it, the start of Ali's transfiguration.

At the same time, the reporters, who were almost as thrilled by Ali as he was by himself, were also learning that he was a complicated man, a kind and gentle soul capable nevertheless of flashes of dismissive cruelty. Malcolm X, who had now taken the Sunni name El-Hajj Malik El-Shabazz, was also traveling in Africa after a trip to Mecca. He was wearing a goatee and the gauzy white robes of the pilgrim and carrying a walking stick. On his trip, Malcolm had encountered many light-skinned Muslims, and decided that all the talk of "blue-eyed devils" amounted to "generalizations [that] have caused injuries to some whites who did not deserve them." Malcolm's trip was life-altering, so much so that when a reporter asked him if it was now true that he no longer hated white people, Malcolm said, "True sir! My trip to Mecca has opened my eyes." Just as Martin Luther King was expanding his critique of American society to include the war in Vietnam and economic injustice, Malcolm was becoming more moderate, more universalist, in his moral outlook. The two vectors of black leadership were converging, and it was Malcolm's trip to the Middle East and Africa that helped make it happen. At the Hotel Ambassador in Accra, just as he was about to leave for the airport, Malcolm crossed paths with Ali.

"Brother Muhammad!" Malcolm called out. "Brother Muhammad!"

Ali looked over at Malcolm, but did not greet him as a friend.

"You left the Honorable Elijah Muhammad," Ali said stiffly. "That was the wrong thing to do, Brother Malcolm."

Malcolm did not want to make matters worse by approaching him, and Ali looked away and moved on.

It was a terrible moment for Malcolm. Despite the appearance of strength and endurance, Malcolm had lived with his losses all his life. "I've lost a lot," he said after the chance meeting. "Almost too much." As a child, he had watched his father, a Garveyite preacher named Earl Little, frightened for his life by white racists; he remembered his father's mysterious death on the trolley tracks and his mother going mad as a result; he remembered, after declaring his intention to become a lawyer, being told by his teacher, "You've got to be realistic about being a nigger"; and now, thrust out of the Nation of Islam, his life threatened by the Fruit of Islam, he had been rejected in the harshest terms by Muhammad Ali, his great protégé and friend.

Shortly before leaving Africa, Malcolm sent Ali a wire that still assumed the tone of their former relationship. "Because a billion of our people in Africa, Arabia, and Asia love you blindly," Malcolm wrote to Ali, "you must now be forever aware of your tremendous responsibilities to them." In the telegram, which soon appeared in *The New York Times,* Malcolm warned Ali not to let his enemies exploit his reputation; Malcolm kept his language vague, but it was clear that the exploiters he had in mind were in the Nation of Islam.

Ali was in no mood to take advice. He joked with reporters that he had come to Africa to find four wives: one to shine his shoes, one to feed him grapes, one to rub olive oil on his muscles, and one named "Peaches." He was not prepared to accept the righteous moralizing of a discredited teacher.

"Man, did you get a look at Malcolm?" he asked Herbert Muhammad. "Dressed in that funny white robe and wearing a beard and walking with that cane that looked like a prophet's stick? Man, he's gone. He's gone so far out, he's out completely. Nobody listens to Malcolm anymore."

Most of the country, especially white America, could not have cared less about the differences between Malcolm and Elijah Muhammad and where a twenty-two-year-old fighter from Louisville came down between them. The split seemed utterly marginal next to the truly epic battle going on between civil rights demonstrators and their opponents on the streets and in Congress and the courts. Only a very few people (outside of the FBI, to be sure) took the time to sort through these differences. But some black nationalists who admired Ali as both a fighter and an independent soul now wondered about his maturity and his choice. The poet and black nationalist LeRoi Jones, who later changed his name to Imamu Amiri Baraka, said that while Ali was now "my man," his choice of Elijah Muhammad over Malcolm X "means that he is a 'homeboy,' embracing this folksy vector straight out of the hard spiritualism of poor Negro aspiration, i.e., he is right now just angry rather than intellectually (sociopolitically) motivated."

Sonia Sanchez, a well-known poet and an activist in CORE, thought Baraka was inflexible and unforgiving, especially considering Ali's position and his age. "Ali had no time for analysis," she said. "He had to make a split-second decision between Malcolm and Elijah Muhammad and there was no gray area, no in-between.

He was surrounded by powerful people from the Nation who could convince him that Malcolm may have been close to him but the real leader was Elijah Muhammad. Also don't forget that the split was not helped by the way outside forces, including the FBI, infiltrated the Nation and other black groups with the idea of weakening them. The establishment saw that now even middle-class people were moving to a more radical position—Malcolm's position—and wanted to undermine it. Ali was a great man, but he was not a thinker, an analyst. You couldn't expect him to make better flash decisions than anyone else."

Robert Lipsyte of the *Times* was disappointed in Ali not so much for splitting with Malcolm as for his all too easy acceptance of the way a small core of Nation of Islam members were now attacking dissidents. Lipsyte knew a Muslim named Leon 4X Ameer, who had acted as a kind of makeshift press secretary for Ali. Ameer had also been a bodyguard and an organizer for Malcolm X before his suspension from the Nation. Ameer's relationship to Malcolm now made him suspect among the Muslims. One day, in the lobby of the Sherry Biltmore Hotel in Boston, the captain of the Nation's Boston mosque and three other Black Muslims attacked Ameer, beating him and clubbing him to his knees. Ameer was lucky to be rescued by a security guard. That night, however, another group of Muslims from the Boston mosque battered their way into Ameer's room and beat him nearly to death. He was found the next morning in the bathtub with his face looking like hamburger; his eardrums were ruptured and several of his ribs were broken.

Lipsyte had planned to collaborate with Ameer on a magazine article about the Muslims. When Ali came to New York to sign a contract for radio rights to a rematch with Sonny Liston, Lipsyte asked the new champion about his old friend's beating.

"Ah-meer? A little fellow?" Ali said mockingly. "I think I remember a little fellow who hung around camp, a little fellow who liked to go downstairs and get me papers. Now I hear he's telling lies, saying he was my press secretary."

Lipsyte persisted, and Ali exploded.

"Any fool Negro got the nerve to buck us, you want to make him a star. Jim Brown said something about the Muslims and they made him a movie star. Ameer was caught with a young girl. He had a wife and nine children. That man stole eight hundred dollars, he was a karate man, and he come down on three officials and he got what he deserved."

Should Ameer fear for his life? Lipsyte asked.

"They think everyone's out to kill them because they know they deserve to be killed for what they did."

Malcolm X, for his part, showed no inclination to end his opposition to the "pseudo-Islamic" sect of Elijah Muhammad. Through his jailhouse discovery of the Nation of Islam, Malcolm had remade himself; he had gone from street hustler to national figure. But he was now reworking himself almost as radically as he had in the mid-fifties. He spoke out on the potential utility of a civil rights bill. He shook hands with Martin Luther King in a corridor of the U.S. Senate. He began to link the struggle of American blacks with those of Africans and other "brothers of the Third World," and, in that spirit, tried to start two new groups, Muslim Mosque Inc. and the Organization of Afro-American Unity.

Elijah Muhammad was surely paying attention. On November 30, 1964, an FBI informant inside Washington's Mosque No. 4 told the bureau that a general announcement had gone out to the Fruit of Islam: Malcolm should be attacked on sight. A week later, Louis X (soon to become Louis Farrakhan) wrote in *Muhammad Speaks* that Malcolm would not escape vengeance. He invited Malcolm to picture his own head rolling along the sidewalk. And in January, yet another article in *Muhammad Speaks* predicted that 1965 would be "a year in which the most outspoken opponents of the Honorable Elijah Muhammad will slink into ignoble silence."

PART FOUR

Las Vegas, 1965. With Joe Louis.

CHAPTER THIRTEEN

"Save Me, Joe Louis . . ."

BOXING IN AMERICA WAS BORN OF SLAVERY. LIKE THE ROMAN emperors who gathered at the Colosseum to watch their warring chattel, Southern plantation owners amused themselves by putting together their strongest slaves and letting them fight it out for sport and gambling. The slaves wore iron collars and often fought nearly to the point of death. Frederick Douglass objected to boxing and wrestling not merely because of the cruelty involved, but also because it muffled the spirit of insurrection.

Even Ali, who would earn millions of dollars in the ring, who became famous and adored because of his skill at beating other men, even he expressed ambivalence about the spectacle of two black men fighting. "They stand around and say, 'Good fight, boy; you're a good boy; good goin',' " Ali said in 1970. "They don't look at fighters to have brains. They don't look at fighters to be businessmen, or human, or intelligent. Fighters are just brutes that come to entertain the rich white people. Beat up on each other and break each other's noses, and bleed, and show off like two little monkeys for the crowd, killing each other for the crowd. And half the crowd is white. We're just like two slaves in that ring. The masters get two of us big old black slaves and let us fight it out while they bet: 'My slave can whup your slave.' That's what I see when I see two black people fighting."

The first acknowledged American champion was a Virginia-born slave named Tom Molineaux. Many Virginia gentlemen acquired

222 | KING OF THE WORLD

their enthusiasm for boxing on their visits to England, where the sport was extremely popular. After Molineaux beat all the other fighters in Virginia, he came to New York as a freeman and went on to defeat all comers, American and foreign, who boxed on the Hudson River piers. He was then sent to England to challenge the great Tom Cribb, a white man, and the putative champion of the British Empire. They met on Capthall Common, Sussex, in 1810. Round after round, Molineaux destroyed Cribb, but Cribb's supporters would not tolerate a loss to a black man. They propped their man up—literally propped him up—and caused long delays in the contest, the better to give Cribb time to recover from his beating. Some in the crowd even attacked Molineaux, punching him, breaking some of his fingers. Finally, Cribb revived himself sufficiently to win in the fortieth round.

The stink of slavery, of rich brutes exploiting the strong and the desperate, did not fade with the Emancipation Proclamation. John L. Sullivan, the first champion of the modern era, established the "color line" in boxing by refusing to fight black challengers. "I will not fight a Negro," Sullivan declared. "I never have and I never shall." Sullivan's successor, Jim Jeffries, also said he would retire "when there are no white men left to fight." And so he did. But Jeffries was lured out of retirement to face Jack Johnson, who had taken the title from a white fighter, Tommy Burns.

Jeffries admitted that he was returning to the ring less for a belt than to redeem the white race. "I am going into this fight for the sole purpose of proving that a white man is better than a Negro," he said. Naturally, he had the full-throated support of the press, including the *New York Herald*'s occasional boxing correspondent Jack London. London thought of himself as a great radical, a friend of the worker, and yet his racism could not have been plainer. "Jeff must emerge from his alfalfa farm and remove that smile from Johnson's face," he wrote. "Jeff, it's up to you." The editors of the popular magazine *Collier's* declared that Jeffries would surely win because of his long history of valor; the white man, after all, "has thirty centuries of traditions behind him—all the supreme efforts, the inventions and the conquests, and whether he knows it or not, Bunker Hill and Thermopylae and Hastings and Agincourt." Jeffries simply could not lose. Someone named Dorothy

Forrester wrote a song in praise of Jeffries called "Jim-a-da-Jeff" and instructing Jeffries thus:

> *Commence right away to get into condish,*
> *An' you punch-a da bag-a day and night,*
> *An'-a din pretty soon, when you meet-a da coon,*
> *You knock-a him clear-a out-a sight.*
>
> *Who give-a Jack Jonce one-a little-a tap?*
> *Who make-a him take-a one big-a long nap?*
> *Who wipe-a da Africa off-a da map?*
> *It's a Jim-a-da-Jeff.*

When Johnson finally climbed into the ring to fight Jeffries in Reno, Nevada, on July 4, 1910, the crowd began its chant of "Kill the nigger!" A band struck up "All Coons Look Alike to Me." If this displeased Johnson, he did not show it in the ring. Johnson destroyed Jeffries, humiliated him both fistically and verbally, taunting him and his cornermen throughout the fight. "Hardly a blow had been struck when I knew that I was Jeff's master," Johnson wrote in his autobiography.

When Johnson's triumph was announced around the country, there were riots in Illinois, Missouri, New York, Ohio, Pennsylvania, Colorado, and the District of Columbia. In Houston, a white man slashed the throat of a black man named Charles Williams for cheering Johnson too enthusiastically. In Washington, D.C., a group of blacks stabbed two white men to death. In the town of Uvalda, Georgia, a gang of white men opened fire on a group of blacks celebrating the Johnson victory; three black men were killed and five wounded. In Manhattan, police rescued a black man who was just about to be lynched. Thousands of whites gathered on Eighth Avenue, threatening to beat any black man who showed up. No racial event until the assassination of Martin Luther King, Jr., in 1968, would set off such a violent reaction. Terrified, Congress passed a bill banning the interstate distribution of fight films. Various religious and right-wing political groups that had never shown much interest in boxing before now wanted to ban it.

Johnson, of course, was persecuted wherever he went with cries of "Lynch him! Kill the nigger!" Even though this was the era of

Booker T. Washington and the strategies of accommodation and gradualism, Johnson was defiant. He was probably the most publicly reviled black man of his time, and he tried not to show he cared. He even flaunted the sexual subtext of the hatred directed at him. He had affairs with young white women and prostitutes; his wife, a white woman named Etta Duryea, shot herself in 1912 after a year of marriage. When he invited reporters to watch him train, he wrapped his penis in gauze and displayed its grandeur under tight shorts. Johnson was magnificently defiant, and defiantly magnificent. He owned preposterously expensive cars and sipped vintage wines through a straw. He read widely in English, French, and Spanish (he was especially fond of the novels of Dumas) and played the bass viol. When he opened the Cabaret de Champion in Chicago he equipped the place with silver cuspidors.

Eventually, the white establishment had its way with Johnson, forcing him into prolonged exile. Johnson was prosecuted under the Mann Act, which was enacted to prevent commercial prostitution and the transport of women across state lines for immoral intent. Johnson avoided jail by wandering through Canada and Europe. Finally, he returned to the United States and served time in Leavenworth; in 1915, he lost his title in Havana to Jess Willard, claiming later that he had taken a dive. He ended his career as promoter of his own legacy and a raconteur in a dime museum. Muhammad Ali was keenly aware of the parallels with his own life. Years later, when talking with James Earl Jones, who played Johnson in *The Great White Hope*, Ali said his own exile from the ring after refusing the draft was "history all over again."

"I grew to love the Jack Johnson image," he said. "I wanted to be rough, tough, arrogant, the nigger white folks didn't like."

After Johnson's eclipse, white champions held the crown until the early thirties. So obvious was their systematic avoidance of black challengers that the leading black heavyweights fought among themselves for the honor of becoming champion of the race. When Jack Dempsey took the title from Jess Willard in 1919, he quickly assured the nation, at Tex Rickard's urging, that he would not entertain the challenges of any of the great black boxers of the time, including Sam McVey, Sam Langford, and Harry Wills. Wills and Langford were left to fight each other eighteen times while the official world championship belonged for two decades to a string of Caucasians: Willard, Dempsey, Gene Tunney, Max Schmeling, Jack Sharkey, Primo "the Ambling Alp" Carnera, Max Baer, and Jim Braddock.

The era of unending whiteness finally came to a close with Joe Louis, who beat Braddock in 1937 to capture the heavyweight championship. Louis retained the title until his first retirement in 1948. Some organs of the sporting press were so shocked by the development that they were convinced that Louis had won *because* of his race, as if he had some sort of unfair advantage. An editorial in the New York *Daily Mirror* said that "in Africa there are tens of thousands of powerful, young savages that with a little teaching could annihilate Mr. Joe Louis." Paul Gallico of the New York *Daily News*, another legendary sportswriter admired for his enlightened views, could think of Louis only as an ignorant, if glorious, brute, a beast who "lives like an animal, fights like an animal, has all the cruelty and ferocity of a wild thing."

"I felt myself strongly ridden by the impression that here was a mean man," Gallico wrote, "a truly savage person, a man on whom civilization rested no more securely than a shawl thrown over one's shoulders, that, in short, here was perhaps for the first time in many generations the perfect prizefighter. I had the feeling that I was in the room with a wild animal."

Louis was the son of an Alabama sharecropper, whose broken family came to Detroit in 1926. Louis never went further in school than the sixth grade—a fact that allowed nearly all sportswriters to deduce that he was a sullen ignoramus. Louis said little in public, but, in fact, this was due mostly to the careful calculations of his black handlers. The team of Jack "Chappie" Blackburn, the trainer and father confessor, and the managers John Roxborough and Julian Black groomed Louis as both a fighter and a public figure. They did not want their fighter to alienate white America—the level of routine racism in the thirties was such that even the Northern press still referred to blacks as "darkies," "animals," and "sambos"—and, toward that end, they drew up a set of rules for Louis.

1. He was never to have his picture taken alongside a white woman.
2. He was never to go to a nightclub alone.

3. There would be no soft fights.
4. There would be no fixed fights.
5. He was never to gloat over a fallen opponent.
6. He was to keep a deadpan in front of the cameras.
7. He was to live and fight clean.

Louis, in other words, was designed to be the anti–Jack Johnson. His talent was so undeniable and his behavior so deferential that in time he won over even the Southern press, which deigned to call him a "good nigger" and an "ex-pickaninny." Unlike Johnson, Louis seemed to know his place. He offended no one. He did not flee the country, as Johnson had, he served it. He enlisted in the army during World War II and donated his fight earnings to the government. Of course, at the first opportunity, much of the Southern press was ready to withdraw its peculiar brand of support. When Louis lost to the German Max Schmeling in June 1936, William McG. Keefe of the New Orleans *Times-Picayune* wrote that the fight was proof of white supremacy. Keefe was relieved that "the reign of terror in heavyweight boxing was ended by Schmeling."

Louis's revenge match with Schmeling on June 22, 1938—a one-round knockout—was an even more complicated metaphor than Johnson's defeat of Jeffries. For all Americans, Louis had conquered the specter of the Aryan, the self-declared Nazi superman; once more, he was worthy of white admiration, of Jimmy Cannon's famous accolade "a credit to his race—the human race." For black Americans, the celebration was more intense and even subversive. First, there was the satisfaction of seeing at least one black man celebrated by the entire country, even its most glaring racists. The work of nonathletes, of black activists and scholars as distinguished as A. Philip Randolph and W.E.B. Du Bois, was invisible to nearly every white American, but here was an achievement that even the Grand Dragon of the Ku Klux Klan could not overlook. The white press would forever be obsessed with Louis's color—he was "the tan tornado," "the mahogany maimer," "the saffron sphinx," "the dusky David from Detroit," "the shufflin' shadow," "the coffee-colored kayo king," "the sable cyclone," "the tan Tarzan of thump," "the chocolate chopper," "the murder man of those maroon mitts," "the sepia slugger," and, most famously, the "brown bomber"—but they could not attack him as they had Jack Johnson.

His behavior, or rather his utter absence of misbehavior, was unassailable.

Louis was a god in the black communities, including the West End of Louisville. He was a surrogate and a redeemer. "We loved him in our family," Cassius Clay, Sr., once said. "It doesn't get bigger than Joe Louis." In 1940 Franklin Frazier wrote that Louis allowed blacks "to inflict vicariously the aggression which they would like to carry out against whites for the discriminations and insults which they have suffered." Similarly, the poet Maya Angelou recalls that as a child she was devoted to "the one invincible Negro, the one who stood up to the white man and beat him down with his fists. He in a sense carried so many of our hopes, maybe even dreams of vengeance."

The worshipers of Joe Louis ranged from Count Basie, who wrote a song in his honor ("Joe Louis Blues"), to Richard Wright, who covered his fights for *The New Masses* ("Joe Louis Uncovers Dynamite"). In *Why We Can't Wait,* Martin Luther King recalled, "More than twenty-five years ago, one of the southern states adopted a new method of capital punishment. Poison gas supplanted the gallows. In its earliest stages, a microphone was placed inside the sealed death chamber so that scientific observers might hear the words of the dying prisoner to judge how the victim reacted in this novel situation. The first victim was a young Negro. As the pellet dropped into the container, and gas curled upward, through the microphone came these words: 'Save me, Joe Louis. Save me, Joe Louis. Save me, Joe Louis. . . .' "

BY THE EARLY SIXTIES, AS THE CIVIL RIGHTS MOVEMENT GENERated varied strands of militant politics, many blacks felt that Americans were paying too much attention to sports heroes and too little to the suffering of millions of ordinary people. On the day of the first Patterson-Liston fight in 1962, Bob Lipsyte covered for the *Times* a march protesting housing discrimination in New York City. One of the young African-Americans on the picket line told him, "We're beyond the point where we can get excited over a Negro hitting a home run or winning a championship."

But the excitement over sports has been a twentieth-century constant in America. Boxing as a racial metaphor intensified in the sixties. And while Ali may not have read every article written about him, he was deeply aware of his position in relation to both Jack Johnson and Joe Louis. Ali could endure the predictable insults: the newspapers that continued to call him Clay, the epithets of Jimmy Cannon and Dick Young. What grated on him, however, was the disapproval of his childhood hero Joe Louis.

"Clay will earn the public's hatred because of his connections with the Black Muslims," Louis told reporters. "The things they preach are just the opposite of what we believe. The heavyweight champion should be the champion of all people. He has responsibilities to all people.

"Clay has a million dollars' worth of confidence and a dime's worth of courage," Louis went on. "He can't punch. He can't hurt you, and I don't think he takes a good punch. He's lucky there are no good fighters around. I'd rate him with Johnny Paycheck, Abe Simon, and Buddy Baer. . . . I would have whipped him. He doesn't know a thing about fighting on the ropes, which is where he would be with me. I would go in to outpunch him rather than try to outbox him. I'd press him, bang him around, claw him, clobber him with all I got, cut down his speed, belt him around the ribs. I'd punish the body, where the pain comes real bad. Clay would have welts on his body. He would ache. His mouth would shut tight against the pain, and there would be tears burning his eyes."

Ali could have ignored Louis. By the early sixties, Louis was addicted to cocaine, the victim of bad romances, mental deterioration, and horrific tax problems. To pay his debts, Louis tried to become a professional wrestler, a career that ended the day a three-hundred-pound blob named Rocky Lee landed on his chest, broke two of his ribs, and bruised the muscle around his heart. Ash Resnik, Sonny Liston's good friend, eventually brought Louis to Caesars Palace to work as a "greeter." Louis drew a salary and ate and gambled on the house in exchange for hanging around and being Joe Louis. To anyone with a memory and a heart, Louis was a beaten man, and a man who never really recognized his own contribution. "Sometimes," he once said, "I wish I had the fire of a Jackie Robinson to speak out and tell the black man's story." When Louis finally died in 1981 at the age of sixty-six, he lay in state at Caesars Palace.

It was hard for the proud young Ali to forgive Louis his wound-ing criticisms. And so Ali answered in kind. He called Louis an Uncle Tom and loudly vowed that he would "never end up like Joe Louis." In a documentary film, Ali answered Louis's boxing chal-lenge, saying, "Slow-moving, shuffling Joe Louis beat me? He may hit hard, but that don't mean nothing if you can't find nothing to hit. I'm no flat-footed fighter. . . . Joe Louis had a thing called the bum of the month club. The men that Joe Louis fought, if I fought them today in Madison Square Garden, they'd boo them out of the ring."

With time, as Ali no longer needed Joe Louis to confirm his greatness, and as Louis himself grew weaker, the terms of the rela-tionship shifted. Louis recognized Ali's skills as a fighter, reckoning that he would still beat him, but not as easily as he had disposed of Johnny Paycheck. In the mid-seventies, Ali invited him to his train-ing camp and offered him a gift of thirty thousand dollars.

When Louis died, a reporter reminded Ali of his earlier difficul-ties with the great champion. He would hear none of it. "I never said that, not that way, anyhow," Ali said. "That's demeaning. Look at Joe's life. Everybody loved Joe. He would have been marked as evil if he was evil, but everybody loved Joe. From black folks to red-neck Mississippi crackers, they loved him. They're all crying. That shows you. Howard Hughes dies, with all his billions, not a tear. Joe Louis, everybody cried."

NO MATTER HOW RUINOUS BOXING IS TO BOXERS, IT IS UNDENI able that part of Ali's appeal derived from boxing, from going into a ring, stripped to the waist, a beautiful man, alone, in combat. It is perfectly plausible that as a basketball player or even as a swad-dled halfback, he would have been no less famous and quicksilver. But the boxer represents a more immediate form of super-masculinity, no matter how retrograde. For all his verbal gifts, Ali was first a supreme physical performer and sexual presence. "Ain't I pretty?" he would ask over and over again, and, of course, he was. Here Ali was fortunate. If he had had the face of Sonny Liston he would have lost much of his appeal.

When Ali became world champion at the age of twenty-two and announced officially his affiliation with the Nation of Islam, he would never be more sexually magnetic. On the night of the fight, Gloria Guinness, a fixture in the fashion world who covered the first Liston fight for *Harper's Bazaar,* later told George Plimpton, "He was simply to *die* over."

And yet, unlike Jack Johnson, Ali was, at first, a very cautious sex symbol. Before he won the title, his experiences with women were, by all accounts, including his own, extremely limited. Ironically, it was just as he was discovering himself as a Black Muslim that he also discovered his sexual hunger.

"I'm ashamed of myself, but sometimes I've caught myself wishing that I had found Islam about five years from now, maybe," he told Alex Haley. "With all the temptations I have to resist. But I don't even kiss none, because you get too close, it's almost impossible to stop there. I'm a young man, you know, in the prime of life. All types of women, white women, too, make passes at me. Girls find out where I live and knock at the door at one and two in the morning. They send me their pictures and phone numbers, saying, 'Please, just telephone me.' . . . I've even had girls come up here wearing scarves on their heads, with no makeup and all that, trying to act like young Muslim sisters. But the only catch is that a Muslim sister never would do that."

Ali's social life was so restrained before he won the title that some sportswriters idly suspected that he was a closeted homosexual. ("I mean, we all wondered about a guy who had no dates and was always talking about how pretty he was," one of them said.) But it was readily apparent to those close to him that he preferred women. In the semifictional autobiography *The Greatest,* Ali (or, better, his ghost) describes losing his innocence to a prostitute and losing a fight early in his career after unwisely spending the previous night with a woman.

Perhaps. Perhaps not. What is certainly true is that Herbert Muhammad introduced Ali to his first real love, an older, more experienced woman named Sonji Roi.

When Ali was traveling in Egypt in the spring of 1964, Muhammad watched with amusement as the new champion fell in love with yet another pretty waitress. "I got a girl in the States who's better-looking than she is," Muhammad told him. Before leaving for Africa, Muhammad had taken a few pictures of Roi at his photography studio. He had a copy of one of the photographs in his briefcase and showed it to Ali. The champion was impressed and hoped Herbert would introduce him to Roi when they got home.

Sonji Roi was an odd choice for Muhammad, the son of the Messenger, to have made. She was gorgeous and, in the words of Ali's first Muslim instructor, Jeremiah Shabazz, "two cents slick." She was a party girl who spent her nights in bars and nightclubs. Ali would not be the first athlete she had dated. Elijah Muhammad's own sexual behavior was nothing if not hypocritical, but it is odd that Herbert chose a woman so at odds with the Nation's puritan style. Sonji's father was killed during a card game when she was two and her mother died when she was eight; she was raised by godparents. She gave birth to a son when she was still in her teens, dropped out of school, worked in nightclubs, entered some minor beauty contests. After she met Herbert Muhammad at his photo studio, he hired her to do phone solicitations for *Muhammad Speaks.*

Ali went out with Roi for the first time on July 3, 1964, just five months after he won the title. "He asked me to marry him that night," she told Thomas Hauser. "I didn't know if he was serious or not. I didn't know anything about him. But I was alone in the world. I didn't have a mother to go home and ask. I had to make the decision myself. After we spent some time together, I felt needed by him. He was strong, but he didn't know a lot of things. He needed a friend, and what better person than me? I said to myself, there's nothing else I'm doing with my life. I can do this. I can be a good wife to this man. Somebody has to be there for him, and I saw it as a chance for me to really help somebody. I wanted to be his wife and his best friend. I wasn't doing it for the money."

After their first meeting, Ali and Roi were together all the time, which worried the Muslims in his camp and amused the others. Many years later, married for the fourth time, Ali would admit that his greatest weakness and his most flagrant betrayal of Muslim ideology was his insatiable need for women. Married or not, he had so many affairs that Ferdie Pacheco called him a "pelvic missionary." The low point of that history would come in Manila before the third fight with Joe Frazier when Ali, married then to Belinda Ali, introduced his lover, Veronica Porsche, as his wife. Belinda then boarded a plane for Manila, and the ensuing row led to divorce and marriage to Porsche. The persistent myth about Ali and sex is that Sonji was his great tutor. "Rumor always had it," Pacheco said, "that Sonji was an artist who could demonstrate the *Kama Sutra* in all its rich splendors."

"It's like I'm some sort of sex object, and people still believe it," Sonji told Hauser. "A couple of years ago, a friend of mine called from the University of Texas. She was taking a psychology course, and called to tell me that I was in one of her textbooks. . . . The book said how Ali was torn, because he believed in his religion yet he loved me for my beauty and sensuality, and I carried myself in a manner that was unbecoming to the religion, but he was so mesmerized by my sexuality that he had to have me. And if you read this, you picture someone who's like running around in her underwear. So let me tell you, I didn't teach him nothing about sex. He knew what to do when I met him. It's just that I may have made him want to do it."

On August 14, 1964, Ali and Sonji married; she took the name Clay, though she agreed to be a good Muslim wife. Ali also cut an agreement with Sonny Liston: there would be a rematch on November 16, 1964, at Boston Garden.

CHAPTER FOURTEEN

Gunfire

ALI NEVER DOUBTED THAT HIS VICTORY IN MIAMI WAS LEGITI-
mate and repeatable. "In Miami I was Columbus," he would say. "I
was traveling to the unknown. I had to be cautious because I didn't
know what to expect. Now I know."

But even his closest associates felt a shiver of doubt in their
bones. Liston was still so strong and menacing, and Ali was so
young, so difficult to understand, that the event, even in retrospect, seemed like a fantasy. Ali's cornermen and backers ran
through the details of the fight—Ali's easy dominance in the early
rounds, his survival fighting blind in the fifth, Liston quitting on
the stool before the seventh though he had never been knocked
down—and it was still hard to absorb. "You really didn't think you
saw what you saw," Ferdie Pacheco said. "First it ended up in
doubt, because Liston quit. That took the bloom off the rose a lot.
It tarnished the victory. All you knew for sure somehow was that
this kid had survived. There wasn't jubilation like Joe Louis winning the title back and all of Harlem and the country celebrating.
There was some doubt."

That doubt extended to the United States Senate. It turned out
that Ali's backers had made a handshake agreement with Liston's
backers for an automatic rematch in case of an upset. Liston's In-
tercontinental Promotions paid Ali fifty thousand dollars for the
right to promote his next fight, be it a rematch against Liston or

New York, February 21, 1965. Assassination of Malcolm X.

against someone else. Several points occurred to the senators. First, the law prohibited such agreements because it was an incentive for a champion to lose and then fight a rematch for a far bigger purse. Second, Liston the Unconquerable had quit without ever having been knocked down. The senators found this inconceivable. Third, Liston never bothered to follow Estes Kefauver's fatherly injunction to choose his managers more carefully. Carbo was in jail, but Liston was still a property of such men as Pep Barone and Sam Margolis, and friend to Ash Resnik.

And so the Senate antitrust and monopoly subcommittee, now chaired by the Michigan Democrat Philip A. Hart, held a hearing in March 1964. It did not uncover much that the readers of the sports columns did not already know. Jack Nilon testified that Liston was indeed "a difficult man" to handle, a "neurotic" who refused to train very hard or follow instructions. If he had a case of the sniffles, Nilon said, Liston "acted as if he were dying" and stayed in bed. It was also true, Nilon allowed, that Liston kept company in Miami with various unsavories. "Sonny thinks an awful lot of Mr. Barone," Nilon testified. "He thinks Pep Barone's good luck. Sonny's very superstitious. He won't let you throw a straw hat on the bed."

The other Nilon brother, Bob, testified, however, that for all of Liston's recalcitrance, for all his unwillingness to train properly and follow the moral guidance of others, his cornermen and business associates had no advance notion whatsoever that a rematch with Muhammad Ali would be necessary. "Never at any time did I consider as a remote possibility that Cassius Clay could beat Sonny Liston," Bob Nilon testified. "Before my God, I didn't think he had any more chance of beating Sonny Liston than if he were in the ring with Grandma Moses. But I thought Clay represented a great show business property, the greatest thing since Jenny Lind."

Hart's subcommittee was scolding, but not entirely censorious. The senators uncovered no evidence of unseemly collusion, to say nothing of an outright fix, and did nothing to stand in the way of a second Ali-Liston fight. Its only result was a series of familiar resolutions to increase the level of regulation—not right away, of course, but sometime very, very soon.

.   .   .

LISTON TRAINED FOR THE REMATCH AT A KARATE AND JUDO CLUB in south Denver. For the first time since the early days of his career, he seemed determined to prepare himself for a long fight. In the early morning he often drove out to the mountains and ran to the Shrine of Mother Cabrini. He'd run up the 350 steps to the statue of the Sacred Heart and shadowbox there, all alone, breathing the cool mountain air. When it came time to move his camp to New England, Liston set himself up at White Cliffs, a fine old country club near Plymouth Rock with a golf course overlooking the Atlantic. Every morning Liston ran at least five miles up and down the dunes, and in the afternoons in the gym he went through his exercise routines and sparred. He even worked out with a martial arts instructor to improve his agility. Willie Reddish, his trainer, had been furious with Liston in Miami; he could not bear the way his fighter had dissipated his talent with whiskey and prostitutes. But now Liston was in a monastic mood, angry, focused on beating Ali. Reddish saw a new Liston, or at least the old Liston, the ferocious fighter who had demolished Floyd Patterson twice in less than five minutes, total.

One late-October afternoon, Liston worked over a sparring partner named Lee Williams so thoroughly that he left him reeling and sporting an ugly gash between his eyes that needed eight stitches. That left Liston, if not Williams, in a regal mood. "Blood is like champagne to a fighter," Al Lacey, an old trainer, remarked. "It gives his ego bubbly sensations. It helps the fighter's inner man. They used to feed Dempsey old has-beens in the last days of his training just so he could knock them down, and it never failed to pick up his spirits." Other sparring partners in Liston's camp quit because, as one of them, Dorsey Lay, put it, "some guys don't see the point in risking their faces for fifty bucks a day."

Ali was training no less hard. He quickly peeled off the weight he had gained on his trip to Africa. He began a running regime that was even more rigorous than before. Ali also looked stronger, broader, than he had in Miami; his body was maturing, and yet as he got stronger, he was not slowing down. Dundee, of course, heard that Liston was working with more discipline, but it didn't seem to bother him. Liston was not going to be any younger in Boston, Dundee reasoned. Also, the stylistic difference between the two fighters—to say nothing of the age difference—had not changed, and neither, Dundee said, would the result: "Liston buys everything. He's a one-way fighter. He can't lick a two-way, let alone a four-way fighter, a guy that can go forward and back, side to side."

The bookmakers believed that the Miami fight had been an aberration. The world, they calculated, would soon right itself. One week before the fight was set to go off at the Boston Garden, the Vegas odds were nine to five Liston.

The promoters were also in a buoyant mood. Unlike the commercial disaster in Miami, this fight promised profits. Fans would be curious to see a matchup between a wounded Liston and an ascendant character as fast and as loud as Ali. Boston Garden officials predicted a sellout crowd and a record gross of five million dollars from closed-circuit and radio rights. Good news all around.

Three days before the fight, on Friday the 13th of November, Ali was in room 611 at the Sherry Biltmore relaxing. In the morning he'd gone out on a five-mile run, but that was all. He was not sparring anymore. Mainly he stayed around the hotel with his growing entourage—with his brother, now called Rahaman Ali, and Bundini, Dundee, Captain Sam, and several new Muslim friends. From time to time ministers and hangers-on like Clarence X, Louis X, Thomas J., Brother John, and Minister George stopped by to say hello. It was a Muslim fast day, but because the fight was coming up, Ali ate a moderate dinner—a steak, greens, a baked potato. Afterward, he turned on a 16-millimeter projector and watched a rented film: *Little Caesar,* with Edward G. Robinson.

Suddenly, just after six-thirty in the evening, Ali sprang from the bed, ran to the bathroom, and started vomiting. He was in terrible pain.

"Oh, something is awful wrong," Ali said weakly as he came out of the bathroom. "You better do something."

"I'll call a doctor so the press won't find out!" Rahaman said.

"Damn the press," Ali said. "Get me to a hospital, man. I'm real sick."

Captain Sam, Rudy, and a few others helped carry Ali on a stretcher down the halls of the hotel to a service elevator. They covered his face with a towel, the better not to attract any press. They carried him through a laundry room and out the exit. Within a few minutes, Ali was headed toward Boston City Hospital in an ambulance, a boxy vehicle that looked more like an ice cream truck. By the time the ambulance arrived at the hospital, a photographer for the *Boston Herald* was already there, ready to take pictures. He was dissuaded from doing so by a cadre of the Fruit of Islam.

"Keep away," Louis X shouted. "Nobody goes through these doors. Somebody will get hurt if they try."

The doctors soon discovered the source of Ali's pain: a swelling the size of an egg in the right bowel, a dangerous condition known as an incarcerated inguinal hernia. If Ali had waited longer to call an ambulance, the hernia could have been life-threatening; as it was, he required an immediate operation.

As he was being prepped for surgery, a nurse told Ali in her best soothing voice, "Remember now, you're the greatest."

"Not tonight I'm not," he said.

The surgeon announced that it was a terrible shame to cut open such a splendid torso, but there was no choice. Now there was a big crowd at the hospital, including all of Ali's cornermen. Dundee had been at a theater watching a college football game on closed circuit when someone told him the news. He raced to the hospital, and as he was being interviewed by a local television station, he wept. Bundini looked over at Dundee and told a reporter, "I wish the Black Muslims could see Angelo now. Those are tears, real tears of love from a white man for a Negro. They don't think anything like that can happen. It ought to be a lesson to them."

When the wires put out the news of Ali's illness and the inevitable postponement of the fight, rumors circulated that Ali had been poisoned. It was all part of the war between the Nation of Islam and the followers of Malcolm X. Ali was faking injury on orders from H. L. Hunt or Robert Kennedy or Elijah Muhammad. It was the Mafia. It was Ali who had brought the hernia on himself because he was afraid of Liston.

Geraldine Liston heard the news on television, and everyone in camp could hear her cry out, "Chaaaarles! Come quick! Do you know what that boy's gone and done?"

Once Sonny had absorbed the news, he cracked open a bottle of vodka and made himself a screwdriver. Training was officially over. "If Clay wouldn't run around the streets the way he does," Liston said, "he wouldn't have anything wrong with him. When he opens his mouth a lot of wind goes in. That's what gave him the hernia. I'm sorry, it could have been worse. It could have been me." But for all his joking, Liston was crushed. He had worked himself to a physical peak, and there was no telling if he had the strength or the discipline to start all over again. All night, Liston kept muttering to no one in particular, "That damned fool. That damned fool."

The promoter, Sam Silverman, would end up losing hundreds of thousands of dollars. His reaction to the news of Ali's hernia was only slightly different from Liston's. He poured himself a tall bourbon.

The rematch was put off until May 25, 1965.

BY THE END OF 1964, MALCOLM X HAD EVERY REASON TO BE-lieve that he would not survive another year. The Nation of Islam had declared war on him; various ministers declared it everywhere from the pulpits in Chicago and Boston to the pages of *Muhammad Speaks*. Malcolm took what precautions he could. When he went to a television studio in New York to give an interview, the building was guarded by men carrying shotguns. Before going on the air, he called his wife at their house in Queens and said, "Keep those things near the door and don't let anyone in until I get there." Six weeks later, on Valentine's Day 1965, Malcolm's house was firebombed. The entire family, Malcolm, Betty, and their four daughters, escaped without serious injury. As the fire tore through the house, Malcolm stood out on the street, barefoot and in his pajamas, holding a .25-caliber pistol. He was furious, but not surprised. For months, Malcolm had been hearing that the Nation had set up murder squads to kill him. There had been rumors of car bombs and hit men; the articles in *Muhammad Speaks* only confirmed what he already knew. Malcolm even believed that Elijah Muhammad's men were working together with the Klan and the American Nazi Party to get rid of him. On February 18, he called the FBI—the same agency that had monitored him and harassed him with such diligence for so long—and said that there was a conspiracy to murder him.

"It's time for martyrs now," he told the photographer Gordon Parks. "And if I'm to be one, it will be in the cause of brotherhood."

On February 21, Malcolm was scheduled to speak at the Audubon

Ballroom in the Washington Heights section of Manhattan. After flashing his anger and jangled nerves backstage, ostensibly because there were no preliminary speakers ready, Malcolm came out to the rostrum and opened with the traditional Islamic greetings. As the crowd answered in kind, a driver from Newark's Mosque No. 25 ignited a smoke bomb and yelled, "Get your hand out of my pocket!" As most of the crowd turned to look at this theatrical diversion, three gunman crouched in front of the stage.

"Hold it!" Malcolm shouted.

Then came the shooting. Malcolm was hit with at least one shotgun blast and died almost instantly. He was thirty-nine years old. One gunman, Talmadge X Hayer, was apprehended, and the other two ran off.

A few hours after the shooting, there was a fire in Ali's apartment on the South Side of Chicago. The fire was ruled an accident. "Some fellow's bedspread on the floor caught on fire," Ali told the press. "Elijah warned that there would be bad publicity and it will test the weak followers. There will be more tests to come and the true believers will survive. The white people have got all the airplanes and all the bullets, and I'm not afraid of them. Why should I be afraid of the black man?" Two days later, a bomb went off at the Nation's New York mosque, and the ensuing fire nearly leveled the building.

Neither Elijah Muhammad nor Muhammad Ali expressed satisfaction at Malcolm's death, but they didn't express any sympathy, either. "Malcolm X was my friend and he was the friend of everybody as long as he was a member of Islam," Ali said. "Now I don't want to talk about him. All of us were shocked at the way he was killed. Elijah Muhammad has denied that the Muslims were responsible. We are not a violent people. We don't carry guns."

"Malcolm died according to his preachings," Elijah Muhammad said at a rally in Chicago on February 26. "He preached violence and violence has taken him away."

AFTER ALI RECUPERATED FROM HIS OPERATION HE DID SOME preliminary training in Miami, then decided to leave for New England on April Fool's Day. The idea was to drive his bus from Miami to the training center in Chicopee Falls, Massachusetts. In addition to a twelve-person entourage that included his sparring partners Cody Jones and Jimmy Ellis, his wife, Sonji, and various friends, cooks, and adjutants, Ali also invited along a few writers: Edwin Pope of *The Miami Herald*, Mort Sharnik and George Plimpton of *Sports Illustrated*, Bud Collins of *The Boston Globe*. Everyone gathered at Ali's house in northwest Miami and waited for the champion to get ready.

"Don't need no map," Ali told everyone. "Just going to point that old bus north and be in Boston in nothing flat."

Sonji came out of the house and interrupted her husband's monologue.

"Ali," she said, "you see about my dry cleaning?"

"All sent."

"How 'bout my shoes at the shop?"

"Done."

"Then take out the garbage."

Ali put a finger to his mouth.

"Champs don't take out the garbage," he protested, but he took it out all the same.

Once the bus was loaded with distilled water, soda, and baskets of chicken, everyone got on board and headed for the Sunshine State Turnpike. The bus itself was still decorated on the outside with Ali's advertisements for himself—"World's Most Colorful Fighter" and so on—but inside it was nothing special. Half the seats were broken. "From the moment we set out, the atmosphere was like an old-fashioned circus caravan," Pope said, "and, of course, Muhammad was the lead entertainer." Ali was often behind the wheel (a somewhat terrifying experience, especially when he would push the bus to seventy or eighty while turning around in his seat and lecturing the passengers). Sometimes Ali would leave the driving to one of the men in his entourage and perform without the handicap of holding the wheel. Early in the trip, he got up in the door well of the bus and, struggling to keep his balance, danced a soft-shoe in his workboots while Howard Bingham sang "The Darktown Strutters' Ball."

"I have to admit that before that bus ride," Ed Pope said, "I didn't understand Ali even though I'd been around him quite a bit in Miami. He seemed hostile and strange to me. But on that bus I got a sense of how complicated and how sweet he could be and how funny he was, always funny."

In the evening, they stopped in Sanford, Florida, Bundini's hometown. Bundini told everyone that when he was growing up, on the nights of Joe Louis's fights, people in the black part of town, Goose Hollow, would string up loudspeakers in the pines to listen to the action.

Then they moved on, shoving on north into the night, until Bundini announced, at around eleven, that his hunger was fierce. "Let's stop and eat," he said. "I empty." They stopped in the town of Yulee not far from the Georgia border beside an old, broken-down roadside luncheonette. Bundini and the four white journalists headed out of the bus. The others stayed back.

"You're goin' watch a man face reality—that's what you're goin' to see," Rahaman said.

"I might not be welcome," Ali told Bundini, "and besides, I don't believe in forcing integration. You go ahead, though, Jackie Robinson."

Bundini had grown up in Florida, but after so many years abroad and up North, he thought he could avoid an incident. But in the luncheonette, the manager told them in the plainest terms that there was a separate place, a window "out back," where they could get something to eat if they insisted on eating together.

"You mean the champion of the world can't get served like other people if he wants to come in here?" Bundini said.

"That's right."

"Isn't this discrimination against the law?" Bud Collins said.

"Not in Nassau County," the manager answered.

"Isn't this county in the United States?"

"Not yet."

Ali went in and grabbed Bundini by the collar and started shouting, "What's the matter with you—you damn fool! I told you to be a Muslim. Then you don't go places where you're not wanted. You clear out of this place, nigger! You ain't wanted here!"

Ali kept it up, haranguing Bundini all the way back onto the bus. The writers looked on amazed. Bundini was on the edge of tears.

"You got *showed*, Bundini. You got *showed*!"

The bus moved on, but Ali did not. He kept it up for a long time, demanding Bundini admit that he had faced reality at long, long last, shouting "Uncle Tom! Tom! Tom!" and whacking him over the face with a pillow.

Bundini could only answer feebly, "I'm a free man. No slave chains around my heart."

Bundini was crying now; Plimpton thought Bundini's face resembled the traditional mask of tragedy. Finally, when Ali saw how upset Bundini was, he calmed him down, joked with him, until eventually they were brothers again.

Ali's rickety bus held out until Fayetteville, North Carolina, where it collapsed and had to be abandoned. The group would have to make the rest of the trip courtesy of Trailways.

"My poor little red bus," Ali said. "You was the most famousest bus ever in the history of the world."

Fifty hours later, they reached Chicopee Falls.

"I'm Cassius Clay," Muhammad Ali announced at the front desk of the best motel in town. "Give me the sixty-dollar-a-day suite."

"But somebody is in there right now," the clerk said.

"Well, get him out. The Greatest is here."

IN EARLY MAY, WITH ONLY A FEW WEEKS TO GO BEFORE THE fight, the Massachusetts boxing authorities, in an odd rush of moralism, decided the fight could not occur in the Commonwealth for fear of infection from promoters with ambiguous credentials and perhaps (who knew?) organized crime. Instead, officials in Maine, eager for the publicity and the money, offered up St. Dominic's, a schoolboy hockey arena in the impoverished textile town of Lewiston. Lewiston is thirty-five miles from Portland and far from glamorous. The population was 41,000, mostly French Canadians; there were precisely two small hotels and one nightspot. Henry Hollis of the Hotel Holly's Leopard Room hired an extra stripper for the month of May. "We call 'em dancers," he said. "It sounds better. This town's small. It can only support one strip—ah, *dancer.*"

St. Dominic's could seat only five thousand souls. Not since Independence Day 1923, when Jack Dempsey fought Tommy Gibbons in Shelby, Montana, had there been a smaller venue for a heavyweight title fight. Shelby was a run-down cow town with a population of five hundred. Dempsey's manager, Jack "Doc" Kearns, tricked the city fathers into paying a $300,000 guarantee to Dempsey in advance (and nothing for Gibbons). Only seven thousand people showed up for the fight, and Dempsey put on a dismal performance, punching just enough to take a fifteen-round decision. When the fight was over, Kearns and Dempsey escaped on a train that Kearns had kept waiting in case of such a disaster.

But while the Dempsey fight led to the virtual bankruptcy of Shelby, Lewiston was not risking much; most of the money for the Ali-Liston fight would come from ancillary media rights anyway. There was even some advantage in holding the fight in Maine. Now the state of Massachusetts would not be blacked out from closed-circuit broadcast.

The twenty-four-year-old mayor of Lewiston, Robert T. Courturier, found boxing distasteful but figured the publicity would be invaluable. He soon discovered that his quiet town was now the focus of a more morbid kind of attention: grave rumors of assassination were soon splashed across every newspaper in the country. All kinds of rumors were circulated by the police, the reporters, the townspeople, the fight camps, and, not least, the irrepressible publicist Harold Conrad, who was only too glad to give the event an aura of menace, the better to sell tickets at theaters showing the fight on closed circuit. One rumor had it that Malcolm X's followers were sending a hit squad to Lewiston in a red Cadillac to kill Ali, possibly while he was in the ring, possibly before. Jimmy Cannon went for that rumor after hearing it from Conrad, and featured it prominently in his column. This, of course, occasioned a phone call to Milton Gross from the sports editor of the *New York Post*, Ike Gellis, wondering where his menace-and-mayhem story was. It's coming, Gross assured him, and you haven't heard *half* the story.

Another rumor had it that the Nation of Islam had threatened to kill Liston unless he took a dive. Liston's cornerman Joe Pollino told Jack McKinney that Liston had indeed been visited by two Black Muslims and afterward Liston had looked almost "catatonic." McKinney, who was not in New England with the Liston camp this time, said, "Sonny had been sparring with Thad Spencer and Amos 'Big Train' Lincoln and he'd been going through them like shit through a goose. But after that meeting, Sonny was a zombie and the two sparring partners were beating up on him. Finally, Joe told them he'd pay them double to let Sonny do well, to let Sonny feel good." Many of the other columnists, however, dismissed the idea that Liston could be intimidated by the Muslims. "Sonny had the goddam *Mafia* in his corner," said Larry Merchant, then of the *Philadelphia Daily News*. "Why would he get scared about two guys in bow ties when he was the product of the toughest guys in the country?"

The white reporters in town were uneasy about the new and obvious presence of Muslims surrounding Ali. Cannon and Gross, and even some of the younger reporters, found the Muslims, with their bow ties and steely, theatrical stares, unconducive to the gay carnival atmosphere they expected at a heavyweight title fight. Even Angelo Dundee, always so accommodating, was uneasy. At one point he went to thank one of the Muslim women in Ali's camp for sewing up his shirt; as he expressed his gratitude he lightly put his hand on the woman's arm. Rahaman Ali sternly called Dundee aside.

"Come out here a minute," he said. "Don't you ever put your hand on one of the sisters again."

"The vibe of the Black Muslims had been pretty subtle in Miami but it was enormous in Lewiston," Robert Lipsyte recalled. "There were these tall, strong, sober, shining-eyed Muslims. They even tried to shake down reporters for money for interviews with Ali. Most of them were ex-cons, because that's where the recruiting was going on at the time."

As the reporters wrote more and more dispatches about the atmosphere of dread, the Lewiston authorities reacted by increasing security. There were careful searches at press conferences and later at the fight itself. Melvin Durslag of the *Los Angeles Herald-Examiner* wrote that police even confiscated his wife's knitting needles. The Lewiston police chief, Joseph Farrand, put 250 officers on the street, including sheriff's deputies, state troopers, and ninety reserves from neighboring counties. He arranged for forty-five more men for security on fight night. A special homicide detail arrived from New York. No precaution, it seemed, was too much. "I don't want to go down in history as the place where the heavyweight champion was killed," Chief Farrand said.

There were moments of strange comedy, too. In Chicopee Falls, Ali trained in a ballroom at the Schine Inn. The makeshift gym was just above a bowling alley, and all during the training sessions the crash of bowling balls and pins could be heard over Ali's voice. His

246 | KING OF THE WORLD

entourage ranged from hardened members of the Black Muslims to the old vaudeville comic Stepin Fetchit. Ali called Fetchit his "secret strategist," so named, it was said, because Fetchit was old enough, at seventy-three, to have known Ali's historical hero Jack Johnson. Fetchit, who was born Lincoln Theodore Monroe Andrew Perry because his father wanted to name him after four presidents, was the warm-up act and master of ceremonies. Fetchit had starred in dozens of movies from the twenties to the fifties, including *Steamboat 'Round the Bend* and *The Sun Shines Bright*. He took his name from the horse that had beaten the one he'd bet all his worldly possessions on when he was living in Texas in the early twenties. Fetchit made a sizable fortune in the movies ("I had one mansion so big that when it was three o'clock in the kitchen it was five o'clock in the living room"), but by the early sixties he had become a charity case in Chicago. In the days before a big fight, writers desperate for feature stories troll around the camps looking for an angle. Unlike the grim Muslims, Fetchit filled their notebooks. Perhaps because he had such a sly notion of acting, Fetchit understood Ali's ability to transform himself. "People don't understand the champ, but one of these days he'll be one of the country's greatest heroes," he told one reporter. "He's like one of those plays where a man is the villain in the first act and then turns out to be the hero in the last act. That's the way it'll be with the champ. And that's the way he wants it, because it's better for the box office for people to misunderstand him than to understand him."

In the knowing eyes of the white reporters in camp, Fetchit was also the epitome of the Uncle Tom Negro, forever saying "Yassuh, I'm a-comin', suh!" At one press conference, when the phrase "Uncle Tom" came up, Fetchit interrupted Ali and said, "Uncle Tom was not an inferior Negro. He was a white man's child. His real name was MacPherson and he lived near Harriet Beecher Stowe. Tom was the first of the Negro social reformers and integrationists. The inferior Negro was Sambo."

The reporters were stupefied.

"What's the matter?" Ali shouted. "Write it down. Your pencils paralyzed?"

"You tell it, brother!" came the unlikely shout from the Muslims. "Oh, make it plain!"

"The truth was," Robert Lipsyte recalled, "that Stepin Fetchit was very funny and insisted that his head-scratching and foot-shuffling was just a way to get over, the sly civility of the colonial Indian in British-ruled India." Fetchit, as it happened, converted to the Nation of Islam a few years later.

Most papers still referred to Ali as Clay. Many of the reporters agreed with their editors and would not have thought to challenge them on the issue. Lipsyte, however, was embarrassed that the *Times* was still calling the champion Clay ("who is sometimes known as Muhammad Ali") and came over to Ali one day to try to explain. Ali patted his head and told him not to worry.

"You just the white power structure's little brother," he said.

Ali, as always, was open to all reporters and all visitors. One day a young Olympic champion arrived at the gym.

"Do you have any advice for me?" Joe Frazier asked Muhammad Ali.

"Yeah," he said. "Lose some weight and become a light heavyweight."

When Ali moved from Chicopee Falls to a Holiday Inn closer to Lewiston a few days before the fight, a dozen uniformed and plainclothes police officers met him at the state line and escorted him to Maine. Ali accepted the protection but laughed it off. "I fear no one but Allah," he said. "He will protect me. White, black, yellow people all love me. Nobody wants to kill me. If they shoot, the gun will explode in their hands. Their bullets will turn against them. Allah will protect me." Besides, Ali reckoned, "I'm too fast to be hit by a bullet." That was all fine for the champion, but the editors of *The Boston Globe* took out extra insurance for their five writers in Lewiston.

Compared to his antic performances before the fight in Miami, Ali was relatively subdued. By his standards, anyway. He vowed to raid Liston's camp in Poland Springs but thought better of it when he discovered that the owner of the hotel there had borrowed two black bears from the state game farm and chained them outside near the entrance.

While Ali had certainly sloughed off the weight he had gained in Africa, he was getting hit pretty hard in the gym, especially by Jimmy Ellis. But that was deliberate. Throughout his career Ali always prepared himself for major fights by allowing his sparring partners to beat him up, as if that sharpened his defensive skills and his endurance.

At home, however, Ali was really suffering. His relationship with Sonji was foundering. Sonji had made some overtures to the Muslims, but she would often wear makeup or clothing deemed inappropriate by the crowd of Nation members who now hung around Ali all the time, and Ali could not bear the embarrassment. At one point he complained loudly when Sonji wore a tight denim outfit. Ali demanded she go back inside and put on something more modest.

Years later Ali would admit that he had been deeply in love with Sonji, and their marriage was often a happy one, especially when they were alone and away from the judging stares of the other Muslims. At night he would sing his favorite song for her, Ben E. King's "Stand by Me." But at times Ali could not bear the gap between them. He would get angry when she questioned the restrictions and the mythologies of the Muslims or when she'd point out how differently he acted when they were alone and when they were with Herbert Muhammad and the other Muslims. Once, Ali even slapped Sonji, something he remembered and regretted thirty-odd years later. "It was wrong," he told Thomas Hauser. "It's the only time I did something like that, and after I slapped her I felt sorrier than she did. It hurt me more than it hurt her. I was young, twenty-two years old, and she was doing things against my religion, but that's no excuse. A man should never hit a woman."

But for all the commotion, the rumors of violence and the discord at home, Ali remained calm, even in the face of the rematch with Liston. As he started winding down his training before the fight to some early-morning runs with Howard Bingham, Ali spent his time just waiting around at the Holiday Inn in his second-floor suite. One afternoon, Bundini and Pat Putnam of *The Miami Herald* were in the room with Ali and Sonji. Bundini was in the bathroom, Ali on the bed. Sonji was sitting at a vanity, brushing her hair. Police guards were a few rooms down the outdoor walkway. All of a sudden, there was a gun blast. "It was crazy fucking Bundini playing with his pistol in the bathroom and it went off," Putnam said. "Everyone else was tight as a drum, except Ali. Ali chewed Bundini's ass off, of course, but then that was it. His mind was on the fight, not hit squads."

LISTON WAS NOW TRAINING IN THE SPA TOWN OF POLAND Spring. The guests at the hotel included more than a hundred Roman Catholic priests in town for a convention and contestants in a massive drum and bugle corps competition. The boxing writers, who thought the sun came up at ten, were displeased in the extreme to be awakened at seven by the drums and bugles and then bewildered at breakfast by the streams of men in black. Nor were they much impressed with the Poland Spring Hotel, which seemed in its amenities to summon the dusty wooden inns of John Ford westerns. The "fire escape" was a long rope in each room. Bathrooms were communal.

In Liston's camp, determination was giving way to lassitude and dissension. Liston had screaming fights with Jack Nilon not only in private but in the hotel lobby; usually the subject was money. Geraldine Liston said years later that Sonny was paid $250,000 for the second fight with Ali, but he never got the $150,000 he was owed for the Miami fight. Liston was miserable in Lewiston.

"It was very disappointing," Geraldine said years later. "The training was bad. It was wet. It was damp. And the little place where they were going to fight was terrible, you know, so Sonny was very disappointed and I . . . I guess he was just to the point that he'd say, well, win or lose, forget it, you know. He was in a very low spirit."

If Liston was visited by members of the Nation of Islam, he did not make an issue of it, and he made a great show of treating Ali with disdain. Once more, he was surrounded by the heavyweight traditionalists—Louis, Marciano, Walcott, Braddock, and Patterson—and he worked out in the traditional way. Under a spectacular chandelier, and as sunlight filtered through green stained glass, Liston skipped rope to Lionel Hampton's "Railroad No. 2," which has a quicker beat than "Night Train." To the untrained eye he was, as usual, dominating the sparring partners who had been brave enough to remain to the end. "Don't tell me I'm afraid of Clay," Liston told reporters at a workout one day. "All I'm afraid of is that if he opens his big mouth wide enough I'll lose an arm. I gotta redeem myself after letting that Clay take my title away. . . . I'll convert him all right—convert him into a stiff." Six days before the fight the Maine Athletic Commission doctor pronounced Liston "the fittest man I have ever examined."

The doctors of Maine may have been accustomed to a relatively low level of fitness. The truth was otherwise. The layoff had thrown Liston out of rhythm. Given his tender psyche and advanced years, throwing away what he had accomplished training the first time around and then doing it all over again after Ali's hernia was intolerable. He was drinking, usually J&B, and staying up all night. To the more experienced ring rats and reporters in camp, Liston was growing old before their eyes. When one sparring partner, Wendell Newton, came into the ring imitating Ali's speed, Liston looked especially weary. What would he do against the real thing? Amos "Big Train" Lincoln did all he could to revive Liston's spirits by providing him with an open target, but it did little good. And as he floundered, Liston was also showing his temper with the reporters around him, prompting Mark Kram, of *Sports Illustrated,* to write, "Liston is still Liston, socially primitive and sadly suspicious and forever the man-child."

A priest in Liston's camp called him "a hurt man, a humiliated man." Gil Rogin, who would eventually take on the editorship of *Sports Illustrated,* had written a prescient article for the magazine describing the disintegration of Liston's spirit and skills even while he was still training in Massachusetts.

"You can see it in his eyes," one of Liston's sparring partners told Rogin. "They don't look so scary anymore."

"One day you are the champ and your friends say, 'Yes, champ, no one in the world can beat you,' " Liston said one day as he and Geraldine were coming back to camp from a trip to the grocery store. "Then you are no longer the champ and you are all alone. After that, your friends and the people who have been making a big payday off of you aren't talking to you but about you, and what they say isn't what they said the day before."

Liston seemed pensive, more reflective and sad than ever before. In Poland Springs, he was openly melancholy. He and Geraldine visited a nineteenth-century burial ground near the hotel. They stopped at one headstone for a man named Richard Pottle that read:

Then fare thee well
Why should I weep
To see thee thus
So proudly sleep?

Geraldine said, "Charles, we ought to get us some pictures of those stones."

"What for?" Liston answered. "You going to be in there soon enough and long enough."

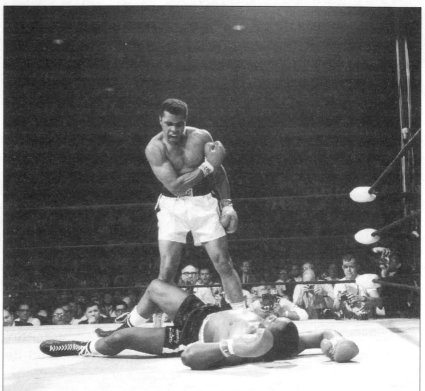

Ali-Liston, the knockout.

CHAPTER FIFTEEN

The Anchor Punch

MAY 25, 1965

THE CROWDS, SUCH AS THEY WERE, STARTED GATHERING AT ST. Dominic's at twilight. The announced attendance was 4,280, but it was clear to anyone in the arena that night that the real total was around three thousand at most. The citizens of Lewiston and the surrounding towns were more interested in the drum and bugle corps competition. The promoters were practically offering to give away the tickets, but no one was taking. This fight was for the cameras and the press. Technicians had erected a set of transmitting towers in the parking lot to beam a heavyweight title fight for the first time to Africa and the Soviet Union. Western Union set up a string of trailers to transmit copy. UPI hired the four fastest sprinters at Bates College to run copy from ringside to the trailers; tonight they would have to run fast, but it would be an early night.

The paranoia in Lewiston had increased. Security men sifted through handbags, briefcases, and pockets. As Red Smith's wife, Kate, entered the arena, an officer of the law checked her pocketbook.

"You won't find anything in there," she said. "I've got the tommy gun in my garter belt."

Jimmy Cannon, still in high-crisis mode, reported breathlessly that two officers of the New York homicide bureau were still sifting St. Dominic's on fight night for explosives. "They were searching for poison gas bombs, which . . . a leg-breaker for the Boston mosque who has a police sheet claimed were planted among the steel bars and spokes," Cannon wrote. "They didn't find them but they stationed themselves at the main entrance afterwards to pick up any black nationalist they made. They know them all."

Cannon went on, "The cement-block building was infiltrated by two hundred Maine policemen from every echelon. They were beat-walkers from Lewiston and county deputies and troopers of the state highway patrols and moving quietly among them were agents of the FBI. Even state liquor inspectors were issued handguns which they wore at their hips in holsters. The purse of every woman who entered the joint was frisked and all bags and packages and bundles and briefcases and satchels had to be opened for perusal. They were assisted in their surveillance by the strong-arm bravos of the Black Muslims who allied themselves with the forces of law enforcement to shield the only famous Negro to support publicly their crusade of black supremacy." Cannon failed to mention that one reason why all the police and special agents were there in the first place was that local officials were reacting to his reporting—and, thus, Harold Conrad's sly rumor-mongering.

Ali waited until around nine to leave his hotel and drive to the arena. He wore jeans and a sweatshirt. Mort Sharnik of *Sports Illustrated*, who rode along with him, found Ali in a somber mood.

"Give me your scenario for the fight," Sharnik asked him.

Usually Ali would go into a three-act performance, complete with mimicry of his opponent and the ring announcers. But now, quiet and serious, he said that it would be a strange fight. "It may start out with me not even throwing a punch. I'm just gonna go backwards and Liston will pursue and then, finally, *bam!*—I'll hit him with the right hand and it's gonna be over."

"That's a short fight," Sharnik said.

"It will be a short fight," Ali said. "That's the way fights are. There's no plan. It's like no other sport. But I think I can take him. I would've knocked him out last time in the rounds I predicted."

Ali was not merely improvising with Sharnik. Three weeks earlier he had told a reporter about a recurring dream in which he rushed across the ring at the opening bell and hit Liston with a quick right hand. "That's a psychological trick old Archie Moore taught me," he'd said, "and it lets the bear know right now who's in charge. I don't see in the dream if it knocks him out, but he never recovers and I go on to win in an early knockout."

Back in his dressing room, Liston got a short visit from José Torres, the light heavyweight champion, who was in Lewiston to do the Spanish-language broadcast. Torres asked Liston if he had seen his victorious fight against Willie Pastrano for the title. Liston said he had.

"Well, you gotta do the same thing," Torres said. "Cut off the ring. You gotta cut off the ring on Ali."

Maine's boxing officials did not assemble an especially distinguished cast to coordinate the fight. The referee, Jersey Joe Walcott, had, of course, been heavyweight champion in his time, but now in his new role could not offer much expertise. He was a "celebrity referee," hired on the assumption that it does not require a genius to wave two heavyweights together and, eventually, count to ten. The knockdown timekeeper was Francis McDonough, a sixty-three-year-old retired printer. The referee always coordinates his count with the knockdown timer, and yet Walcott never found out where McDonough was sitting. The official timer was a fifty-five-year-old schoolteacher named Russell Carroll, who had been timing fights for thirty-odd years, including the fastest fight in boxing history, a ten-and-a-half-second extravaganza in which a boxer named Al Couture ran across the ring a split second before the opening bell and clubbed his opponent just as he was turning to face him. There is usually a clock somewhere near the ring, if not above it; there was not in Lewiston. All questions of time would be determined by the stopwatches in the hands of McDonough and Carroll.

The honor of singing the national anthem went to Robert Goulet, a slick heartthrob singer made for Las Vegas and fight nights. But this would not be his finest night in the ring. As Goulet walked from his dressing room, he fumbled around in his pockets and discovered that he had lost his "palm notes," the lyrics to "The Star-Spangled Banner."

"What am I going to do?" Goulet murmured to himself as he stepped through the ropes and into the ring. Then it turned out that he could barely hear the organ music accompanying him. He flubbed the lyrics and had a hard time keeping pace with the tune; it was as if he were a small child struggling to keep step with a parent in a rush. There were smiles along press row and in the celebrity seats: Elizabeth Taylor, Jackie Gleason, and Frank Sinatra were there.

In his corner, Ali looked more confident than he had in Miami. There was nothing nervous in his bounce or in his gaze. Would he ever look more magnificent? He wore white trunks with black trim. He weighed 206 pounds and looked stronger now in his chest and arms.

Liston, on the other hand, looked faraway, spacey. He took off his robe and stretched his torso, back and forth, side to side. Liston weighed 215 pounds and wore black trunks with white trim.

At the sound of the opening bell, a reporter for UPI handed a bulletin over to one of the Bates College runners that read, "The Clay-Liston fight has begun and the following is a round-by-round report. . . ."

By the time the boy from Bates made it to the transmitter trailer outside with his news, the Western Union man, who was watching the fight on a monitor, had news for him.

BOXING AFICIONADOS HAVE STUDIED THE FILMS OF THE ENSU- ing minute or so of action with the same fanatical attention Kennedy assassination scholars have given the Zapruder film. But unlike the Zapruder film, with its bleeding colors and blood clouds, the films of the Ali-Liston fight actually erase some of the mystery that supposedly enveloped the event as it happened.

The film is best seen, of course, in slow motion:

As in his dream, Ali crosses the ring, and opens the fight with a right lead. But Liston absorbs the blow easily, and thus begins a minute's worth of dancing, or rather Ali dancing clockwise, his gloves at his hip points, and Liston plodding along after him. Twenty seconds of ring time go by without a blow being struck or even attempted. Then Liston decides he must fight and strikes out with four lefts. All of them land, but glancingly, their force erased as Ali keeps moving backward and muffles the punches with his gloves and forearms. Liston jabs and jabs and not once does he hit Ali cleanly.

Then comes the moment that would bewilder so many in the arena. With Ali skimming along the ropes, Liston lunges forward with a left. Ali yanks back his chin just enough to avoid any damage, and then, as he pivots forward, throws a short, chopping overhand right to Liston's temple. Liston's head snaps to the side and he goes straight down to the canvas. It is possible that later in the fight, the punch might not have been enough on its own to floor Liston, but Liston is off-balance from missing the jab, frustrated, and, since it is still just a minute into the fight, cold.

Now all this, of course, is with the benefit of a projector that slows the two fighters the way the photographer Eadweard Muybridge reduced the gallop of racehorses to discreet, comprehensible still images. Replayed in real time, in "fast motion," there is a minute or so of uneventful dancing and pawing followed by a moment in which Ali obviously does *something*—his arm suddenly becomes a whipping blur—but it is not completely clear what has occurred except that it profoundly affects Sonny Liston, who is now flat on the floor. So confusing is the moment, and so quick is Liston's drop, that one imagines there might have been a few people at St. Dominic's who were suddenly terrified that Liston had been shot from ringside. Yet some observers who were there and were without the benefit, at least for a while, of slow-motion replay said they saw the punch clearly.

"It was just like Ali had envisioned it on the bus," said Mort Sharnik, who had a prime press seat. "Liston overloaded on the left, threw it, Ali rode the punch back and away, and Liston fell in toward him, and Ali rose up and brought his right hand up and dropped it as Liston was falling forward. Liston never saw the punch to his cheekbone, and it's the punch you never see that causes you the problem. People say it was a 'phantom punch.' You started hearing that phrase right away. Well, I was sitting with Floyd Patterson and Cus D'Amato. And there was an old Maine state trooper in what looked like a Smokey the Bear hat screaming, 'Dammit, he hit him right smack on the chin!' And the bunch of us saw what happened. There was no question in our minds. Not later, but right away."

In slow motion, one can see that the downward force of the blow not only snaps Liston's neck, it also makes him lift his left foot off the ground before he finally tumbles onto the canvas. "I teach that punch," said Angelo Dundee, as he watched the tape thirty-odd years later. "Stick, slide right, drop the right hand over. Liston just didn't see it—and that's the punch that gets you out of there." As Liston was falling, Ali tried to follow up with a left hook but he missed. Liston was already down.

"That shot shivered Liston," Chicky Ferrara said at the time. Ferrara was an experienced trainer whom Dundee had placed near Liston's corner to discourage a repeat of the blinding incident in the last fight. "He blinked his eyes three times, like he was trying to clear his head, and I looked at Willie Reddish. I could see Reddish looked sick because he knew his fighter was in trouble."

LISTON WENT DOWN AND ROLLED TO HIS BACK, HIS ARMS stretched over his head. The rules of the game demand that the upright fighter retreat immediately before the referee starts his count, but Ali would not retreat. Jersey Joe Walcott was too deferential. He didn't force Ali away but should have.

Instead, Ali stood directly above Liston. He kept his right hand cocked and started shouting down at Liston:

"Get up and fight, you bum! You're supposed to be so bad! Nobody will believe this!"

At that moment, a young photographer for *Sports Illustrated* named Neil Leifer clicked his shutter. The photograph—Ali above Liston, Ali fierce and beautiful—was the lasting image of the fight; it may even be the most lasting image of Ali in the ring, period. Leifer had idolized the great sports photographers of the previous generation: Mark Kaufman, John Zimmerman, and Hy Peskin at *Sports Illustrated* and George Silk at *Life*. By the early sixties the photographers were no longer using the boxy Speed Graphics favored by WeeGee; they were using twin-lens reflex cameras or 35-millimeters. "Boxing, for the photographer, was a matter of anticipation," Leifer said. "With the Rolleiflex and strobe lights you had one shot and then you wind and wait three to five seconds for the light to recycle. You didn't have the supertechnology yet, but even in the early Ali days it was better for a photographer than it would be years later. There were three ropes, not four. There were fewer lights, so you got a black background. There was no advertising for the MGM Grand or Bud Lite on the ring apron. People smoked and so you got a dramatic haze. And this was before TV got rid of the strobe lights so you could light more dramatically. The images were more poetic then."

Leifer had the advantage of both poetry and luck. "I was just in the right place," Leifer said. "A clear shot, no referee blocking the way. We'd spent three days lighting the ring and greasing the local electricians. We borrowed the lights from Roosevelt Raceway on Long Island—forty condensers at eighty pounds each—and had them trucked up to Maine and used that for a fish-eye of the whole arena at the moment of the knockdown. So everything was perfect. The instant I took the picture I knew the spot was perfect. Except one thing. They used one of George Silk's punching pictures for the cover and mine with the article inside."

Ali finally backed away from the fallen Liston and allowed Walcott to shove him toward a neutral corner. But by now, everything was out of kilter. The crowd was screaming, "Fix! Fix!" Liston was lolling around on the canvas and Walcott was utterly confused. "The reason I stayed with Clay and kept pushing him away was because I was afraid he was going to kick Liston in his head," Walcott told reporters. "Clay was like a wild man. He was running around the ring and shouting for Sonny to get up. Can you imagine what they would have said about me if Clay had kicked Liston in the head? And you know he might have hit Sonny as he was getting up. . . . Like all referees I was in there to protect the fighter on the floor. Liston was a whipped man. I could see by that glassy look in his eyes. It didn't make any difference if I counted or not, I could have counted to twenty-four, Liston was in a dream world, and the only thing that could have happened was that he'd be seriously hurt." Walcott never counted over Liston, he said, because Ali never gave him the chance to start. Nor could he get the count from the knockdown timekeeper. "They should have had a loud speaker," Walcott complained.

Those with the presence of mind to think historically thought immediately of the 1927 Tunney-Dempsey fight in which Dempsey neglected to go to his neutral corner when Tunney was down; Tunney got up at what would have been "fourteen" and went on to win.

Francis McDonough, the knockdown timer, would be persecuted for years by doubting reporters until he finally stopped talking to them. He died in 1968. "If anyone was to blame for the fiasco it was that bum Clay," he said. "If that bum Clay had gone to a neutral corner instead of running around like a maniac, all the trouble would have been avoided. I started my stopwatch when I saw Liston hit the canvas and banged off the count until the watch showed twelve seconds elapsed, and I shut it off. When the referee came over to me I told him I had stopped the watch at twelve seconds and that Liston by that time had been on the canvas for at least twenty seconds."

And yet after Ali was safely in a neutral corner, Liston finally got to his feet. Walcott cleaned off Liston's gloves against his shirt and then called the fighters back in to resume fighting. Ali moved in on Liston, eager to finish him off. He immediately started hitting Liston without much thought to choreography or self-defense. He was looking for a knockout.

But at the same time, just as the two fighters engaged, Walcott started walking *away* from the action and toward the ring apron. He was responding to the summons of the grand elder of the boxing press, Nat Fleischer, the editor of *Ring* magazine, who was shouting his name.

"Joe! Joe, the fight's over! The fight's over!"

"What?"

"The fight's over!" Fleischer was sitting next to McDonough, and he told Walcott that Liston had been on the floor for well over ten seconds. Thus instructed, Walcott turned around and waved off the fighters. It's over, he told them, and he declared Ali winner and still heavyweight champion.

Liston was confused and groggy. Willie Reddish had to steer him by the elbow to the stool.

Dundee crossed the ring to console Liston and his corner.

"I looked at Sonny and said, 'Tough fight, Sonny,' and Sonny just looked right through me," Dundee said.

"The whole thing was a disaster," said Ferdie Pacheco. "We were in a state where they knew nothing about boxing. It was a comedy of errors. But don't think for a minute the result would have been any different. Liston had trained himself like old fighters do, to a fine point. But more than that, old fighters can't take it. It's like your gas tank is filled and you can't put more in. After Ali had the hernia, Sonny couldn't maintain his edge. As an old man your muscles can't take it. They're not young muscles anymore. You overtrain and you're dead. In the meantime, Ali had a nice rest. It was the same thing in Zaire a decade later. Ali wasn't quite ready, Foreman got cut in camp, they postponed the thing, Ali got really ready, and won. When you think about Ali's career, one factor you should never discount is good fortune. At least until he went on too long and paid for it, he was truly blessed."

But it wasn't only Ali's cornermen who could see that Liston had been stunned. Liston went back to the locker room and softly asked his cut man, Milt Bailey, for smelling salts. "Smelling salts is nasty—you don't ask for smelling salts if you haven't been hit and hit hard," Bailey said. "I felt so bad for him. The shame of it is that Sonny really was ready when the fight was supposed to go off in Boston, but the next time around he wasn't in shape. He'd just lost it."

Floyd Patterson, who knew something about losing and about shame, went to Liston's dressing room, an incredible gesture considering how humiliating his losses to Liston had been. Patterson was stunned that Liston had lost so quickly. He had seen Liston in the ring against some tough fighters—Machen, Williams, lots of them—and he had never seemed to mind getting hit. And now he'd gone down on a flash overhand right. Liston was alone now and sat on a rubbing table.

"I know how you feel," Patterson said in his soft deferential way. "I've experienced this myself."

Liston did not respond, not right away, and it struck Patterson that Liston still wore that terrible expression of his, that "mean look." Patterson said a few more consoling things, but he decided after a while that he just couldn't reach Liston. It would be foolish to go on trying.

"Okay, I'll see you later," Patterson said and turned to the door.

Liston got up and ran after Patterson and put an arm around his shoulder.

"Thanks," Liston said, and Patterson felt better.

"I knew then that I had reached him."

Back in the arena, Ali wandered to his corner. His brother, Rahaman, took the mouthpiece out.

"He laid down," Ali said quietly.

"No, you hit him," Rahaman said.

"I think he . . ."

"No, man, you hit him," Rahaman said.

Eventually, Ali was taken over to a television monitor and asked to look at the round in slow motion. Now he could see what his reflexes and strength had done. Soon Ali alternated between calling the blow "my karate punch" and crediting Stepin Fetchit for passing along Jack Johnson's "famous anchor punch." Nat Fleischer would later say that after a long scholarly search he had determined that Johnson never had such a punch. Instead, Fleischer compared the blow to one used by turn-of-the-century middleweight champion Charles "Kid" McCoy, the "corkscrew punch."

No matter what the tag, Ali said later that his punch was "timed with rhythm and balance. It had the force of two moving cars coming together and that makes it twice as hard as if one was standing still in a collision." Liston later said that he stayed on the canvas for a while longer than might have been necessary because Ali was still there and Ali was "a nut." He feared that Ali would hit him as he struggled to his feet. Besides, before the knockdown he'd had no success in hitting Ali. As Jerry Izenberg of the Newark *Star-Ledger* put it, "If Ali had not thrown this punch and the fight had gone on for three more rounds of the same thing, [Liston] would not have gotten close to him. Sonny could not have hit Muhammad in the ass with a canoe paddle."

Liston never denied that Ali had reached him with a sharp, true punch. "I didn't think he could hit that hard," he said. "I didn't quit. I got hit and hurt good. Clay's right hand caught me high on the left cheekbone and I felt all screwed up. I figured I could beat the count but you don't figure so good when you get clobbered. It wasn't the hardest punch I ever took, but it was hard enough."

DOUBTS WILL LIKELY REMAIN ABOUT THE SECOND ALI-LISTON fight for as long as anyone cares about fights. Even after taking into account that Ali really did hit Liston a sharp, unseen blow, and even allowing for the confusion in the ring and Liston's willingness to continue the fight once he was on his feet, it would be foolish to dismiss entirely the possibility that Liston took a dive—or was preparing to take a dive.

Johnny Tocco, a fight trainer who worked with Liston in both St. Louis and later in Las Vegas, told journalists before he died in 1997 that he, too, had heard the rumor that the Black Muslims had tried to intimidate Liston. "I asked him about it," Tocco said, "and all Sonny told me was 'Let's not talk about that—it was the way the fight had to go.' " Tocco claimed that John Vitale had told him that the fight was going to last just one round. But somehow the hearsay evidence that runs from a St. Louis mobster to a Las Vegas ring rat seems less than conclusive.

In old age, Geraldine Liston took to demanding money from interviewers—an arrangement I declined. But in the last free interview she gave, to producers for HBO in 1996, she denied that there had ever been a fix.

"He said, 'You win and you lose. . . . There has to be a winner in everything, you know.' And he was that type of guy. . . . He said it was just one of those things. . . . If he throwed the fight, he went to his grave, he never told me. And if he throwed it, I didn't see none of the money."

Ali never believed there had been a fix, and his disbelief was not merely a way to preserve his own reputation. What he said made sense. "Sonny is too dull and too slow to be a fixer in a fight," he said. And besides, Liston would have waited more than just a minute if only "to make it look good. . . . I hit him flush with all of my two hundred and six pounds and they hated to give me credit. . . . Didn't you hear the people hollering fix? Didn't you hear them hollering fake as soon as he hit the floor? I wanted the world to know I wasn't satisfied with him falling. I wanted the world to know I had nothing to do with them thinking it was a fix. . . . Let me have my day, because when something happens to me you will have your day. . . . Give me justice, but the people are still trying to say fake. My mouth has overshadowed my ability."

MOST OF THE REPORTERS WERE IN NO MOOD TO GIVE ALI THE benefit of the doubt, not after enduring a week of conspiracy rumors and a fight that lasted a minute or so. Gene Ward of the *Daily News* led his story thus: "A right-hand punch, thrown with phantom force and landing with the thud of a cream puff, knocked out Sonny Liston at one minute of the first round here tonight as a screaming crowd filled little St. Dominic's Arena with cries of 'fake' and 'foul.' "

Jimmy Cannon blamed Liston. He wrote that the Ali-Liston fight—"this swindle of a charade"—might have been the last straw, the "murder" of boxing. "The slayer is Liston who once worked for the mobs of St. Louis as a head breaker. The hell with it. Let it go. It has earned a passport to oblivion. There is no reason for its existence."

The august voices of *The New York Times* seized on the event to attack boxing itself.

Under the headline "A Hollow Ring," the *Times* ran an editorial reading, "On the theory that it is unsportsmanlike to attack an adversary when down, we postpone our usual morning-after demand for the abolition of professional prizefighting. Who, deploring beastly brutality, could find any fault with the brief and gentle Clay-Liston encounter at which only the customers suffered any damage? Not for many years have so few traveled so far to see so little. Cassius Clay and Sonny Liston, instead of 'murdering' each other, as the quaint language of the ring has it, have presided at the beginning of the end of commercial boxing—we hope. A sport as sick as this one surely cannot survive much longer."

Russell Baker wrote in his column that the fight had "done for boxing what Paris has done for women's fashion. They have made the public pay through the nose for the charm of being bilked. . . . This criticism has been heightened by the fact that fighters usually come from the hungry classes and were risking their brains for the titillation of the overfed. It can be highly corrupting to be so overfed that you have to pay two hungry boys to beat each other to keep you from yawning. Muhammad and Sonny saved the crowd from all this. Some critics of their encounter have called their show a farce. They are wrong. There was nothing funny about the main characters. It was a morality play in which two of life's losers—the exploited—turn the tables and exploit their exploiters.

"What was funny was the wounded fury of the mob. Believing in Santa Claus. Heads full of childish notions about the clash of good and evil. Duped by a pair of canny codgers who, except for rare musculature and reflexes, would have been doomed to toil for peanuts at a shoeshine stand or cracking skulls on a picket line."

For a couple of days, at least, while the outrage was still fresh, Cannon and Ward were in the majority. But after a few days of watching replays, other members of the press were more apt to believe their eyes. There was some debate at the offices of *Sports Illustrated* over what had happened in Lewiston—Bud Schrake was the loudest in proclaiming the bout a fraud—but the lead story, by

Tex Maule, reflected the majority opinion in the office: that the fight, and the punch, were legitimate. Even Arthur Daley of *The New York Times,* who had rarely written a kind word about Ali, now wrote, "Kinetics is a branch of physics dealing with the effects of forces. There is absolutely no method, however, of applying kinetics to boxing so that the force of a punch can be measured."

THE FBI DID NOT CONDUCT A FULL FIELD INVESTIGATION OF the Lewiston fight, but, at the request of the U.S. attorney in Maine, agents did interview a wide range of informants about a possible fix. The bureau came back with a vague report that the state attorney felt did not warrant further investigation. "He did not feel we had developed sufficient information," William Roemer of the FBI told an HBO producer shortly before Roemer's death. The report, the U.S. attorney felt, had no "prosecutive value."

Three years after the fight, however, Roemer and his partner John Bassett interviewed the Chicago mob front man Bernard Glickman, who had since become a cooperating witness for the government. Glickman, who knew Liston well from the days when the St. Louis mob ran him, claimed that he heard Liston tell his wife that he was going to take a dive, and Geraldine, in turn, Roemer recounted, "said to Liston that as long as he was going to dump the fight, then don't take the chance of getting hurt. As long as you're going to lose anyhow, go ahead, go down early." The problem for the FBI was that Glickman's uncorroborated testimony had little value as the basis for further investigation. Glickman had perjured himself already on other mob-related issues. What was more, the FBI investigators may have been suspicious of the Lewiston fight, as many columnists were, but in the end they never discovered any betting bonanzas that would have suggested a fix. Nor could they even answer why the Mafia would have wanted to give up the heavyweight championship of the world, the biggest money-making title in sports, for a short-term gain.

Years later, when Liston was living in Las Vegas, he ran into Jerry Izenberg of the Newark *Star-Ledger,* one of the few reporters whom he seemed to like and to trust. They exchanged pleasantries and agreed to sit down and have breakfast together. They ordered and began to talk. The first thing out of Liston's mouth was "I don't want to talk about Lewiston."

"Fine," Izenberg said. "We'll talk about something else."

And so they did for a while. But then Izenberg put duty before deference and said, "But we've got to talk about it. What's it like? I mean, tell me in one sentence and I'll never ask you again."

"In Lewiston I lost the world heavyweight championship," Liston said. "I lost it because Nat Fleischer said I lost it."

"What makes him the arbiter of conduct in boxing? What gave him that authority?"

"Because," Liston said, "he could count to ten faster than Joe Walcott."

CHAPTER SIXTEEN

What's in a Name?

ON JUNE 23, ONE MONTH AFTER THE FIGHT, ALI FILED A COM-
plaint in the Dade County, Florida, circuit court asking that his
marriage to Sonji Clay be annulled. The Muslims told him that he
had to choose: membership in the Nation of Islam or marriage to
a heathen. Never mind that Herbert Muhammad had introduced
Ali to her in the first place. The plan had not included marriage.
When Ali and Sonji were dating and driving to a Muslim convention in Arizona, Captain Sam married them "Islamically" by turning around in the front seat to the young couple in the back and
saying, "I wed thee, I wed thee, I wed thee." They later received the
blessings of the state of Indiana through a justice of the peace in
Gary.

Ali's complaint cited Sonji's pledge to follow the tenets of the
Nation of Islam and her failure to do so. His complaint was especially detailed in her refusal to follow the Muslim dress code. He
cited, as evidence, their dispute over an outfit she had worn to a
press conference in training camp before the Lewiston fight.

"You could see all of her! The seams of her underwear!" Ali
would say in court. "Tight pants around all those men was wrong!"

Sonji's lawyers actually brought the outfit to court and asked the
judge, "Would there be any objection to the court if she put on the
dress now during the recess?"

"I don't think it is necessary," the judge said. "The court has a
vivid imagination."

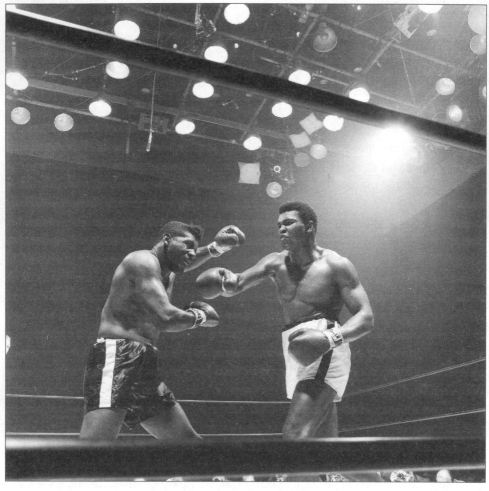

Muhammad Ali vs. Floyd Patterson, 1965.

Sonji had worn a knee-length red dress to the hearing, and her lawyer asked Ali, "Is the dress Mrs. Clay is wearing today acceptable to Muslims?"

"No, it's too tight," Ali said. "Her knees are showing and her limbs are showing. She's wearing false eyelashes and lipstick. It's lust to the eye and embarrassing to me."

It came out that Sonji irritated Ali with her irreverence. When he would recount for her the story of Black Muslim cosmology, that the great flying wheel would drop bombs on the world, she'd needle him, ask him why Elijah Muhammad's house in Chicago would survive apocalypse when the rest of the South Side would burn. And, like Cassius Clay, Sr., she had little respect for the grim-faced Muslims and wondered aloud if, while preaching the puritan ethic, they were not off chasing women and ripping off the heavyweight champion for his money.

Sonji left Lewiston in anger right after the fight and did not see Ali again until June 11, when they met in Chicago. That day Ali tried to drive her to a dressmaker to buy some "plain and simple" floor-length dresses. Sonji exploded and demanded he pull the car over to the curb and let her out. They did not live together again.

In his suit, Ali said that the theme of immodesty had been a constant in their year-long marriage. Once, after he had taken a washcloth to her face to wipe away her lipstick, Sonji left home. "Baby, I can't take it no more," her note to him read. "I'm not happy. I've never really been happy."

"I just love my husband and I want to be with him," Sonji told reporters. "It's just this religion. I have tried to accept it, and I have explained this to him but I just don't understand it. It's very hard to change to the way they want me to be. . . . We've always had our little arguments about clothes. I told him if I was embarrassing him I would just stay out of the picture. I just want to be his wife and I won't let them take him away from me just like that. . . . Cassius said that Elijah Muhammad told him I was embarrassing the entire Muslim nation by not wearing the long white dresses the Muslim women are supposed to wear. I don't drink, I don't smoke, I attend meetings and services and observe dietary laws. I was baptized in his religion. All except the dress. I never joined that part. I am not accustomed to wearing stuff like that. I'm normal like other women. I don't like to wear that stuff."

Ali's suit declared that the marriage had gone awry right away, within a day of exchanging vows. It said that Sonji's promise to practice the faith was a "mere sham," a deception to help bring her all the material wealth promised by a champion. "Every girl dreams of finding a Prince Charming who can afford the things she wants," she had said once. "I looked up one day and there was mine." And yet, according to all the non-Muslims around, Ali and Sonji seemed to have a loving marriage which went wrong only when leaders of the Nation started putting pressure on Ali. They were affectionate with each other; Sonji even got along well with Ali's parents. In time, Ali would become a world-class woman-izer—the "pelvic missionary"—but while he was with Sonji he was faithful.

When the divorce decree was finally issued, Sonji came out of it heartbroken and only modestly enriched. The court ordered Ali to pay her $15,000 a year for ten years and a one-time payment of $22,500 to cover her legal costs. When it was over, Ali left Sonji a bitter note reading, "You traded heaven for hell, baby." But he was heartbroken, too. He was surrounded by sexual opportunity—flunkies offering to find him women, and women offering them-selves. But for months Ali stayed away. He once said that he stayed in his room, still smelling Sonji's perfume. It was only when the air cleared of her scent that Ali returned to the world of women.

"Of course, when Muhammad went back to the women he did it with world records in mind," Pacheco said. Unlike Jack Johnson, however, he never went near white women. A strict adherence to Islamic law would have precluded any sex at all outside of mar-riage, but Ali, as always, cut his own deals. For him, an avoidance of white women was a moral and political necessity, a form of strength and purity. He was rarely as vehement about anything as he was about interracial sex and marriage.

"Man, I was in Chicago a couple of months ago and saw a white fella take a black woman into a motel room," he told an interviewer for *Playboy.* "He stayed with her two or three hours and then walked out—and a bunch of brothers saw it and didn't even *say* nothin'. They should have thrown rocks at his car or kicked down the door while he was in there screwing her—do *something* to let him know you don't like it. How can you be a man when another man can come get your woman or your daughter or your sister—

and take her to a room and screw her—and, nigger, you don't even *protest?* But nobody touches our women, white *or* black. Put a hand on a Muslim sister and you are to *die*. You may be a white or black man in an elevator with a Muslim sister and if you pat her on the behind, you're supposed to die right there."

"You're beginning to sound like a carbon copy of a white racist," the interviewer said. "Let's get it out front: Do you believe that lynching is the answer to interracial sex?"

"A black man *should* be killed if he's messing with a white woman," Ali said. "And white men have always done that. They lynched niggers for even looking at a white woman; they'd call it reckless eyeballing and bring out the rope. Rapping, patting, mischief, abusing, showing our women disrespect—a man should die for that. And not just white men—black men, too. We will kill you, and the brothers who don't kill you will get their behinds whipped and probably get killed themselves if they let it happen and don't do nothin' about it. Tell it to the president—*he* ain't gonna do nothin' about it. Tell it to the FBI: we'll kill anybody who tries to mess around with our women. Ain't *nobody* gonna bother them."

"And what if a Muslim woman wants to go out with non-Muslim blacks—or white men, for that matter?" asked the man from *Playboy*.

"Then *she* dies," Ali replied. "Kill her, too."

As a fighter, Ali was suddenly alone. The heavyweight division was not quite barren, but damn close. Liston had been thoroughly demystified. There were no calls for a third fight. Who had the stomach for that? And who else was there to challenge Ali? Cleveland Williams? Eddie Machen? Liston had destroyed them. Ali joked that he was dying to find a Great White Hope to fight; a strong white contender, he said, would jack up the purse as no black opponent could. In fact, in 1966, he would fight, and defeat, four white wannabes: George Chuvalo (the toughest of the lot), Henry Cooper, Brian London, and Karl Mildenberger.

Ali, however, had a more serious challenger to deal with first, one who had genuinely angered him—Floyd Patterson. After enduring his humiliating losses to Liston and then Ali's victories, Patterson had appointed himself the avenger, all in the good name of boxing and Christendom. The antagonism had been brewing for more than a year. When Ali had his interview with Alex Haley for *Playboy* just a few days after the first Liston fight, he let his good humor lapse just once. "It's going to be the first time I ever trained to develop in myself a brutal killer instinct," Ali said. "I've never felt that way about nobody else. Fighting is just a sport, a game, to me. But Patterson I would want to beat to the floor for the way he rushed out of hiding after his last whipping, announcing that he wanted to fight me because no Muslim deserved to be champ. I never had no concern about his having the Catholic religion. But he was going to jump up to fight me to be the white man's champion."

To Ali, who had learned from Malcolm X, Patterson represented the toadying posture of old-style Negro politics. Patterson was the integrationist, the accommodationist, the symbol of sit-ins and interracial marriage. This was late 1965, not long after the riots in the Watts ghetto in Los Angeles—an event that signaled the deep dissatisfaction with integrationist, reform politics, an event that seemed to endorse Malcolm's call to seize power "by any means necessary." To many young blacks, especially, the Patterson model was an object of pity. Ali mocked Patterson for buying a house in a white neighborhood only to move after discovering that his neighbors didn't want him. "I ain't never read nothing no more pitiful than how Patterson told the newspapers, 'I tried to integrate—it just didn't work,'" he said.

While Ali was recuperating from his hernia surgery and waiting for the second fight with Liston, he dropped by Patterson's training camp in upstate New York with an armful of lettuce and carrots, shouting that he wanted nothing more than to drive "the rabbit" back into his hole. "You're nothing but an Uncle Tom Negro, a white man's Negro, a yellow Negro," Ali taunted. "You quit twice to Liston. Get into the ring and I'll lick you now."

As always with Ali his undertone of humor saved his taunts from sounding vicious. Ali repeated this sort of performance many times. In order to promote a fight and psych himself up, he would customarily gin up some sort of seriocomic animosity against his opponent and find a way to cast him as the dupe of the white establishment. The performances became ritual: the "surprise" visit to the opponent's gym; the nicknames; the taunts; the hold-me-back let's-get-it-on-right-now melee; the imagined vendetta. Some, like Joe Frazier, would resent these performances for many years to come; Frazier, especially, took it to heart when Ali called him an ignorant Tom and made him out to be the fighter of the "white power structure." Others, who were more self-assured, or who were pleased simply to be on the same card with the most famous athlete on the planet, went along with the joke; they were happy and well paid for having played the foil.

But Ali's anger at Patterson, even when it took humorous shape, was genuine, even visceral. Patterson really had begun to see himself as the Christian savior of boxing. Ali scheduled a fight with Patterson for November 22, 1965, in Las Vegas, but well in advance of that Patterson had showed himself eager to play the part of redeemer. In the October 19, 1964, issue of *Sports Illustrated,* he collaborated with his close friend Milton Gross of the *New York Post* in the first of three articles staking out his position. He wrote:

> I am a Negro and I'm proud to be one, but I'm also an American. I'm not so stupid that I don't know that Negroes don't have all the rights and privileges that all Americans should have. I know that someday we will get them. God made us all, and whatever He made is good. All people—white, black, and yellow—are brothers and sisters. That will be acknowledged. It will just take time, but it will never come if we think the way the Black Muslims think. They preach hate and separation instead of love and integration. They preach mistrust when there must be understanding. Clay is so young and has been so misled by the wrong people that he doesn't appreciate how far we have come and how much harm he has done by joining the Black Muslims. He might as well have joined the Ku Klux Klan. . . .
>
> One letter I'll always remember, because it showed me how evil can be turned into good and misunderstanding into understanding by living properly. It was from a man who owned a restaurant in the South. He wrote me that he never liked Negroes, but after reading about the way I conducted myself as the champion, he had changed his mind. He said I could come into his restaurant with anybody I chose to and sit down for a cup of coffee and he would sit down with us. From that point, he said, he would serve any person. Sure, it's a small thing, and it may

sound condescending on his part, but I think it's important. . . .
Would this man write to Clay as a member of the Black Muslims? I don't think so.

Patterson's yearning for acceptance by his inferiors seemed pathetic to Ali. It was as if Patterson were grateful for the most pa-
tronizing treatment imaginable. Patterson was the troubled boy
from Bedford-Stuyvesant who had been saved and endorsed by
kindly white liberals: by Eleanor Roosevelt's Wiltwyck school, by
Cus D'Amato, by President Kennedy. Ali's refusal to beg for acceptance reflected the new attitude popularized by Malcolm X. But at
the same time, it would be worse than condescending to dismiss
Patterson. His impulse, like Bundini's at the restaurant in Yulee,
Florida, was to insist on his humanity, to demand service and voice
his grievance when refused. To dismiss Patterson as nothing more
than sniveling would be to dismiss the civil rights movement as it
was conceived by King. In the end, nonviolent resistance was far
more effective than anything tried by the Nation of Islam and
other nationalist groups—and no less dangerous. Part of the brilliance of James Baldwin's 1962 book *The Fire Next Time* was to
identify the Nation not as a particularly effective political group,
but as a symptom of continued oppression and as a warning that
limited change in society would lead to conflagration—to what was
to come, in fact, soon enough.

And yet what was remarkable about Patterson was the degree to
which he felt he was on a mission to beat Ali, not simply to prove
his boxing superiority to a dubious public, but to prove the superiority of a religion and the liberal rhetoric of equal opportunity.
Certainly Patterson yearned to rid himself of the embarrassment of
losing twice to Liston in less than five minutes of ring time. He
could do that only by regaining the title, or at least by fighting
valiantly in that quest. Usually, boxing writers try to squeeze some
greater meaning out of an athletic contest, if only to enlarge the
focus of their attention. But Patterson had made that task easy and
real. Patterson even offered to fight Ali for nothing and turn his
purse over to the NAACP. One had the feeling that his offer was
only half in jest. Patterson actually said that beating Ali—beating
Clay, as he insisted on calling him—"would be my contribution to
civil rights."

Patterson never doubted that Liston had been hit solidly in Lewiston; what he could not fathom was how so powerful a fighter could have quit—and to a non-Christian!—in Miami. "It was almost as much a blow to me as being knocked out by him," Patterson wrote. "He, of all people! The unbeatable man, the press called him, quitting on his stool. . . . If Liston couldn't punch with one arm, what was wrong with the other? . . . I can't leave things that way. I can't leave people remembering that I lost to a man who quit cold to another man who's taken the championship that belongs to the whole world and given it to the Black Muslims, who don't want to be a part of our world."

Six weeks before the fight, in the October 11 edition of *Sports Illustrated*, Patterson launched an even more self-dramatizing assault in the magazine. The article opened with a photocopy of a kind of declaration of intent handwritten and signed by Patterson:

"I love boxing. The image of a Black Muslim as the world heavyweight champion disgraces the sport and the nation. Therefore, CASSIUS CLAY MUST BE BEATEN by Floyd Patterson."

Patterson began modestly, but soon turned shrill:

You could get the idea that the entire sport depends on me and that if I, as some sort of homemade Sir Galahad, do not defeat the villain, Clay, boxing will most certainly die. That is nonsense. On the other hand, and I feel very strongly about this, boxing most certainly could use a new image right now. I say it, and I say it flatly, that the image of a Black Muslim as the world heavyweight champion disgraces the sport and the nation. Cassius Clay must be beaten and the Black Muslims' scourge removed from boxing.

By calling me a "Black White Hope" and by several other ill-advised and intemperate remarks, he has continually damaged the image of American Negroes and the civil rights groups working on their behalf. No decent person can look up to a champion whose credo is "hate whites." I have nothing but contempt for the Black Muslims and that for which they stand. . . . I am a Roman Catholic. I do not believe God put us here to hate one another. I believe the Muslim preaching of segregation, hatred, rebellion, and violence is wrong. What religion teaches that? By preaching such propaganda and not flatly condemning the murder of Malcolm X, who quit the Muslims, Cassius Clay is disgracing himself and the Negro race.

There was no limit to Patterson's righteousness. But unlike Ali, who would always undercut his taunts with a smile and a quip, Patterson never let on that he was engaged in some sort of political dozens, a rhetorical so's-your-mama face-off. He meant every word, from the reasonable attack on Ali's treatment of Malcolm X to his bizarre vision of what could happen in the ring.

"To be perfectly frank," Patterson went on, "I have even thought about an assassination attempt on Clay while our fight is in progress. If the late President Kennedy can be assassinated, it should not be too difficult to kill Clay, for he is nowhere near as important as our late president. Suppose someone did try to kill Clay while we were fighting. I'm not joking. Two fighters move around quickly, and if a bullet is fired I *might* move right into the range and get killed instead of Clay. If the possibility of assassination has occurred to me, I guess Clay has thought about it, too."

Patterson gave himself an excellent chance to win because he considered Ali inexperienced, a poor in-fighter, a light puncher ("I am sure I punch harder than he does").

"This is both a personal goal and a moral crusade," Patterson declared. "I am convinced, now that he wants to get rid of his wife because she will not embrace the Muslim faith, that Clay is really a dedicated Black Muslim and has no intention of quitting them." But while Ali had the right to choose his own religion, "I have rights, too. I have the right to call the Black Muslims a menace to the United States and a menace to the Negro race. I have the right to say the Black Muslims stink. If I were to support Black Muslims, I might just as well support the Ku Klux Klan."

Ali read these stories in *Sports Illustrated* and answered in a rage. "I want to see him cut, bruised, his ribs caved in, and then knocked out," he said. "I'm American, but he's a deaf, dumb, and blind so-called Negro who needs a spanking. You can play up that the fight is going to be a good one. I plan to make him an example to the world. I'm going to punish him for the things he's said about me in magazines."

. . .

IF ALI WAS PLAYING THE DEFIANT ROLE OF JACK JOHNSON, PAT-
terson was summoning the memory of Peter Jackson. When John
L. Sullivan was champion he drew the color line against Jackson,
who was acknowledged as one of the greatest fighters of his time.
He was born in the West Indies and moved with his family to Australia, winning the national heavyweight title in 1880. Observers at
the time believed Jackson surely would have won the world heavyweight title had he not been denied the opportunity to fight for it.
One of his most valiant efforts came in 1891, when, at the age of
thirty, he fought "Gentleman Jim" Corbett to a sixty-one-round
draw. To make money Jackson even played Uncle Tom in a theatrical production of Harriet Beecher Stowe's novel; when the performance was over, Jackson would strip to the waist and fight
three-round exhibitions as an "extra added attraction."

Frederick Douglass and, later, the writer James Weldon Johnson
were among the black leaders who admired Peter Jackson for his
forbearance, for the dignity with which he bore the racism of his
era. "Peter Jackson was the first example in the United States of a
man acting upon the assumption that he could be a prizefighter
and at the same time a cultured gentleman," Johnson wrote in his
book *Black Manhattan*. "His chivalry in the ring was so great that
sportswriters down to today apply to him the doubtful compliment
'a white colored man.' He was very popular in New York. If Jack
Johnson had been in demeanor a Peter Jackson, the subsequent
story of the Negro in the prize ring would have been somewhat different."

By 1965, however, black intellectuals were far from unanimous in
endorsing the cultured gentleman as a model. "There were to be no
more Peter Jacksons, no more tragic black gentlemen whom whites
found to be spiritual mulattoes ('black skin, white heart')," wrote
Gerald Early. "This is ultimately why both [Eldridge] Cleaver and
[Amiri] Baraka so vehemently condemn Floyd Patterson, for he
seems to be someone who yearned to be, finally, the modern Peter
Jackson. The sixties was the age of the reacceptance of Jack Johnson (in the guise of Muhammad Ali), who was, of course, the inevitable historical revision of Jackson." Patterson yearned to prove
himself worthy of integration; the white man, in Ali's rhetoric, did
not deserve integration after all he had done to blacks. With the
Patterson-Ali matchup, the issue of Good Negro–Bad Negro may

have been clear once more to much of the white public, but it was far different for blacks.

Perhaps what infuriated Ali most was Patterson's implication that as a Muslim he was somehow not an American. And while it was true that Ali had been inspired by his trip to Africa, while it was true that when he was there he called Africans "my people" and talked about the pleasures of coming "home," he was a thoroughly American man fast on the road to becoming a thoroughly American folk hero. Ali may not have read W.E.B. Du Bois, but he was a living example of the "two-ness," the "double-consciousness," described in *The Souls of Black Folk*.

"Patterson says he's gonna bring the title back to America," Ali told the journalist and biographer John Cottrell. "If you don't believe the title already is in America, just see who I pay taxes to. I'm American. But he's a deaf dumb so-called Negro who needs a spanking. I plan to punish him for the things he's said, cause him pain. The man picked the wrong time to start talking to the wrong man. When Floyd talks about me, he puts himself on a universal spot. We don't consider the Muslims have the title any more than the Baptists thought they had it when Joe Louis was champ. Does he think I'm going to be ignorant enough to attack his religion? I got so many Catholic friends of all races. And who's me to be an authority on the Catholic religion? Why should I act like a fool? He says he's going to bring the title back to America. I act like I belong to America more than he do. Why should I let one old Negro make a fool of me?"

Ali was extremely confident that he would be able to handle Patterson in the ring. He was younger than Patterson, stronger than Patterson. He had an enormous eight-inch reach advantage. In all the ways that Patterson was strong—his hand speed, his footwork—Ali was far stronger.

In preparation for the fight, Ali stayed at the El Morocco Hotel in Las Vegas and trained harder than he had to. He had not yet reached that stage of his career when he would parcel out his time and energy carefully; what was more, he really did want to destroy Patterson. He had one of his sparring partners, Cody Jones, ape Patterson's signature moves: the peekaboo defense, the kangaroo punch. Sometimes, just for fun, Ali reversed the roles, imitating Patterson's stance and leaping hook. Ali's brother Rahaman then came in to pound away at the champion's body even though Patterson was not likely to do so.

Meanwhile, Bundini and Ali were having one of their fights. The Muslims in Ali's camp frowned on Bundini's drinking and his penchant for white women, and when Bundini admitted pawning Ali's championship belt, dismissal became inevitable. He would not return to Ali's corner until Ali himself had returned from exile. And so Ali was without his principal cheerleader. He didn't seem to need him this time. Five days before the fight, Ali took the day off and visited Elijah Muhammad in Arizona, where he'd bought a house to help ease his bronchial ailments.

Since losing to Liston, Patterson had beaten an Italian coffee merchant named Sante Amonti, Machen, Charlie Powell, George Chuvalo, and Tod Herring. He was especially emboldened by the win over Chuvalo, a hard puncher from Toronto. He felt he had straightened out his style, and his head, since the two Liston fights. He felt ready. "I wasn't really ready for Liston," Patterson said. "I was ready for Clay."

Usually, Patterson was the most available of men for reporters, but as fight week approached he became shut off, aloof. Rumors circulated around town that Patterson had once more brought his old disguises to the arena. Patterson denied it.

"I had such high hopes for this fight, so much riding on it, so many people cheering for me," Patterson told Gay Talese later. "I remember how, on the morning of the fight, Frank Sinatra had asked to see me, and I was escorted over to his suite in the Sands Hotel by Al Silvani, a friend of Sinatra's who was one of my trainers. I really did not know Silvani very well before the fight, but Sinatra had called me up earlier in the year after the death of my trainer, Dan Florio, and said that if I wanted Al Silvani to help me I could have him. I did not say yes at first. I thought it over, and decided to wait. Then Sinatra called again and said I could have Silvani, who was then working in Sinatra's film company, and finally I said okay, and Silvani, two days before the fight, arrived in Las Vegas to help train me for Cassius Clay, and on the morning of the fight Silvani escorted me to Sinatra's suite, and Sinatra was very nice that morning, very encouraging. He told me I could win, how many people in America were counting on me to win back the championship from Clay."

Once more, Floyd Patterson entered the ring stamped with prestigious endorsements.

ON THE NIGHT OF THE FIGHT, THE SECOND ANNIVERSARY OF the assassination of John Kennedy, it rained in the desert, torrential rains that cut down on the walk-up trade at the Convention Center. The gate was around eight thousand, grossing just over a quarter million dollars, though the promoters would be pleased by ticket sales at the theaters, especially in Europe. Ali had wanted a black performer to sing the national anthem; the promoters went with Eddie Fisher. Patterson wore an elaborate red velvet robe into the ring, while Ali wore the sort of white terry-cloth robe one of the old men on Collins Avenue, back home in Florida, would wear to the beach. Ali seemed to approach the affair with a sense not of spectacle and occasion but of grim duty. He was intent on proving to Patterson just how badly he had miscalculated, what a serious mistake he had made in supposing the way to the public's heart in 1965 was to declare oneself the champion of accommodation.

"Ali was a beautiful warrior and he was reflecting a new posture for a black man," said Toni Morrison. "I don't like boxing, but he was a thing apart. His grace was almost *appalling*." Patterson, however, was misreading Ali. He would pay for it now.

The fight would be painful to watch, and the first round was the worst of all. Like a superb flyweight, Ali darted around the ring, a waterbug skimming the canvas and the ropes. For the entire three minutes he threw not a single serious punch. His intention was humiliation, athletic, psychological, political, and religious. What could have been more demoralizing for Patterson? As Ali danced, as he easily leaned away from Patterson's lugubrious attempts at attack, the champion taunted the challenger:

"Come on, American! Come on, *white* American!"

Ali was so fast and wanted so badly to rile Patterson that he moved around the ring *faking* punches, feinting, bobbing, jerking his shoulders, all to make Patterson respond and reveal his reflexive fear.

Then in the second round, Ali added the jab to this humbling recipe, flicking it at Patterson's face every time he dared come near.

"I took a swing at him and missed, and got a muscle spasm, and after that I could not swing without great pain," Patterson said later. "In fact I could not even stand up straight, and the pain was unlike anything I've ever felt, and in the later rounds I was hoping that Clay would knock me out. It is not pleasant admitting this, but it's the truth."

Patterson was not fibbing. His back really was bothering him, and between rounds his cornermen, Buster Watson and Al Silvani, tried to relieve his pain by picking him up and massaging the muscles in his neck and lower back. Patterson moved well enough, perhaps three quarters as well as usual, but that was not near well enough to come close to Ali.

Round after round, Ali circled Patterson, jabbing, throwing left hooks from the hip, throwing right leads, doing whatever he felt like, and at the same time chattering away at Patterson, taunting him to try harder, to punch harder.

"Cut the cackle!" the referee, Harry Krause, told him, but Ali did not.

Ali was beating Patterson badly, hammering him with hooks to the head, and yet he seemed content to keep Patterson on his feet, keep the spectacle going. He would not—or could not—end it. By the sixth round Patterson was so exhausted and battered that after absorbing a left hook he simply dropped to one knee for a few seconds, accepting an official knockdown. But he would not stop, and Ali would not put an end to it. At the end of each round, Ali waved at Patterson in disdain. In the clinches he called him Uncle Tom, Uncle Tom, white man's nigger.

"No contest!" he shouted at Patterson. "Get me a contender!"

"Ali, knock him out for Christ's sake!" Dundee shouted through the ropes.

Sitting at ringside, Robert Lipsyte of the *Times* thought that Ali was treating Patterson the way a cruel child might treat a butterfly, picking off the wings. He used that image to lead his story in the next morning's paper.

Harry Krause moved in to stop the fight after the eleventh, but Patterson would not let him. Patterson was still the only man in history to hold the heavyweight title twice, and now he was fighting for it a third time. Krause was not likely to overrule him. It was only in the twelfth round that it became obvious that to allow Patterson to go on would be to be complicit in his permanent injury.

"I wanted to go down with something that would be worthy of a knockout," Patterson admitted later to Talese. "But in the tenth and eleventh rounds Cassius Clay wasn't landing anything good. He was just jabbing. Then in the twelfth round, Clay became a punching maniac. He still took no chances but he came in and began landing punches here, here, here, here—punches began to land all over my head, and a very, very strange thing began to happen then. A happiness feeling came over me. I knew the end was near. The pain of standing up in the ring, that sharp knife in my back that accompanied every move I made, would soon end and I would soon be out. And as Clay began to land these punches, I was feeling groggy and happy. But then the referee stepped in to break us up, to stop Clay's punches. And you may remember, if you saw the fight in the films, seeing me turn to the referee, shaking my head, 'No, no!' Many people thought I was protesting his decision to stop the fight. I really was protesting his stopping those punches. I wanted to be hit by a really good one. I wanted to go out with a great punch, to go down that way."

Krause stopped the fight at 2:18 of the twelfth round. Patterson's seconds practically carried him from the ring. As always after a loss, he was in the mood to apologize. "I can do much, much better, that I know," Patterson said.

The crowd had not liked the fight at all. As Ali climbed through the ropes and headed down the steps, the boos rolled in once more. Like many of the writers at ringside, the fans had obviously seen cruelty in Ali that night. They thought he had carried Patterson round after round. Ali denied it, somewhat lamely, when he said, "I hit him so regular and so hard I had to back off to keep from wearing myself out."

Ali went to the victory party at the Sands Hotel in the company of twenty members of the Nation and three Muslim women from Pakistan. His right hand was so sore that he accepted congratulations only with his left.

Off in a corner, Sonji watched Ali. She was crying, and it was left to her fellow exile, Bundini, to console her.

"Go to the living room and fix yourself," he told her. "You don't want all these people to see you crying. It isn't the end of the world."

As Sonji left, Ali's eyes followed her across the room.

"She loves him and he loves her," Bundini told a friend from

Louisville. "It's a shame the Muslims had to separate them. She clings to the hope that Cassius will eventually renounce them and take her back. If he would, she would be the happiest woman in the world and he would be happier, too. I know him better than anybody."

Sonji made a good show of recovering. Harold Conrad's wife asked her to show off her slinky red dress, and she got up and took a turn. Ali looked over, but not for long. Later, while Ali sat at a table with the Muslims and the girls from Pakistan, Sonji sat in Cassius Clay, Sr.'s, lap. Finally, Ali went home to sleep and Sonji went out with Bundini to hear Dean Martin at one of the hotels. "He sang 'Agita,' " Bundini said. "A perfect song."

PATTERSON VISITED FRANK SINATRA IN HIS SUITE AND APOLO-gized for his performance. No heavyweight champion had ever done more apologizing in his life. The singer was having none of it. "Sinatra was a very different guy after I lost to Clay," Patterson said at the time. "I was talking to him in his suite and then he did a strange thing. He got up and walked all the way over to the other side of the room, and he sat down there, so far away that I could hardly talk to him. I got the message. I left."

In fact, it was left to Ali to console the loser. Now that he had proved his superiority in the ring, Ali was free to be magnanimous. At a session with photographers for the April 1966 issue of *Esquire*, he asked how Patterson's back was feeling and whether it was responding to treatments.

Patterson told the reporters that they should appreciate the champion. "He's only twenty-four years old," he said, "an entertainer, a very individualistic young man whose life is far from easy. They should make allowances for him."

"Floyd, you should get honors and medals for the spot you was on, a good, clean, American boy fighting for America," Ali said. "All those movie stars behind you, they should make sure you never have to work another day in your life. It would be a disgrace on the government if you had to end up scuffling somewhere."

Then Patterson paid the champion the highest compliment he could think of. He called him by his proper name.

Berrien Springs, Michigan, 1989. With Lonnie.

EPILOGUE:
OLD MEN BY THE FIRE

Three months after Ali beat Patterson, he began his fight with the United States government. An already complicated history with his draft board was about to become more so. In 1960, when he was eighteen, he had registered in Louisville. In 1962, he was classified 1-A. Two years later, just a few weeks before the first Liston fight, he was ordered to go to an army induction center in Coral Gables to take the physical and written examinations given to all draftees. He failed the fifty-minute-long aptitude test, registering a score so low that the army declared his IQ to be 78.

Afterward, he sheepishly explained that not only could he not get the answers, he did not know how to approach the questions. He was humiliated by the experience, but, as always, tried to undercut it all with humor. "I said I was the greatest," he told everyone. "Not the smartest." The army put him at the sixteenth percentile—fourteen points below passing—and reclassified him 1-Y, ineligible for active service. Two months later, with Ali now world champion, the army retested him to make sure he wasn't feigning ignorance. He wasn't.

A couple of years later, after the Patterson fight, Bob Lipsyte came down to Miami to do some feature stories on Ali and cover the start of spring training. "I remember waking up that morning in my hotel and watching a session of the Senate Foreign Relations Committee on TV, the first really sharp debates on Vietnam," Lipsyte recalled. "William Fulbright was chairman and he and Senator Wayne Morse were really going at it with Maxwell Taylor, the general. Taylor had that jock certainty that generals had. This was early 1966. The mood in the country was still anti-peacenik, pro-war. The tide had not yet turned. But with this debate you could feel the pulse of something happening."

In the early afternoon, Lipsyte drove over to Ali's house, a low-slung concrete house in a black neighborhood. The two men sat outside in plastic lawn chairs. Ali was training but he was finished working for the day. School had just let out and Ali watched the high school girls go by, commenting on each one in a harmless, pass-the-afternoon sort of way. Several of Ali's Muslim friends were around—Captain Sam and some of the others—and one came out and told Ali he was wanted on the phone. It was one of the wire services. The reporter told Ali that in the midst of escalating its troop levels in Vietnam, the army had changed its policy: his score on the qualifying exam was now good enough. Ali had been reclassified once more. He was 1-A. He could soon expect a call from his draft board. Did he have any comment?

"Ali came back outside and his mood had changed completely. He was fuming," Lipsyte said. "Until that moment, I was thinking how wonderful this was, how you could step into this sanctuary, this time warp, where nothing had anything to do with the war. I'd been in the army, at Fort Dix, where I wrote about brave cooks in New Jersey. I'd been the valedictorian of the clerk-typist school. I was already a *Times* reporter. My dispatches were so brilliant that *The Philadelphia Inquirer* called me and asked if I wanted a job. I didn't really understand the war. I dimly thought Fulbright was right and the war was wrong but I wasn't into it yet. I was a twenty-eight-year-old careerist sportswriter.

"Ali knew even less about the war than I did. It wasn't on his radar screen at all," Lipsyte went on. "As he kept going back inside for more phone calls and the TV trucks started appearing, the Muslim chorus was chortling. They had all been in the army. They came to the Muslims after hard times, after jail, after the army, and they started telling Ali, 'Of course, the Man is gonna do whatever the fuck he wants to do with you.' They told him how some cracker sergeant would drop a hand grenade in his pants and blow his balls off."

The calls were coming nonstop now. This was a big story, evoking memories of other young athletes and pop stars drafted at the peak of their careers: Joe Louis, Ted Williams, Elvis Presley. But this was different, this was Vietnam, a far more ambiguous and confusing event. It was confusing, not least, to Muhammad Ali. By now he was accustomed to being asked about racial politics, but now he was hearing new questions: What do you think of LBJ? What's your view of the draft? What do you think about the war? What about the Vietcong? For a while, Ali stumbled.

"Then all of sudden he hit the note," Lipsyte remembered.

"Man," Ali finally told one reporter, "I ain't got no quarrel with them Vietcong."

The line came and went so quickly that Lipsyte missed it when he sat down to write. "No question that I blew that story." But enough papers and television stations did pick up the quote that it became the stuff of instant folklore. Eventually, *The New York Times,* too, ran the quote. As he had been before and as he would be again and again, Ali was the lead actor in his own improvisational American drama. He may not have been able to locate Vietnam on a map yet, and he knew almost nothing about the politics of the war, but when he was thrust into the midst of the national agony, he reacted, as he did in the ring, with speed and with wit: *I ain't got no quarrel with them Vietcong.*

"It was *the* moment for Ali," Lipsyte said. "For the rest of his life he would be loved and hated for what seemed like a declarative statement, but what was, at the time, a moment of blurted improvisation." As he had before and would again, Ali had showed his gift for intuitive action, for speed, and this time he was acting in a way that would characterize the era itself, a resistance to authority, an insistence that national loyalty was not automatic or absolute. His rebellion, which had started out as racial, had now widened in its scope.

In the coming days and months, Ali's phones rang incessantly, with calls not only from reporters, but from people who wanted to express their hatred, to tell him they hoped he'd die. But others called in their support, including the British philosopher and pacifist Bertrand Russell.

"In the coming months," Russell wrote to Ali later, "there is no doubt that the men who rule Washington will try to damage you in every way open to them, but I am sure you know that you spoke for your people and for the oppressed everywhere in the courageous defiance of American power. They will try to break you because you are a symbol of a force they are unable to destroy, namely, the aroused consciousness of a whole people determined no longer to be butchered and debased with fear and oppression. You have my wholehearted support. Call me when you get to England."

At about the time Ali got Russell's letter, the government confiscated his passport. From then on, Ali took a fiercely political stand and went from one college campus to the next, speaking out against the war. He learned more about Vietnam and deepened his understanding of what was happening both to the country and to himself. He would not kill Vietnamese on behalf of a government that barely recognized the humanity of his own people. In the short term, the decision not to serve cost Ali everything: his title, his popularity among millions of people, and, undoubtedly, millions of dollars. The members of the Louisville Sponsoring Group knew they were on their way out as Ali's business management team, but all the same they quickly helped line up cushy ways for Ali to get credit for army service: the reserves, National Guard duty. If worse came to worst, they figured, the army would have Ali put on boxing exhibitions for the troops. This way, they thought, Ali, like Joe Louis before him, could enhance his public image without risking his life and fortune. "But to his credit, Muhammad refused all that," said the Louisville Group's lawyer, Gordon Davidson. "This was a real point of principle for him and he wasn't about to make it easy on himself. He created this sense of himself and he stuck to it."

Ali, of course, was instantly denounced by Jimmy Cannon, Red Smith, Arthur Daley, all those columnists whose notion of how a heavyweight champion should behave had been formed in the Louis years. "Cassius makes himself as sorry a spectacle as those unwashed punks who picket and demonstrate against the war," Red Smith wrote. Various senators and congressmen declared Ali a traitor and a pariah. Even his hometown legislature, the Kentucky state senate, felt compelled to issue a proclamation saying he brought "discredit to all loyal Kentuckians and to the names of the thousands who gave their lives for this country during his lifetime."

Over the next year, Ali fought a series of contenders—George

Chuvalo, Henry Cooper, Brian London, Karl Mildenberger, Cleveland Williams, Ernie Terrell—while his draft drama played itself out. Ali's defeat of Terrell, on February 6, 1967, was especially brutal, not least because, like Patterson, Terrell refused to call Ali "Ali." Terrell accused Ali of thumbing him and fighting dirty in the clinches, which Ali denied. As Ali jabbed Terrell, he chanted "What's my name? What's my name?" The columnists who were furious at Ali for his position on Vietnam seized on the Terrell fight, a lopsided fifteen-round decision, as a metaphor for the champion's evil. "This, the Black Muslims claim, is one of their ministers. What kind of clergyman is he?" wrote Jimmy Cannon in a particularly perverse piece for the *New York World-Journal & Telegram.* "He agrees with the people who are the enemy of ministers. The Black Muslims demand that Negroes keep their place. They go along with the Klan on segregation. It seemed right that Cassius Clay had a good time beating another Negro. This was fun, like chasing them with dogs and knocking them down with streams of water."

All the while, Ali was under surveillance by the Federal Bureau of Investigation, getting the same treatment that Malcolm X and Martin Luther King, Jr., had been getting from the bureau for years. J. Edgar Hoover got regular reports on everything from Ali's travels and phone calls to his appearances on television talk shows. He was now, in the eyes of the bureau, a greater subversive than Jack Johnson had ever been. His legal advisers were certainly giving him little hope; jail was a real possibility and the end of his fighting career almost a certainty. Ali's lawyer, Hayden Covington, told him, "It looks like trouble, Champ. This isn't like any case I've had before. Joe Namath can get off to play football and George Hamilton gets out because he's going with the president's daughter, but you're different. They want to make an example out of you."

As time passed and the government put pressure on him, Ali made his stance firmer, clearer. He would not fight exhibitions for the army. He would not move abroad. "Why should they ask me to put on a uniform and go ten thousand miles from home and drop bombs and bullets on brown people in Vietnam while so-called Negro people in Louisville are treated like dogs?" he said to a reporter for *Sports Illustrated.* "If I thought going to war would bring freedom and equality to twenty-two million of my people, they wouldn't have to draft me. I'd join tomorrow. But I either have to obey the laws of the land or the laws of Allah. I have nothing to lose by standing up and following my beliefs. We've been in jail for four hundred years."

On the morning of April 28, 1967, Ali appeared at the U.S. Armed Forces Examining and Entrance Station on San Jacinto Street in Houston, where he had been summoned to face induction. On the sidewalk, a group of protesters, mainly students but some older people, too, was already there chanting, "Don't go! Don't go!" "Draft beer—not Ali!" H. Rap Brown, one of the leading activists from the Student Nonviolent Coordinating Committee, was shouting, "Hep! Hep! Don't take that step!" Brown flashed Ali the raised fist, the black power sign, and Ali answered in kind. Then he went inside to face army induction.

"It's hard now to relay the emotion of that time," said Sonia Sanchez, the poet and civil rights activist. "This was still a time when hardly any well-known people were resisting the draft. It was a war that was disproportionately killing young black brothers, and here was this beautiful, funny, poetical young man standing up and saying no! Imagine it for a moment! The heavyweight champion, a magical man, taking his fight out of the ring and into the arena of politics, and standing firm. The message that sent!"

Ali and twenty-five other potential recruits were told to fill out papers, undergo physical examinations, and then wait for the long bus ride to Fort Polk, Louisiana. In the early afternoon, the recruits lined up in front of a young lieutenant, S. Steven Dunkley, for one last formality. The officer called each man's name and told him to take another step forward—and into the armed forces. Finally, Ali's name was called—"Cassius Clay! Army!" Ali did not move. He was called "Ali" and again he remained still. Then another officer led Ali to a private room and advised him that the penalty for refusing the draft was five years imprisonment and a fine. Did he understand? Yes, he did. Ali was given another chance to respond to his name and step forward. Again he stood still. There was no fear in Ali, none of the anxiety he'd felt in those few minutes warming up in the ring before facing Liston for the first time. Finally, one of the induction officers told Ali to write out a statement with his reasons for refusal.

"I refuse to be inducted into the armed forces of the United States," Ali wrote, "because I claim to be exempt as a minister of the religion of Islam."

Ali stepped outside the building and into a hive of reporters. The protesters were still there, too, and shouted encouragement. But even years later, Ali also remembered a woman carrying a small American flag and shouting, "You're headin' straight for jail! You get down on your knees and beg forgiveness from God! My son's in Vietnam and you no better than he is. I hope you rot in jail."

Ali's refusal to go to Vietnam touched young people, especially young African-Americans, profoundly. Gerald Early, a professor of literature who has written deeply on the "culture of bruising," recalled that moment in 1967 in his essay "Tales of the Wonderboy": "When he refused, I felt something greater than pride: I felt as though my honor as a black boy had been defended, my honor as a human being. He was the grand knight, after all, the dragon-slayer. And I felt myself, little inner-city boy that I was, his apprentice to the grand imagination, the grand daring. The day that Ali refused the draft, I cried in my room. I cried for him and for myself, for my future and his, for all our black possibilities."

Ali was sentenced to five years in prison and a ten-thousand-dollar fine—the maximum. Eventually, in June 1971, the Supreme Court would vindicate him in a unanimous decision, but after knocking out Zora Folley one month after refusing the draft, he would not fight for three and a half years, the prime of his boxing life. He would not regain the heavyweight championship until 1974, when he outfoxed George Foreman on the ropes in Kinshasa, Zaire. "I figure that decision cost him ten million dollars in purses, endorsements, and the rest," said Gordon Davidson. It also cost him the goodwill of many Americans who thought that he was a rich young man in perfect health avoiding military service and using religion as an excuse. But Ali would never regret the price. He watched his old friend from Louisville, Jimmy Ellis, and then Joe Frazier, take his title. *His* title, which he had coveted from the time he was twelve. But even for a young man in love with his fame, there were greater priorities. "I was determined to be one nigger that the white man didn't get," he told *Black Scholar* magazine. "One nigger that you didn't get, white man. You understand? One nigger you ain't going to get."

. . .

As Ali fought the courts, his old antagonist Sonny Liston stumbled toward oblivion. In 1966, Liston bought a house on Ottawa Drive in Las Vegas. The house was a pastel-green split-level just off the sixteenth fairway of the Stardust Country Club. The business magnate Kirk Kerkorian had lived there. The Listons had two Cadillacs: black-and-green for Sonny, pink for Geraldine. Geraldine had her silver tea service plated with gold. You didn't have to polish it as often. There were two pairs of boxing gloves in the living room: a bronzed pair from one of Liston's fights and a mink pair in honor of Geraldine.

Liston renewed his friendships with Ash Resnik and assorted undesirables. He played a lot of blackjack, and at night he either drank at the casinos or drank at home in front of the television. In Las Vegas, the police gave him the sort of breaks he never got in St. Louis, Philadelphia, or Denver. When they pulled him over in his black Fleetwood and could smell the J&B on his breath, they let him go on home.

"It's really nice for us here, I gotta say that," Liston told a reporter from *Sports Illustrated*. "At all the hotels I never have to pay for nothin', they always pick up the tab."

For a while Liston talked about regaining the championship, but the truth was that after the Ali fights he defeated a string of second-raters and then got knocked out by one of his old sparring partners, Leotis Martin. For his next—and last—fight, Liston took on Chuck Wepner in Jersey City, a brawl that left Wepner, "the Bayonne Bleeder," with gashes requiring fifty-seven stitches. The purse was thirteen thousand dollars. "The trouble was that Sonny had bet ten thousand on another fight—Jerry Quarry–Mac Foster—and lost. Plus, he owed three thousand to his corner," said his friend the gambler Lem Banker, who flew back home with Sonny. "He handed over the cash in brown paper bags and went back to Vegas with zip. Zip exactly."

Liston would often drive out to Lake Mead and, sitting alone in a small motorboat, drink beer and drop a line for fish. Perhaps the sweetest moments of his last days were the early mornings when he took long runs with his friend Davey Pearl, a referee, who had worked his corner in Jersey City. "We'd be out there, running in the morning light with the sprinklers going on some deserted golf course, and I think for that time, anyway, Sonny was in good shape," Pearl said. "But the thing with Sonny was that no matter how close you got to him—and we were close—you always got the feeling that there was sadness there that he wouldn't talk about." Liston was a man of severe limitations and an acute awareness of them. When his old friend Father Edward Murphy asked him why he didn't get involved in the civil rights movement, Liston dropped his old sarcasm ("'Cause I ain't got no dogproof ass") and said, more poignantly, "If I was to get involved, I'd find myself at the head of some march and have to say something, and I wouldn't know what to say." Especially now, without the glitter of a championship belt to attract all manner of leeches, Liston was a lonely man. "Many times I was around with Sonny Liston and he said, 'You like me, don't you?' Like a little kid would," his old sparring partner Ray Schoeninger once said. "I says, 'Sure, I like you.' And he says, 'You know, I like you, too.' I think because of his terrible background, he was looking for someone who didn't criticize him and who didn't hit him with a club or a stick."

According to friends who are still around, Liston was always hard up for cash and worked, on the side, in his old job, as an enforcer—this time for loan sharks and, possibly, drug dealers. Banker, who was one of the most successful gamblers in town and a close friend of Liston's, said that in the last weeks of 1970 he got a call from a Las Vegas sheriff who told him that Sonny was getting involved with the "wrong people" and that he'd better watch it if he didn't want to get caught up in an imminent drug raid.

In late December, Geraldine left Las Vegas to visit her mother in St. Louis. When she came home on the evening of January 5, 1971, she found a corpse. Sonny lay dead in his underwear on a bench at the foot of their bed. His body was bloated and dried blood came from his nose. Geraldine had not spoken to Sonny since she'd left. Newspapers were stacked up outside the door. Police estimated that Liston had been dead around six days. Las Vegas police sources said that Geraldine called her lawyer but may have waited as long as two hours to call the police. The police found a small amount of marijuana, a syringe, and a "balloon" of heroin, a few hits' worth, in a cabinet. They also found a .38 revolver and a glass of vodka on a table near the bed. The autopsy revealed traces of morphine and codeine of a type produced by the breakdown of heroin in the body, and yet the report listed the cause of death as lung congestion and heart failure.

The most prevalent theory of Liston's death, among both his friends and the police, is that he was murdered, that he was given a "hot shot"—a lethal dose of heroin—by someone he'd crossed, someone who wanted him out of the way. Gary Beckwith, a sergeant and an undercover narcotics detective on the scene, said that the police were never satisfied with the death report and began investigating the possibility that a former Las Vegas police detective might have been involved in a hit on Liston. The detective in question, Beckwith said, was also convicted of some robberies in the area. The theory had it that the detective killed Liston on behalf of Resnik, who was furious at Liston for not taking a dive in one of his last fights.

"We tried every way in the world to prove that," Beckwith said. "We went after this former detective for the robberies and we tried to corroborate this part of his story, but we were never able to come up with a shred of evidence along these lines. I have doubts myself."

Harold Conrad talked to various mobsters and cops in Las Vegas in the years after Liston's death, and he, too, heard the theory of a bad cop killing him on contract. But Conrad was sure only that Liston had come to the sort of end that was always expected, the end Sonny Liston always expected himself. "I talked to a guy I knew in the Vegas sheriff's office, and here's what he said: 'A bad nigger. He got what was coming to him,' " Conrad said. "I don't buy that. He had some good qualities, but I think he died the day he was born."

LISTON GOT A TRUE LAS VEGAS FUNERAL. GERALDINE SAID that Sonny had always said that if "anything happened to him," his last wish would be to go down the Strip one last time. The funeral began with a service for four hundred people at the Palm Mortuary. The pews were filled with Vegas royalty and near-royalty: Nipsy Russell, Ed Sullivan, Ella Fitzgerald, Jerry Vale, Jack E. Leonard, Doris Day. Joe Louis came a little late because he was shooting craps. "Sonny would understand," he said before putting down the dice. Father Murphy flew in from Denver to deliver the eulogy.

"We should only speak good of the dead," he said. "Sonny had qualities that most people didn't know about." A choir sang "Just a Closer Walk with Thee." The Ink Spots sang "Sunny."

As the funeral cortege inched down the Strip, gamblers came out of the casinos, blinking in the sunlight, to watch the heavy-weight champion in his steel coffin go by for the last time. "People came out of their hotels to watch him pass," Father Murphy said. "They stopped everything. They used him all his life. They were still using him on the way to the cemetery. There he was, another Las Vegas show. God help us."

Liston was buried in Paradise Memorial Gardens, a green oasis in the desert at Patrick Lane and Eastern Avenue. The cemetery is right near the airport landing strip. The grave is in row one of the "Peace" section. A plaque one foot square reads, "Charles 'Sonny' Liston, 1932–1970. A Man."

TWENTY-SIX YEARS LATER, ANOTHER FORMER HEAVYWEIGHT champion and former inmate, Mike Tyson, went out to Paradise Memorial Gardens to lay a bouquet of flowers on Liston's grave. They were the only flowers there and they baked and dried quickly in the early summer sun. Tyson was fighting for the title in a few days against Evander Holyfield. When he was not watching gang-ster movies late into the night, Tyson would occasionally slip a tape into the VCR and watch Liston working out to the tune of "Night Train." To watch Liston work, Tyson said, was "orgasmic."

"Sonny Liston, I identify with him the most," Tyson said one af-ternoon at Don King's house on the edge of Las Vegas. "That may sound morbid and grim, but I pretty much identify with that life. He wanted people to respect him or love him, but it never hap-pened. You can't make people respect and love you by craving it. You've got to *demand* it.

"People may not have liked him because of his background, but the people who got to know him as an intimate person have a to-tally different opinion. He had a wife. I'm sure she didn't think he was a piece of garbage. . . . Everyone respected Sonny Liston's ability. The point is respecting him as a man. No one can second-guess my ability, either. But I'm going to be respected. I demand that."

It was uncanny, the similarities between Tyson and Liston: both poor kids who grew up in unstable homes, criminals at an early age, who learned that their only way out of a humiliating life was through fighting. They were men who trusted no one, not when they had the title and not later. Tyson did his time for rape, Liston did his for armed robbery. Like Muhammad Ali, Tyson had the advantage of fluent speech and money (he made tens of millions), but he wasn't Ali-like in any way. There was no pleasure in his talk; his wit was acid, self-lacerating. Tyson felt alone and headed toward a bad end. He felt like Sonny Liston.

"I have no friends, man," Tyson said. "When I got out of prison, all my old friends, they had to go. If you don't have a purpose in my life, man, you have to go. . . . Why would you want someone around in your life if they have no purpose? Just to have a pal or a buddy? I got a wife. My wife can be my pal and buddy. I'm not trying to be cold, but it's something I picked up. . . . If I'm gonna get screwed, I'm not gonna get screwed over by the people that screwed me before. I'm gonna get screwed by the *new* people. . . .

"I've been taken advantage of all my life," Tyson went on. "I've been used, I've been dehumanized, I've been humiliated, and I've been betrayed. That's basically the outcome of my life, and I'm kind of bitter, kind of angry at certain people about it. . . . Everyone in boxing makes out well except for the fighter. He's the only one who suffers, basically. He's the only one who's on Skid Row. He's the only one who loses his mind. He sometimes goes insane, he sometimes goes on the bottle, because it's a highly intensive, pressure sport, and a lot of people lose it. There's so much you can take and then you break."

A few nights later, Tyson went into the ring with Holyfield, and when he discovered that he was no longer what he once was, that he could not muscle Holyfield around the ring, he snapped. He bit off a chunk of Holyfield's ear. And then he bit him again.

"My career is over," he said in the locker room after the fight. "It's over. I know that."

AFTER HIS FIGHTING DAYS WERE DONE, FLOYD PATTERSON RE-tired to New Paltz, New York, where he ran the Huguenot Boys'

Club and trained young boxers at no charge. "That's what kept me off the street when I was a kid, so I wanted to do the same for someone else," he told me. In 1995, the new governor, George Pataki, appointed Patterson head of the New York State Athletic Commission, which handled the state's boxing and wrestling shows. The salary was $76,421 and the job was not very demanding. Boxing had long ago faded from New York and migrated to Las Vegas and Atlantic City. There wasn't very much for Patterson to do. And yet it was clear that he could barely handle his duties, and did so mainly through the efforts of a few discreet aides in the various state offices. There had been rumors for years that Patterson's memory was failing, that he was feeling the effect, at last, of sixty-four professional bouts and countless knockdowns, but no one was eager to embarrass a decent man. Patterson's condition was an open secret among boxing reporters, but for a long time no one printed anything. So what if he held the office? It was a patronage sinecure for a guy who deserved it.

When I interviewed Patterson, he looked, at sixty-three, almost exactly as he had as heavyweight champion: the same trim, sinewy build, the same wide, pleading eyes, the same little pompadour. To meet him was to realize how incredible it was that he had ever been heavyweight champion or that he had ever been in the ring with Liston or Ali. He was of mortal size. Only his hands, which were swollen, sandpapery, and huge, gave any hint of power. As we talked, Patterson repeated himself occasionally and forgot names and places and dates, but he wasn't "out of it" so much as he was insecure about his ability to stay on a subject and remember details.

"Do I sound to you like someone who's been damaged by boxing?" he said at one point. "Don't I sound perfectly normal? I love boxing. Boxing is wonderful. Boxing's given me everything in the world."

A few months later, in March 1998, Patterson was called on to give an extensive deposition in a legal case involving the promoters of "ultimate fighting," a brand of organized mayhem banned in New York. The deposition was a disaster for Patterson. He was questioned under oath by a lawyer named David Meyrowitz for more than three hours:

Question: Who did you fight [for the heavyweight title in 1956]?

Patterson: I'd have to think about that. . . . I can't remember the opponent I fought, but I wound up beating him to become heavyweight champion of the world. . . .

Q: Where did the fight take place?

Patterson: I really don't know. I think it was in New York. . . .

Q: Do you know the name of your predecessor?

Patterson: Yes, I am going to get that out. Just a minute. (Searches his pockets.) I have it here. (He is unable to find it.)

Q: Mr. Patterson, do you know the name of your predecessor, chairman of the New York State Athletic Commission?

Patterson: Yes, I do know, but, uh, I didn't get that much sleep last night to tell you the truth and I am very, very tired and it's hard to think when I'm tired. . . .

Q: Do you know the names of the other two commissioners who were commissioners at the time you were appointed?

Patterson: No. . . .

Q: Do you know the names of the other commissioners of the New York State Athletic Commission?

Patterson: Uh, yes and no. I know them, but it's hard for me to think. I didn't get to bed till very late last night. . . .

Q: The other two commissioners?

Patterson: One's a lady and one's a man.

Q: Do you have the telephone number of that office [the commission in Poughkeepsie]?

Patterson: I have the number at home.

Q: Would you know it here?

Patterson: No. . . .

Q: What's the secretary's name?

Patterson: Oh boy. . . . I see her quite often, I know her very well. I just forget the name. . . .

And so on. The painful session took place on March 20 and made the papers ten days later. Patterson couldn't place the name of the commission's lawyer, he didn't know the most basic rules of boxing (the size of the ring, the number of rounds in a championship bout), and he generally seemed lost. The fact that he could not remember the greatest night of his life—his win over Archie Moore in Chicago, in 1956, to win the title—devastated him.

"What are we talking about?" he said at one point. "I'm lost." He allowed that when he was tired he was bad with names: "Sometimes, I can't even remember my wife's name, and I've been married thirty-two, thirty-three years."

When the *New York Post* made it clear that the paper was going to publish a story about the deposition, Patterson quickly wrote a letter to Governor George Pataki resigning his post.

"It's hard for me to think when I'm tired," Patterson said. "Sometimes, I can't even remember my own name."

ALL THE BEST HEAVYWEIGHTS DURING ALI'S TIME AND AFTER— Patterson, Liston, Joe Frazier, George Foreman, Larry Holmes, Mike Tyson, Evander Holyfield—have languished in his shadow. They have all been good fighters, even excellent ones, but they could never hope to achieve Ali's resonance, his brilliance. "I came to love Ali," Patterson told me. "I came to see that I was a fighter and he was history."

Ali may turn out to have been the pinnacle of boxing and also its end. His successors came at a time when boxing itself is fading away. One by one, the most famous gyms in the country are shuting down. The Fifth Street Gym, the Gramercy Gym, Stillman's, the Times Square Gym: all gone. Arenas like Madison Square Garden put on, at most, a few shows a year. Boxing is becoming the anachronistic entertainment of gambling towns, on a par with Wayne Newton and Siegfried and Roy. More and more women are watching and participating in sports like basketball, baseball, even hockey, but they will not watch boxing; as a result, the networks show almost no boxing at all on the Olympics broadcasts. And, not least, boxing, a sport designed to stun the brain, is finally indefensible. Boxing has come to represent an utter lack of opportunity, not opportunity itself. There is beauty in it—there is terrible beauty in battle, too, particularly for the noncombatant—but if you meet enough former boxers, if you try to decipher their punch-drunk talk, you begin to wonder. What beauty is worth this? What is worth Floyd Patterson's confusion? What is worth Jerry Quarry left so damaged after all the pounding or Wilfred Benitez left raging at his ghosts? And these were the *top* fighters, the men who meted out more punishment than they got. What of the would-bes, the professional opponents with records of 47–44, their ears cauli-flowered and their minds forever rattled? What of them?

Ali, like so many before him, was sure he would have the sense to get out of boxing in time. "I don't intend to leave it with ugly sou-venirs of my career," he said when he was in his mid-twenties. "I won't retire from boxing with cuts, cauliflower ears, and a busted nose. I'll leave boxing physically intact, just as I am now. I will do this because my style of boxing protects me from cuts and injuries, yet it wins. I beat my opponents, you might say, gently. . . ."

Ali thought his style would go a long way toward saving him from the usual injuries and indignities. "I cannot be touched!" he always shouted. But when he returned from his long exile, his speed was limited; it came only in short bursts. He had to learn dif-ferent ways to fight. Perhaps his most vexed discovery in his sec-ond career was that he could take a punch. And he took hundreds of them: from Frazier, Foreman, Ken Norton, Ernie Shavers, Holmes, Leon Spinks; from a parade of second-rung heavyweights like Jean-Pierre Coopman, Alfredo Evangelista, and Trevor Berbick; from a platoon of sparring partners who were instructed to bang away at Ali in the gym, the better to toughen him up for the bouts themselves. Learning to take a punch was a form of short-term survival for Ali—it was the secret to the great triumphs in Zaire and the Philippines—but it was a long-term disaster.

One spring afternoon, I visited Ferdie Pacheco, who lives in a gated community in Miami. He spends most of his time painting, writing fiction, and doing television commentary for the occa-sional fight. Pacheco resigned from Ali's camp after the Shavers fight in 1977, which Ali won by decision only after absorbing enor-mous punishment. Pacheco learned after that fight that Ali's kid-neys were deteriorating; in fact, he had been convinced since the third Frazier fight in Manila in 1975 that Ali was in real danger of suffering brain damage if he didn't retire. Pacheco sent medical re-ports to Ali, to his wife, Veronica, and to Herbert Muhammad. None of them responded except to brush him off. So Pacheco de-cided it was time to go. The rest of the entourage, including Angelo Dundee, stayed on. Everyone concerned—Ali included—was hooked on the money and the mainline thrills of the fights them-selves.

"Angelo had a feeling—misguided—but a feeling that if you start out with a fighter you should end up with him," Pacheco said. "Okay, but the fighter should listen to you when it's time to leave. And if he doesn't listen, then you should leave. With all great athletes, there comes a day when Babe Ruth is no longer Babe Ruth, when Joe Louis gets knocked out by an Italian sausage maker, and when John Barrymore can't do the soliloquy from *Hamlet*. There comes a day when you're through, when age knocks you out."

By the time Ali fought his last bouts, in 1981, against Larry Holmes in Las Vegas and against Trevor Berbick in the Bahamas, it is more than likely that his neurological deterioration had already begun. His speech was already slurred, and his reflexes were certainly not what they had been. Those fights were nothing short of criminal.

"But blame is a hard word," Pacheco said. "I'm not blaming anybody. They all slid into what they did, because of their belief that somehow, as he always did, Ali would find a way to win. They didn't understand that these victories were costing him physically, they didn't accept it, in spite of the fact that the punch-drunk syndrome is common in any boxing gym you walk into. They couldn't relate that to this big, wonderful, handsome guy who still looked the same. That's the problem. They *look* the same. I worked in Sugar Ray Robinson's corner in one of his last fights. He *looked* the same.

"The last time I saw Ali [medically] was in 1977. But I've watched his decline. Now I see him all the time. When I see him now, he says, 'Hi, Doc, how ya doing,' and he tells me that he's responsible for my success, which I agree with one hundred percent. He says he's surprised how we've progressed, he and I. But he says nothing. Platitudes and jokes and gags. I don't try to have a conversation with him. I've had all the conversations with him I want. There's nothing he can say to me or that I can say to him that can change what I know is going to happen to him.

"Luckily, he has what all of us would like to have: spiritual serenity. He's the only guy I know who's got it. He's got total peace of mind, because he's convinced himself that *here* isn't where it's at. Heaven is where it's at. And he's working hard as hell to get there, and he has the absolute knowledge he's going. See, Ali was unique. Ali and boxing are two different subjects. The only thing that Ali did that was pure boxing was the tragic end, which all boxers have if they've been too good and they won't quit. Joe Louis, Sugar Ray Leonard, Sugar Ray Robinson, George Foreman, Larry Holmes, Tommy Hearns. They just won't stop! So their end is tragic. That's the one thing, the *only* thing, that makes Ali just another boxer."

UP IN MICHIGAN, ALI SITS IN THE OFFICE ON HIS FARM. THE office is on the second floor of a small house behind the main house, and it is the headquarters of the company known as GOAT—the Greatest of All Times. Outside, geese glide along the pond. A few men are working in the fields. Someone is mowing the great lawn that rolls out from the house and up to the gates of the property. There are various fine cars around, including a Stutz Bearcat. There is a tennis court, a pool, and playground equipment sufficient for a small school in a well-taxed municipality. Ali is father to nine children; his oldest is Maryum, who is twenty-eight, and the youngest is Assad Ali, a six-year-old boy, whom Lonnie and Muhammad adopted. "Muhammad finally found a playmate," Lonnie said. "He wasn't around much for his other children, but now he gets to play with Assad all the time." The Alis have loved living on the farm, but they are looking for a buyer. They talked to some people who wanted to buy the place and convert it into a wellness center; they even tried to unload it on a television home-shopping network. Eventually, Lonnie said, the family will move back to Louisville, where they hope a Muhammad Ali center will be built. Ali's parents have died, but his brother still works in Louisville.

Ali's days begin before six with the first of five daily prayer sessions. Sometimes he prays in a gazebo out on the lawn or inside in the living room. Lonnie is also a Muslim believer and generally wears modest, if not entirely traditional, clothing. Ali's religious course has shifted with time. Elijah Muhammad died in 1975 and the Nation of Islam split between the followers of Muhammad's son Wallace, who sought to soften the Nation's doctrine by denying his father's divinity and moving closer to traditional Islam, and Louis X (now Louis Farrakhan), who considers Wallace a soft-minded heretic. Ali stayed with Wallace Muhammad, and one of Wallace's first gestures of reconciliation was to rename the New York mosque in honor of his father's old antagonist Malcolm X. In many ways, Ali has followed Malcolm's path. At first, Ali's membership in the Nation was largely political—a gesture of self-assertion and racial solidarity—but, like Malcolm, he has become more inclusive in his rhetoric and more devout. Everything about the Nation of Islam that was once so threatening or obscure—the separatist rhetoric that was greeted so heartily by the KKK, the talk of "big-headed" Yacub and mysterious spaceships—all that, for Ali, has been forgotten long ago.

Ali is intensely proud of his past, but if there is anything he looks back on with regret it is his cruel and hasty rejection of Malcolm. One of the first things Ali did when I met him in Berrien Springs was to open an enormous attaché case and pull out a photograph of himself and Malcolm taken by Howard Bingham in Miami just before the first Liston fight.

"That was Malcolm, a great, great man," he said in his low, whispery voice.

At home and on the road, Ali plays out certain routines with the people he meets every day. He certainly played them out with me. He likes to do magic tricks: he "elevates" on one foot; by rubbing two fingers together, he makes you think you're hearing a very annoying cricket behind your ear; he makes a small ball disappear. It's as if in doing these simple tricks he is reminding you, and himself, of the greater stunts of his career: the mock nervous breakdown at the weigh-in before fighting Liston, the pop-eyed poetry recitals, his sleight of hand in the ring. But then, because a Muslim cannot deceive anyone, he deflates his own magic, he explains to you how the tricks are done, he shows you how to raise yourself on one toe to "elevate."

But tricks are tricks, they are nothing much for him anymore. Ali is serious about faith. One way he likes to talk about faith and Islam is to prove the "consistency" of Islamic texts compared to the Bible, which he does in a deadly serious scholastic sort of way. He carries around a long list of textual "inconsistencies" in the Old and the New Testaments. When I was with him, he spent at least as much time slowly thumbing through his worn Bible looking up these inconsistencies as he did talking about race or boxing or anything else. He would point out a difference between, say, the gospels of Mark and Matthew as if, in one stroke, he had undermined an eon of Christian belief.

"There are thirty thousand of these!" he said. "Someone found them."

Ali's religion orders his life and helps him cope with his illness. A lesser man could be forgiven some hours of darkness, for here is a performer who was robbed of what had seemed to be his essence—his physical beauty, his speed, his wit, his voice—and yet Ali never betrays self-pity. "I know why this has happened," Ali said. "God's showing me that I'm just a man like everyone else. Showing you, too. You can learn from me that way."

It's not as if Ali has put the past behind him. He earns his living signing pictures that are then sold at auction and at dealerships. He has various agents and lawyers working on his behalf, and Lonnie coordinates everything.

Sometimes, when he is sleeping, Ali dreams about his old fights, especially the three fights with Joe Frazier. He is not immune to celebrating the past. When the documentary film about his triumph in Zaire, *When We Were Kings,* opened, Ali watched the tape many times over. He was there in Hollywood when the film's director, Leon Gast, collected an Academy Award. As always now, Ali stood and wordlessly accepted a standing ovation.

His greatest triumph in retirement came on the summer night in Atlanta when, to the surprise of nearly everyone watching, he suddenly appeared with a torch in his hands ready to open the 1996 Summer Olympics. Ali stood with the heavy torch extended before him. Three billion people watching on television could see him shaking, both from the Parkinson's and from the moment itself. But he carried it off. "Muhammad wouldn't go to bed for hours and hours that night," Lonnie Ali said. "He was floating on air. He just sat in a chair back at the hotel holding the torch in his hands. It was like he'd won the heavyweight title back a fourth time."

Ali is an American myth who has come to mean many things to many people: a symbol of faith, a symbol of conviction and defiance, a symbol of beauty and skill and courage, a symbol of racial pride, of wit and love. Ali's physical condition is shocking not least because it is an accelerated form of what we all fear, the progression of aging, the unpredictability and danger of life. In Ali we see the frailty even of a man whose job it was to be the most fearsome figure on the globe. But Ali's illness is no longer news, no longer quite so shocking, and even though he is stiff in his movements, even though he barely speaks in public settings, he can still inspire every person in every room, every arena or stadium he is in, anywhere he goes. By the time Ali returned from exile and became champion once more, nearly all of the anger directed at him had dissipated. Partly, that was because most people could see how sincere he was, even if they could not accept the Nation of Islam or his reasons for refusing the draft. He made them laugh. And, after all, the times had changed, *they* had changed, or some had. For instance, Red Smith, whose columns had been so hostile to Ali early on, was just one of many Americans who came out of the late sixties and early seventies seeing the world in a different way, seeing Ali in a different way. After Ali became champion again in 1974, DC Comics published a special issue in which he took on Superman and won. Ali is a living symbol, as ambiguous and free-floating as many symbols are, but he remains important.

"Clay was my slave name," he said quietly to me as the afternoon wore on and he grew more tired. He was beginning one of his oldest riffs. "You hear 'Khrushchev' and you know it's a Russian. 'Ching' and its Chinese. 'Goldberg,' Jewish. What's 'Cassius Clay'? So plain. So true. George Washington is not a black man's name. So plain. So true. Islam was something that was powerful and strong. It was something I could touch and feel. I grew up and learned that everyone was white. Jesus Christ was white. Everyone at the Last Supper, white. Now these Muslims, they come along and question things. And I think I helped. Now you see a commercial on TV. There's three kids—two black, one white. Or the other way around. It wasn't like that back then. Things changed. Things changed. And I helped. Cassius Clay was my grandfather, Cassius Clay was my father, too. But I changed that. I changed that, too."

While we were still watching tapes of the Liston and Patterson fights, I asked Ali how he'd like to be remembered. He didn't answer. But a long time ago, when his body still allowed him free speech, Ali answered the same question:

"I'll tell you how I'd like to be remembered: as a black man who won the heavyweight title and who was humorous and who treated everyone right. As a man who never looked down on those who looked up to him and who helped as many of his people as he could—financial and also in their fight for freedom, justice, and equality. As a man who wouldn't embarrass them. As a man who tried to unite his people through the faith of Islam that he found when he listened to the Honorable Elijah Muhammad. And if all that's asking too much, then I guess I'd settle for being remembered only as a great boxing champion who became a preacher and a champion of his people. And I wouldn't even mind if folks forgot how pretty I was."

The phone rang. Ali picked up the receiver, though it took several seconds for him to lift it to his ear. He barely had the strength now to say hello. There were many calls, and each time Ali told whoever it was to call later, call tomorrow, call next week, Lonnie'll be here later. It took him a long time to return the phone from his ear to the cradle. It took him a long time to do nearly everything.

"The only thing important now is to be a good Muslim," he said. "Help others."

Then he stopped talking entirely. He closed his eyes. And for a few minutes it seemed he was sleeping. Then he opened his eyes and smiled. He was joking.

"Got you!" he said.

He paused awhile and then he said, "Sleep is a rehearsal for death. One day you wake up and it's Judgment Day. I don't worry about disease. Don't worry about anything. Allah will protect me. He always does." He has said this many times.

Then Ali said he was tired. It was a nice way of saying goodbye. He walked with me down the stairs and out to the driveway.

"This your car?" he said.

"Well, it's mine for today," I said.

"Not even that," Ali said. "You don't own nothing. You're just a trustee in this life. Take care of yourself."

I said goodbye and drove down the long road to his gate. In the mirror, I could see Ali still standing out on the gravel. He waved once, very slowly, then turned around and walked back inside the house for his afternoon prayers.

NOTES ON SOURCES
AND ACKNOWLEDGMENTS

The heavyweight championship fights of the early sixties fall in a strange crevice between history and recent events. To readers over forty, the early Ali fights are the stuff of early (or not-so-early) memory. To those who are younger, they are as distant as Agincourt. Many participants and witnesses who figure in the story of the rise of Muhammad Ali have died, including Sonny Liston, Malcolm X, Elijah Muhammad, Betty Shabazz, Willie Reddish, Jimmy Cannon, Cus D'Amato, Joe Martin, Odessa Clay, and Cassius Clay, Sr. But with the exception of a few living sources who refused to be interviewed, the main actors who are still alive were uncommonly generous with their time and recollections. I am especially grateful to Muhammad and Lonnie Ali, who invited me to their farm in Michigan, and to Howard Bingham and Thomas Hauser for helping to make that meeting possible.

I am grateful for interviews to Maury Allen, Dave Anderson, Teddy Atlas, Milt Bailey, Lem Banker, Gary Beckwith, Jack Bonomi, Kirby Bradley, Dennis Caputo, Gil Clancy, Foneda Cox, Stanley Crouch, Gordon Davidson, Angelo Dundee, Henry Ealy, Gerald Early, Beverly Edwards, Jimmy Ellis, Ralph Ellison, Sam Eveland, Leon Gast, Truman Gibson, Pete Hamill, Tom Hauser, John Horne, Jerry Izenberg, Lamont Johnson, Murray Kempton, Neil Leifer, Robert Lipsyte, Jack McKinney, Larry Merchant, Archie Moore, Toni Morrison, Jill Nelson, Jack Newfield, Gil Noble, Ferdie Pacheco, Floyd Patterson, Davey Pearl, George Plimpton, Ed Pope,

Pat Putnam, Gil Rogin, Harold D. Rowe, Jeffrey Sammons, Sonia Sanchez, Dick Schaap, Mort Sharnik, James Silberman, Bert Sugar, Gay Talese, Ernie Terrell, José Torres, Mike Tyson, and Dean Weidemann.

I am grateful to the librarians at *Sports Illustrated*, the Louisville *Courier-Journal*, and *The New Yorker* for opening their files to me; to the boxing historian Hank Kaplan for free run of his shoe boxes filled with clippings on Ali, Liston, and Patterson; to the New York Public Library; to Bill Vourvoulias for helping to find old materials and conducting a few interviews about Liston's death; and to Pete Wells for fact-checking the manuscript.

The reader undoubtedly understands that the passage of time could not help but make its mark on the research. Ali no longer speaks as well as he once did and Liston is gone. The quotations in the body of the book are mainly from newspapers, magazines, and broadcasts of the time, or from publications that came later. There are several books that are especially important to understanding the early Muhammad Ali. Foremost are Thomas Hauser's excellent oral biography, *Muhammad Ali: His Life and Times*; John Cottrell's *The Story of Muhammad Ali, Who Once Was Cassius Clay*; and Jack Olsen's *Black Is Best: The Riddle of Cassius Clay.* Cottrell and Olsen are especially good on Ali's background and early fights, and Hauser provides unique material on, among other subjects, Ali's complicated introduction to the Nation of Islam and his self-creation. To Hauser, Cottrell, and Olsen, I am indebted and grateful.

Other books that were of help were George Plimpton's witty accounts in *Shadow Box*; José Torres's *Sting Like a Bee*; A. S. "Doc" Young's moving early portrait of Liston, *The Champ Nobody Wanted*; Rob Steen's *Sonny Boy*; Robert Lipsyte's *Sportsworld*; Gerald Early's incisive essays in *Tuxedo Junction* and *The Culture of Bruising*; Joyce Carol Oates's *On Boxing*; Floyd Patterson's *Victory Over Myself* (with Milton Gross); Harold Conrad's *Letters to Muffo*; *The Autobiography of Malcolm X* (with Alex Haley); A. J. Liebling's *A Neutral Corner*; Norman Mailer's anthologies *The Long March* and *The Time of Our Time*, which includes his *Esquire* article "Ten Thousand Words a Minute" and other boxing pieces; Jeffrey T. Sammons's fine academic study *Beyond the Ring: The Role of Boxing in American Society*; *Nobody Asked Me, But . . . The World of Jimmy Cannon*, a compilation of columns edited by Jack Cannon and Tom Cannon; Taylor Branch's *Pillar of Fire*, the second volume of his history of the King years; Gay Talese's *Fame and Obscurity*, which includes his great *Esquire* profile of Floyd Patterson, "The Loser"; *Muhammad Ali: The People's Champ*, edited by Elliot J. Gorn; *The Muhammad Ali Reader*, edited by Gerald Early; LeRoi Jones's *Home: Social Essays*; and Eldridge Cleaver's *Soul on Ice*.

Also helpful were Bruce Perry's biography *Malcolm*; Elijah Muhammad's *Message to the Blackman in America*; C. Eric Lincoln's *The Black Muslims in America*; Claude Andrew Clegg III's *An Original Man: The Life of Elijah Muhammad*; Nick Tosches's profile of Liston in the February 1998 *Vanity Fair*; James Weldon Johnson's *Black Manhattan*; Henry Hampton and Steve Fayer's *Voices of Freedom: An Oral History of the Civil Rights Movement from the 1950s Through the 1980s*; Leon F. Litwack's *Trouble in Mind: Black Southerners in the Age of Jim Crow*; *The Eyes on the Prize Civil Rights Reader*, edited by Clayborne Carson et al.; Harold Cruse's *The Crisis of the Negro Intellectual*; *Classical Black Nationalism: From the American Revolution to Marcus Garvey*, edited by Wilson Jeremiah Moses; Chris Mead's *Champion: Joe Louis, Black Hero in White America*; *The Autobiography of Jack Johnson*; and James Baldwin's *The Fire Next Time* and *Nobody Knows My Name*.

Sports Illustrated is the most comprehensive and accurate contemporaneous guide to the world of boxing in the early and middle sixties. The magazine helped make its name with its coverage of the Ali story. I'm grateful to the writers: W. C. Heinz, Huston Horn, Robert H. Boyle, Jack Olsen, Mort Sharnik, Gil Rogin, George Plimpton, and, later, Pat Putnam, Gary Smith, Bill Nack, and Mark Kram.

Thanks to Jack Bonomi for providing thousands of pages of transcripts from the Kefauver committee's hearings on boxing, to HBO for its documentary *Sonny Liston: The Mysterious Life and Death of a Champion*, and to both the Classic Sports Network and Bill Cayton's company, Big Fights, which provided me with videotapes of dozens of fights.

I owe a real debt to David Halberstam, who helped with the idea for the book and sets a standard for journalism and generosity, and to my friend and agent Kathy Robbins for making a vague notion a reality. I am also grateful to Jeffrey Frank, Thomas Hauser, Jack

Newfield, Michael Shapiro, Jeffrey Toobin, Malcolm Gladwell, Ted Johnson, and Robert Lipsyte, who all read the manuscript with great care, and to Joy de Menil for constant help at Random House.

I am especially grateful to Tina Brown, who made a home for me at *The New Yorker,* to all of my colleagues at the magazine, and to Jason Epstein, who has been a force of integrity, generosity, and wit in publishing for forty-eight years.

My parents and grandmother were, as usual, an inspiration. The book is dedicated to my brother, who shared my fascination with my subject to such a degree that he even went with me to see Ali fight a professional wrestler, Antonio Inoki, via closed circuit at the Beacon Theater. And it is dedicated to my dear friend Eric Lewis, who skipped Ali-Inoki—but he is forgiven.

As ever, I owe far too much to recount here to my sons, Noah and Alex, and to my wife, Esther.

INDEX